NO
DISCOURAGEMENT

Exploring Faith

in the Chantry Group

Honor Anthony

Joan Crewdson

Dorothy Emmet

Vera Hodges

David Hughes

Elaine Kaye

Robert Mitchell

Olga Pocock

Anthony Pragnell

Bryan Saunders

Michael Smart

Muriel Smith

Vernon Thomas

Eberhard George Wedell

Rosemarie Wedell

Shirley Wren-Lewis

AVON BOOKS
1 DOVEDALE STUDIOS
465 BATTERSEA PARK ROAD
LONDON SW11 4LR

Printed and bound in the U.K.
First Published 1997
© Chantry Group authors as named 1997
ISBN 1 86033 453 9

The article by Geoffrey Taylor beginning on page 208 is reproduced by kind permission of *The Guardian*.

NO DISCOURAGEMENT

He who would valiant be
'Gainst all disaster,
Let him in constancy
  Follow the Master.
There's no discouragement
Shall make him once relent
His first avowed intent
  To be a pilgrim.

John Bunyan 1628 - 1688

ACKNOWLEDGEMENTS
BY MEMBERS OF THE CHANTRY GROUP

As a group of friends we have no infrastructure except what we can muster ourselves. So this volume would not have seen the light of day but for the devoted work of Bryan Saunders on his computer.

Elaine Kay, James Mark, Michael Smart and Eberhard George Wedell have worked on Parts I and IV. We discussed these at our meeting in Ecton in June 1997, and we think that they command a broad measure of agreement.

Elizabeth Browne made the etching of Brandlehow, Derwentwater that appears on the cover.

Richard Wilkinson kindly agreed to do the bookkeeping for our enterprise.

We are indebted to all of them more than we can say.

CONTENTS

Part I

Part IV

PART I

The Chantry Group

These essays have been written by a group of friends. We came over the years to be called the Chantry Group after the lovely Queen Anne house opposite Knole Park in Sevenoaks where we used to spend weekends together in the 1970s. But our origins go back to the early 1950s when most of those coming to talk about God and the world lived and worked in or around London. They would come to the Wedell's flat in Lower Belgrave Street on the corner of Eaton Square. In those days ordinary people could still afford to live on the 'right' side of Victoria Station.

Arising from the war and the reconstruction period there were several intersecting circles in the 1950's and 60's interested in the role of Christians in the secular realm, almost all of which have since disappeared. Most of us had received our early training in the Student Christian Movement, in those days a powerful agency of intellectual encounter between the Christian faith and modern society. We came into active professional life with articulate assumptions about the duty of the Christian to pursue his or her vocation in the secular realm. So some of us were in touch with the Christian Frontier Council, a group of politicians, senior civil servants and others launched by J.H.Oldham in the darkest days of the war; others with St Anne's House in Soho, created by the Diocese of London in the same period as a 'centre of Christian discourse'. A less intellectual but equally committed group were the Blue Pilgrims, founded by Beatrice Hankey a generation before, at

2

the Chantry in Sevenoaks. The civil servants among us belonged to an informal group of people in what was then still called the First Division of the Civil Service, who met from time to time to talk about theological issues arising from their work. The William Temple Association was another, more tangentially related, circle. William Temple College, the national memorial to Archbishop William Temple, exercised significant influence through Mollie Batten, its principal.

We were not then, nor are we now, ecclesiastical or theological professionals. Our professional expertise lay elsewhere. Our interest in Christian discipleship and theology stems from personal conviction rather than professional engagement. That, we think, may make the essays in this volume of interest to others.

All rules have their exceptions. Stephen Burnett was a solicitor turned parson, who maintained throughout his ministry a healthy regard for the lay life. Rupert Bliss is the most unclerical of priests; and Patrick McLaughlin's vocation was as much histrionic as priestly. Rupert's first wife Kathleen was more of an ecclesiastical pundit, who edited the Christian Newsletter after Joe Oldham, and was Secretary of the Board of Education of the Church Assembly in Archbishop Geoffrey Fisher's time. Others who tried to help the Churches in their secular contexts have included George Wedell who, on secondment from the Ministry of Education launched the Anglican Board for Social Responsibility in 1958,. He was succeeded at two or three removes by Giles Ecclestone a Clerk in the House of Commons. Derek Pattinson from the Inland Revenue became General Secretary of the General Synod, and Michael Smart retired early from the Department of Employment to become Secretary of the International Dept. of the British Council of Churches. For most of those involved these were, however, relatively brief interludes in a secular career

Other early members of the Group were Donald McKay, one of the pioneers of cybernetics, and Claude Curling. At this time they were lecturing in Physics at King's College in the Strand. Donald's denominational background was the Free

3

Church of Scotland and he came with his then student fiancée
Valerie. There were David and Patricia Hughes, from the St.
Anne's House circle and before that parishioners of Joseph
McCulloch. This was also the provenance of John and Shirley
Wren-Lewis. Both John and David were I.C.I. products. John
in the Research Department was developing a lively line in
Christian Apologetics at the time. Some years later he went off
to America and now lives in Australia.

When the Wedells moved to Manchester in 1964 Derek
Pattinson for a time gave the group house-room in his flat in
Manchester Square. When that was no longer available we
decided to meet less often and at greater length. This evolved
into our weekends at the Chantry. Claude Curling, Dorothy
Emmet, Patrick McLaughlin, Vernon Thomas and the Wedells
were Blue Pilgrims; so the connection was easily made. When
the Chantry was sold we moved to the house of the Grey
Ladies, then home of an Anglican order in Dartmouth Row,
Blackheath; and later to the Royal Foundation of St.
Katherine in Stepney for our winter meeting. In the summer
we met for several years at Dunford, Richard Cobden's former
home near Midhurst, by then taken over by the YMCA. Since
that became too expensive we have moved to Ecton House, a
lovely honey-coloured Northamptonshire Rectory, now the
retreat house of the Diocese of Peterborough. This has the
added advantage of being rather closer to those of us who live
in the North.

We have by now met for over forty-five years. Although
there have been changes in membership, a good many of the
original group of friends remain actively involved in it. We
have not set ourselves a sharply defined agenda or precisely
delimited the subject-matter with which we concern ourselves.
Our conversation has, from time to time, included aspects of
government; priorities in the use of economic resources both
within this country and in our relationships with other
countries; and a variety of social questions, as well as current
activity in the arts. One might say that we have concerned
ourselves with any issues in the life of our time which we have
found interesting and important, particularly in the broad

4

religious context. So our conversation has by no means been solely theological. But theology has been the subject to which we have most frequently turned; and the context of our discussion of other subjects has usually been a recognisably theological one. The theology however, does not exclusively express a belief in God, but rather the relevance of what one may call the theological dimension.

In this collection of essays each of the contributors tends, as becomes evident in Parts II and III, to write his or her theology differently, each author refers to God (or does not refer to him) in different ways; and therefore does not always find him or herself in agreement with the others. But there is, in all our contributions, a certain approach, a certain stance which gives this collection an element of coherence. If we ask ourselves 'what are the distinctive characteristics which have moulded this material over the years?' one or two emerge. The 'lay' character of the group is one. We have never avoided our ordained brethren, (or indeed sisters, in recent years). But we have proceeded over the years on the assumption that the Christian life, if it is to be lived at all, is lived in the world at large. It has to prove itself in a certain autonomy vis-à-vis the ecclesiastical structures (though not necessarily the means of grace). It may be that, for some of us, friendship has come over the years to become as important as the community of the religious traditions which nurtured us in our earlier years. It may be that the language of tradition (or of traditions) which is expressed in metaphor and myth has come to replace for us the language of factual statement and assertion but not, we hope, the language of imagination. Dietrich Bonhoeffer (the inspiration of many unorthodox Christians, who nevertheless remained firmly orthodox in his devotion to Christ) has shaped the thought of the group as has no other single theologian. We have all been trying, since his death, to interpret where he was pointing with his haunting phrase about a world come of age, for which there is no way back; about a language which has to be discovered anew, 'perhaps wholly unreligious, but liberating and redeeming'. We have found that the new language has to be discovered in the common life of men and women.

5

The second characteristic is that our group has always seen its work as inter-disciplinary in its interests, orientation and experience. We come from a wide range of academic disciplines: philosophy, political science, economics, medicine, law, psychology, the history of art, classical and modern languages. This range, and the variable extent to which we would apply the adjective "intellectual" to our several modes of thinking and argumentation, have given the group an air of catholicity. We do not write as a group of intellectuals, though some might, with pejorative intent, label us thus. We have, at least, proved by our respective involvement in the affairs of this world that we are not intellectuals in the sense of being disengaged from public affairs. We have sought, whenever we thought it necessary and possible, to get advice from experts and to discuss that advice with them.

Another characteristic of our make-up which has in practice fostered a commonality has been the range of jobs members of the group have done. Even the civil servants among us have done jobs wholly disparate in this context. Health, Social Security, Education, Employment, Transport, Betting & Gaming control, the central administration of the Church of England and the British Council of Churches, Overseas Aid and Technical Assistance, Medicine, Teaching, Psychiatry, Social Work, Housing, Community Relations, Scientific Research, Broadcasting, Higher Education and other commitments have engaged one or more of us. If anything, we have been thin on practising artists of all kinds, even though many of us would claim to enjoy their work. Nor, with one or two exceptions, have we been at the forefront of developments in the natural or applied sciences, though, again, some of us have followed these closely.

During almost half a century when pressures of life have in many ways reduced the scope for leisurely encounter among friends we have been fortunate to be able to keep alive the pleasure of being together without extravagance or exclusivity. This is a fourth characteristic of the group. We are in no way smart or privileged. We have all, over the years, had to bring up our families and/or look after our elderly relatives. For

6

most of us life has not been without struggle or stress. These cares and distractions of the world might well have killed our friendships. The fact that most of us have made the effort to keep them in good repair, often in the face of these difficulties, has made for a continuity rare in these occupationally and geographically mobile (and to that extent unfriendly) times.

The listing of these characteristics might suggest that we are a pretty earnest lot. Nothing could be further from the truth. We have had a lot of fun over the years. In offering our thoughts to a wider readership we are conscious that there must be similar groups up and down the country which contribute to the web and woof of our common culture. It would be splendid to know about their struggles, achievements and failures. Perhaps this volume will encourage them to share with a wider readership their insights into the intellectual and practical challenges of trying to live life responsibly on the verge of the 21st century.

An obvious comment on the essays is that they cover only a relatively small part of the subject-matter with which the group has been concerned. An obvious reply would be that it would have been impossible to cast the net more widely, given the breadth and variety of that subject-matter to which we have turned from time to time. The group has functioned, inescapably, not as a body of experts (for its expertise has been relatively limited) but as a group of people, living their lives in the Western world of the late twentieth century. Our experience has had a theological dimension, though the validity of individual experience has varied, as has any agreement as to the possibility of expressing it. It is not surprising, we think, that the group should have produced a collection of papers on faith, for faith is the concern which, however indirectly, they have in common. Faith - or for the sceptics the need to do without it - underlies all our other concerns. However we define it, we have to recognise it as the ground of our being. It is not surprising, therefore, that although our concerns are varied, most of us have wished to say what we can about it. We have a collection of seventeen papers. It would not have been either possible or appropriate

7

to collect such a symposium on any other subject.

The immediate impulse was given by the need felt by one of our members, James Mark, 'to work out for myself what kind of statement of faith I can make in the situation to which my exploration has led me'[1], both as a member of the group and in other situations, notably as a former member of the Treasury and of the Ministry of Overseas Development and, after his retirement, as one of a trio of editors of Theology with David Jenkins, John Drury and Peter Coleman. He invited the comments of friends (including members of the group, to whom the essay was addressed). The discussion to which the essay gave rise within the group led fairly quickly to a feeling shared by many of its members that they wished to follow James Mark's example, and to formulate their own thoughts on the same theme. The present collection is the result.

Any collection of writings on this subject is likely to be varied, even though the writers or most of them may share a number of convictions. The present collection is no exception. Bonhoeffer's question 'What is Christianity or even who is Christ for us today?' is likely to evoke a variety of responses. James Mark begins by describing the place from which he speaks and goes on to speak of four interlocutors with whom he has been involved - four thinkers who (whether Christian or not) seem to him to have possessed the kind of sensitivity which made it possible for them to see what Christianity is about[2]. Significantly the four are Wittgenstein, Sartre, Bonhoeffer and Simone Weil; but they do not include Marx or Freud. He goes on to specify four problems with which he has found himself confronted: the inescapable paradoxes of the human situation; the nature of religious language; the justice of God, and the impossibility of a portrait of Christ[3]. In what sense, if at all, can we bring in the notion of the transcendent to enable us not to solve, but to live with, these insoluble problems? And in what sense, if at all, is any notion of the transcendent linked with the Christian revelation? These are the problems which James Mark explores in the latter part of his essay.

8

Probably more people will recognise the situation to which James Mark addresses himself than the substance of either his argument or of any conclusions which emerge. This can only be a contribution to a complex debate. It was with this in mind that members of our group were invited both to comment critically on the approach and to offer their own suggestions as to the ways in which our debate might develop. The contributions are very varied, in the length and the extensiveness of their discussion, and in the amount of autobiographical reference they contain. Most contributors have devoted relatively little space to detailed review or criticism of James Mark's essay; rather they have treated it as a source of illumination or of dissent. For all the diversity of thought expressed by the contributors and by those to whom they refer, the essays reveal a sequence of questions and concerns with which those who seek meaning in life find themselves confronted.

References;
1. Page 15
2. Page 22
3. Page 30

PART II

An Essay on Faith

James Mark

I
The Purpose of this Essay

This essay is a personal document.   It is concerned with problems of Christian belief. It is the product of an engagement that has dominated my life since I first turned to the Christian faith in my mid-thirties, over forty years ago. I embark on it after some months of hesitation and a number of false starts. I have asked myself whether I want to try to write anything more and what purpose it will serve: whether it will help me or anyone else who may read it. But there is a challenge which I have always felt that I must face as honestly as I can: a challenge to say what I believe, and what relationship my belief bears to traditional Christian belief, as it is expressed (whatever that term means) in the historic Christian creeds. I see it as an attempt to respond to the question from which Bonhoeffer began the exploration in the *Letters and Papers from Prison*, 'What is Christianity or even who is Christ for us today?'[1].

The question may seem familiar enough; everything depends on the situation in which it is asked, the challenges which it raises and how they are met. What gives these letters their peculiar distinction in the theological writing of our time is the experience that inspired them and the radical honesty with which Bonhoeffer pressed the question: a question which he felt to be addressed in the first instance to himself. None of us, perhaps, has done or is likely to do theology in a situation comparable with that in which Bonhoeffer wrote the letters to Bethge. Few of us could rival him either in theological sensitivity or in radical honesty, though we might feel that there is a good deal more to be said about the contemporary cultural situation in which faith has to be expressed. But Christians who feel the need to think seriously about their faith (and anyone who regards it as an option to be considered) have to face Bonhoeffer's question and return as honest an answer as they can.

This will be, at the least, a personal exercise in intellectual clarification and in discovering the limits of such clarification so far as I am concerned. That is the central purpose of what I write. But is it likely to offer anything of more general interest? In the end that has to reveal itself in the reading, but it may help at the outset to give some indication of my interests and concerns, which may perhaps be shown in what I have to say. I write as an amateur theologian. My academic training and research has been in the discipline of language and literature; I have no professional qualifications as a theologian, a philosopher, or as a sociologist in the field of contemporary culture, though I have been concerned with these subjects, and, as a former joint editor of the journal *Theology* I have been brought into fairly close touch with that subject, especially contemporary theology.

Such a confession of amateurism is relative: one that even the best-informed, the most learned among us must make if he wishes to write in general about his own beliefs or the beliefs of his time; for in our fragmented culture, with its increasingly specialized fields of knowledge, an academic specialist who ventures outside his own specialism becomes an amateur. No one can be an expert over the whole field. Moreover, both the choice of material and the way in which it is presented and interpreted reflect the concerns and the vision of the writer. He must, as a man of his time, take up an attitude to questions of belief, whether or not he writes explicitly about his own, and he must write mostly as an amateur in the great field which no one - as we see more clearly nowadays - can claim to master as a professional. It isn't surprising, therefore, to find the term amateurism uttered as a criticism by more specialized theologians of the efforts of such contributors to the general debate on belief as Tillich, Küng and (on our more modest English scale) Robinson and Cupitt.

I have been much concerned with the understanding of Christian faith in the intellectual and cultural climate of our day, with those aspects of contemporary philosophical and literary discussion which seem to me relevant to this understanding and, of course, with the contemporary theological debate (or at any rate with such of it as I have found myself able to respond to) on these matters. What I have written in this field has been mostly either on the general theme of how we can affirm Christian faith in the cultural climate in which most of us in the West live, or has been comment on individuals whose writings I have found especially relevant to the theme: who have stimulated or challenged me. I have always been conscious, however, that what I was doing was motivated, at bottom, by a search for a statement of faith which I could myself accept.

Thirteen years ago I wrote an essay specifically on this theme, 'A Shape of Faith' [2]. It was shaped to a considerable extent by my references to four people (Bonhoeffer, Wittgenstein, Sartre and Simone Weil) who have, in their different ways, stood on the frontiers of religion and who have influenced my own religious engagement. I have asked myself whether I didn't say then as much as I can say. But, on re-reading it, it strikes me that I didn't either answer the questions with which that essay ended, on natural theology and on the Christian revelation, or (more realistically) reconcile myself to their unanswerability. It doesn't seem premature, after thirteen years, to ask myself whether I have anything more, or anything different to say about the need to think in terms of some kind of order, and the need to say how, within that order, I can speak of the Christian revelation and what it means to me. More fundamentally, have I honestly addressed myself to the questions that I have to ask myself? Have I uncovered what I really believe in? Have I used the exploration of other people's thoughts in order to keep the enquiry in general terms: to avoid the personal challenge?

What I want to do in this essay, at any rate, is to face the questions as frankly as I can: to work out for myself what kind of statement of faith I can make in the situation to which my exploration has led me; to set out my thoughts, however tentatively and unclearly, about what I can say; to say what I can hold to; how I can justify and live by such convictions as I can formulate. I am concerned here with the thoughts of others in so far as they may clarify my own attitudes and beliefs; I refer to them in so far as they illustrate, reinforce or challenge those attitudes and beliefs. I shall refer to a number of people who have, I think, helped to formulate our contemporary awareness. I shall speak of what challenges or makes sense to me. I shall refer rather than discuss; assert rather than argue in detail. All this seems to me appropriate in a brief writing of this kind. I may well expose myself, as I have in the past, to the criticism that what I write is too strenuous for the general reader but insufficiently rigorous and directed for the specialist. That may matter less in an exchange of thoughts of general concern. What I have to say must, in any case, speak for itself, convincingly or not.

Although I shall be primarily concerned with my own beliefs I remain deeply indebted to some whom I have described as standing, in different places, on the frontiers of belief. They seem to me to be witnesses whom we need: people who have made me look again and afresh. I have become, in particular, more and more conscious (as I think others have done too) of the questions, the challenges, the surprising insights which Wittgenstein constantly reveals (for the most part obliquely) when he speaks of religion, as on subjects with which he was more concerned. I have had to come to grips more closely with the thoughts that Bonhoeffer half-expressed in the *Letters and Papers from Prison.* They took him into a new theological world, and left us with unforgettable hints to be explored. And I have encountered, again, the distinctive spirituality of Simone Weil.

What can I hope to offer? Not, I fear, a burning statement of faith from the furnace of experience. I can speak only on questions of theological understanding (my own) rather than with the experience that may stimulate the desire to understand; with what I am doing when I speak of faith and how I justify the impulse to do so; with how faith can help me to understand the life I lead and to reconcile myself to it; and above all, how it helps me (if it does) to speak of hope in terms which take frank account of that world and what happens in it.

These, you may rightly say, are matters of enormous range and complexity on which no individual, whatever the breadth and depth of his understanding, can hope to say much. True, but we all have to define our own attitudes and to live

16

our lives as best we can. I have felt the need to set out what thoughts I can frame, especially in dialogue with the writers whom I have encountered. There is, I hope, a certain irreducible value which the writing of such an essay has for the writer: for me, as for the many others who feel the need at some time to commit such thoughts to paper, on this theme. It may help us to clarify our understanding of them, whatever the limitations of our knowledge and thought. It may, through the empathy of friendship, help some others with whom I have shared a concern with these matters. It may at least tell them and other friends more about what I have been concerned with during these past years.

II
The Place from which I speak

I have, inescapably, to do my theology from where I am. I must operate with the intellectual assumptions which I have evolved, (and shall continue to evolve for as long as I am capable of intellectual activity), in encounter with the culture in which I live, and in exchange with my contemporaries. I do not find that this recognition reduces me either to the determinism that deprives me of individual choice in the situation in which I find myself, or to the relativism that declines to speak of values in an absolute sense, and regards the values upheld in a culture as relative only to that culture. It does not, in particular, make the pursuit of truth (and of theological truth in particular) a vain occupation. It does imply, with inescapable insistence that the limitations of the human situation make an ambiguous concept of truth. We must speak of it if human life (the lives of each of us) is to have meaning; yet to speak of it with sincerity and sensitivity is to recognize that we can only speak, at best, in hints and guesses.

We speak from where we are; we have such encounters with our fellow-creatures as we can - encounters for good or ill. But nothing can transpose me into a culture which is not my own, or the theology which may seem relevant to it. I can feel sympathy for (shall we say?) the Latin American who is inspired by liberation theology. I can come to believe that any

17

valid theology in our time must come to terms with liberation theology: must feel that it is part of any adequate understanding of the world in which we live. But it isn't my theology, because my own situation demands something different. The social and political situation and the concerns which it stimulates are different and perhaps harder to formulate in our different situation. Sympathy is not identity; and I cannot do my theology from someone else's place in the world, though we are both concerned with a truth which, perhaps, lies beyond all theology.

Since, then, we have to come together from where we are, I must sketch, however brashly and briefly, the place from which I see the world: the presuppositions from which I start, which establish the context within which, for me, exploration has to take place. (And theology is necessarily exploration). I write as an intellectually sophisticated individual (a male one) of the late twentieth century. That in itself does not indicate a point of view or refer to the emotions and concerns which function, perhaps powerfully, beneath the intellectual surface.

It does imply certain presuppositions as to the way in which we interpret our experience, and in which we determine its possibilities as helping us to understand ourselves and the world which we inhabit, whether under Divine providence or as a place into which, in Heidegger's phrase, we have been thrown.

I find myself concerned with what appear to be two very different aspects of experience. They are so different as to seem irreconcilable; and yet they have to be reconciled somehow, if that experience is to be interpreted as a whole - as something more than a meaningless chaos. One is the rapidity of cultural change, springing from the vertiginous development of contemporary technologies, which have transformed the material possibilities of life, and the enormous expansion of scientific knowledge on which the technology is based. All this might seem to imply a radical change in the way in which we are to see ourselves in the world: what we can make of it, and what this makes of us and our destiny. Yet I have to see these changes in the perspective of what does not change, because of the unsurpassable limitations of the human condition. All extensions of our knowledge raise further questions; and the field of knowledge itself is limited, for us, by the limitations of our capacity to observe. We live surrounded by the unknowable. Our limitations are not merely the limitations of our physical capacity to observe; they are expressed in the insoluble problems of conceiving a first event; of thinking of the universe as either finite or infinite.

The enormous expansion of our knowledge, in individual fields, makes it more and more difficult to bring together the results of our research in individual fields into a picture of knowledge as a whole: of the world and our place in it. We recognise the impossibility of achieving the kind of synthesis of knowledge which Hegel envisaged as the task of philosophy; even friendly expositors of Hegel (J.N. Findlay, Charles Taylor) do not consider such a synthesis as possible. And, even if the diversity of our knowledge did not militate against such a synthesis, I find a kind of consensus as to the impossibility of getting outside our world so as to be able to see it as a whole. Wittgenstein and Heidegger, logical analysts and existentialists all seem to me to assume, in their different ways, that this is axiomatic. Our legitimate concern, they seem to suggest, is with the specific problems that we can identify in the world that surrounds us; with investigations in different fields (including what kind of activity philosophy is); even, it is sometimes suggested, with the truth of individual investigations rather than with truth in general.

In this situation, I find a conflict between two mental attitudes, each of which is valid within its own context. One is the game of question and answer which is the source of the knowledge which dominates our Western culture. We increase our knowledge by asking questions, the answers to which we can, in some sense, be verified or which have at least not been falsified by testing. Knowledge is something which we master for ourselves; our answers to whatever questions we find it useful to ask are based on whatever consensus can be discerned at present. The appropriate mental attitude is hard-headed, open-minded, sceptical in the valuation of authority, which can only be provisional, and perhaps limited only to a particular field. The methodology and its results are clearly impressive. But it takes no account of those areas of human experience to which the criterion of verification cannot be applied in any definable sense: to the experience of the arts; of human relationships; of moral experience; of religion. The experience of which we speak is often complex and profound, is always imprecise, and certainly not verifiable, but is part (perhaps the most important part) of what it means to be a human being.

So I find three different problems in seeing our situation in the world as an understandable whole, whether or not this is expressed in theological terms. One is the enormous and increasing diversity of our knowledge, and the problem of relating different parts of it to each other. The second is the unsurmountable limitations of that knowledge. The third is the great areas of human experience to which the language of knowledge hardly applies in any demonstrable sense. We may say, for example, that the plays of Shakespeare increase our knowledge of human nature, but in what sense are we using the term 'knowledge' in referring either to the plays themselves or to the studies whose aim is to increase our understanding of them. And, when we speak of moral issues, the governing concept is judgement rather than knowledge, relevant though knowledge is. And we do not speak (if we are wise) of finality in moral or aesthetic judgements.

Believers might feel tempted to argue that these problems show that nothing has fundamentally changed in our ability to understand the world in which we find ourselves, for we remain surrounded by the mysteries of the human condition, both within our experience and beyond it. I do not share that temptation. I am conscious, rather, of the greater difficulty that we find in our Western culture of coming to terms with the problems; of reconciling ourselves to them. Our forefathers could tell stories which gave us, in the language of myth, an orientation in the mysterious and (for most of them) hard, cruel and unpredictable world in which they lived. I can say no more than that the myth may suggest to my imagination things which I cannot, in any verifiable sense, claim to know. It may show (in Wittgenstein's distinction) what cannot be said[3]. Our forefathers could accept more easily than I can the will of a God which they could understand no more than I can, since they could more easily imagine a future life in which God's purpose would be made known and be seen to be fulfilled. By contrast the culture within which I live is sophisticated, critical, sceptical, sustained by the possibilities that seem increasingly open to mankind, but plagued by the possibility of human catastrophe and by the goblins of meaninglessness[4].

Bonhoeffer came to see the intellectual revolution (and it was for him a revolutionary experience) in his prison cell. He spoke of 'the world come of age' - the memorable phrase which has reverberated so unforgettably in the debate about religion and contemporary culture. He saw it as a movement towards human autonomy which may, he thought, have started as early as the thirteenth century: 'the discovery of the laws according to which man can live in the worlds of learning, political and social affairs, ethics, the arts and religion, so that man has learned to come to terms with himself in all important questions without having to avail himself of the working hypothesis - God' (8.6.44). Living as an autonomous being means that you have to stand on your own feet; you have no choice, since there is no one else to whom you can look for aid. Bonhoeffer nowhere suggests that this leads to overweening ambitions, or to a feeling that man can discover the answers to all the questions about the human condition. We must content ourselves with whatever may be the limits of our knowledge and our powers; we must come to terms with our situation: master it as best we can. To speak of those limits has, indeed, become problematic, when men scarcely fear death and hardly understand the notion of sin. It means the withering of the instinct to worship; 'We worship nothing any more, not even idols' (27.6.44). Bonhoeffer neither welcomes nor condemns the cultural (and therefore the moral) situation in which he thinks that Western man lives. He sees the dangers ('Man can master everything except himself'); he simply insists that this is

21

our situation; and he has little patience with those who describe it in terms of condemnation or insist that it reveals mankind as miserable sinners. This is the culture in which we have to rediscover the Gospel. 'The God who lets us live in the world without the working hypothesis of God is the God before whom we stand' (16.7.44). What makes a Christian is not any specific religious action, but 'participation in the suffering of God in worldly life' (18.7.44).

In these letters and papers Bonhoeffer is speaking to us of a theological breakthrough, and this involves an uncompromising rejection both of the intellectual assumptions and of the pastoral practice of traditional Christianity. We are not to be offered ready-made formulae or bullied into submission by theologians or pastors. He rejects both various pietistic approaches which he lumps together as 'Methodism', and existentialism and the practice of psycho-therapy (his own father was a distinguished psycho-therapist) which he describes as 'secularized Methodism' (8.6.44). Contemporary Western men and women know more problems and fears than Bonhoeffer recognizes. And although his explicit references to 'religion' are negative (as in the demand for 'Christianity without religion'), yet there are plenty of observations which can only imply the need for a religious dimension to life, even though it has to be rediscovered. But what matters in his piercing theological exploration is not the over-simplification and the lack of precision which are natural to exploration, but the challenge that he offers. Theology has to find itself again in our complex and rapidly changing world. Bonhoeffer puts the challenge with the radicalism of a minister of the Gospel who had been forced into the life both of a political conspirator and of a prisoner.

III

My Interlocutors

There are, I think, two different, though related problems about speaking of God in our Western world at the present time. One is whether we need to speak of Him; the other is what we can say about Him. Bonhoeffer is certainly concerned with what we can say, but for him the primary question is the need to speak of God at all. He refuses to force such a need on people who do not feel it. For believers Christianity will consist 'in prayer and in doing what is right among men' (Thoughts on the Baptism of D.W.R., May 44). But a time will come 'when men will again be called so to proclaim the Word of God that by it the world will be transformed and renewed'. It will be a new language, but such a language will be spoken.

Simone Weil, for whom the religious quest was a search for truth, answers both questions in the same passage:

> I am quite sure that there is a God in the sense that I am quite sure that my love is not illusory. I am quite sure that there is not a God in the sense that I am quite sure nothing real can be anything like what I am able to conceive when I pronounce this word. But that which I cannot conceive is not an illusion (GG 103).

Both she and Bonhoeffer were, in their different ways, concerned with what we can say about God, but their primary concern was with the nature of the experience; that, for them, would determine the way in which it might be expressed. Certain contradictions, she said, are not errors but 'doors leading to the transcendent' (FLN 269). The speech that she wants to use lies beyond the domain of the intelligence.

For Wittgenstein the transcendent lay beyond the possibility of speech. For him, 'to write or talk ethics or religion was to run against the boundaries of language. This running against the walls of our cage is perfectly, absolutely hopeless'[5]. But ethics (and, I think, by analogy religion also) 'is a document of a tendency in the human mind which I personally cannot help respecting deeply and I would not for my life ridicule it'.

In the *Tractatus* he claimed to have said what could be said. The important part, however, was that which he had not been able to write - it would have been on ethics, but ethics is transcendental and cannot be put into words (T6.421). In his later philosophy he could only recognize religion as a form of life, to be recognized but not evaluated. He insists that religion rests on commitment, but he does not argue for any such commitment. He was intensely concerned with moral problems, but he did not regard them as philosophically discussable. His friend Engelmann describes his attitude as one of 'wordless faith, which cannot be expressed in any doctrine uttered in words, but only shown in exemplary lives'[6]. But faith in what, if it cannot be uttered, Wittgenstein does not tell us.

Sartre's central concern is with human freedom, which he sought to describe in personal, and later in political terms. But the assertion of human freedom is irreconcilable with any notion of the over-riding power of God. Once Orestes (in *Les Mouches*) has discovered his freedom Jupiter's power is at an end. But Sartre never succeeded in defining freedom, for how can you reason about an existentialist decision, and how is mine to be reconciled with yours? Man's aim is to fulfil himself in freedom, in a world in which he is imprisoned. But only God can reconcile in himself the freedom which is always now and the perfection which does not change.

The passion of man is the reverse of that of Christ, for man loses himself as man in order that God may be born. But the idea of God is contradictory and we lose ourselves in vain. Man is a useless passion[7].

After he reached that conclusion Sartre was engaged in trying to overcome it in political commitment. But the existentialist anguish seems to have turned into ironical reflection. He came to accept himself as the traveller without a ticket, who still feels himself to be in the presence of the ticket-collector, but whom no one awaits at his destination[8]. Is this the death of God or a deadening of sensitivity, loss of the concern for the situation, on which he had earlier insisted? He himself came to say, rather, that 'Atheism is a cruel and lengthy enterprise; I think that I have pursued it to the end', before turning to what he described as his real tasks.

I have referred to people who stand on the intellectual frontiers of belief; this is true of all four, though they stand in different places. Bonhoeffer and Simone Weil are both convinced of a religious truth which illuminates the whole of

24

life, but of which little can be said at present. Wittgenstein speaks of the philosopher as descending into ancient chaos and feeling at home there (CV 65). Sartre cannot reconcile the existence of God with human freedom, and finds our contemporary notions of God incoherent. I have been concerned with them because I am concerned with the intellectual problems of belief, and find that they offer challenges which I cannot ignore. I do not suggest that these challenges are all new; some of them are as old as Christianity itself. But these four, from their very different points of view, put them in new ways. They do so because they are our contemporaries or near contemporaries. They are all concerned, in their distinctive ways, with a contemporary world which we share: a world in which religion has to find its language afresh. They are all concerned, in fact, with the dual problems of whether we think it necessary to refer to God and what we can say about him, without positing a world of religious experience which has no relation to the rest of our lives. These problems have meaning for all of them, including the sceptic Wittgenstein and the atheist Sartre. They do not dismiss religion with crude genetic theories like Marx and Freud. I find them relevant to my own concerns as Marx and Freud are not.

They all have significant things to say about religion, but what they have to say differs because their concerns and commitments differ. It isn't easy to imagine a conversation between them. They all share a common sense that the language of religion has become difficult (Bonhoeffer, Simone Weil) or even impossible (Wittgenstein, Sartre). Their concerns are so different that it is hard to imagine their explicitly agreeing on anything. All of them might agree that it is up to us individually to decide whether or not we want to speak of God, except perhaps Sartre, who concluded that it is a mistaken enterprise. But they would have very different views on what we would be doing. For Wittgenstein it would be attempting the impossible though an impossible to which many have been drawn. For Simone Weil it could only be the expression of supernatural love. For Bonhoeffer we need new language which must be reborn out of prayer and action. They all speak of something that has been important in human life. Only Sartre would accept Nietzsche's aphorism that God is dead. But those who wish to speak of God would agree that at present not much can be said, and it cannot be said in the language of description.

I have concerned myself with these four since they have all confronted me with necessary challenges: Wittgenstein to speak of a language that cannot, he thinks, be spoken, though it is, in fact, spoken; Sartre to speak of a God in whom being and becoming are (impossibly) reconciled; Simone Weil to see how the God whom she cannot conceive is shown in the suffering of Christ; Bonhoeffer to see how we discover Christ as Lord of the world. All of them have helped to form whatever answers I have been able to devise to the two questions with which I began this section of my essay: Do we need to speak of God? and what can we say about Him? The first is primary, since what we say about God is determined by the need we have to speak of Him at all, even if we decide that we must keep silent. What kind of theology do I want and what seems possible?

IV
What kind of Theology do I need?

In speaking of theology in positive terms I lay myself open to the criticism that I am indulging in wish-fulfilment: that there is no relationship between the need that I feel and what is actually the case; that I am setting aside the search for truth and the desolation that this might reveal, and seeking comfort in a friendly fiction. Such criticism has always been and always will be made of all theological statements, of all talk of God. There is no conclusive reply to it, for we have no language in which such a reply could be made: human experience does not extend to the point at which such language would be possible. The only reply to such a challenge that I can make is to be as honest as I can in what I say, and in recognizing what I cannot say, what cannot be said, and what kind of meaning I can claim for whatever I may claim to say - or, in Wittgenstein's phrase, to show, when it cannot be said. I can refer only to pointers towards truth, to intimations of what makes for life.

There is a second recognition also. I have to recognize that my search is not yours. To each his own, inescapably, since whatever weight I may give to authority, whatever fellowship I may find with others in my search, whatever shared vision it may lead to, my need is inescapably mine and can, ultimately, only be met by my own prompting. What I need to do, therefore, is to explore as honestly as I can both what kind of theology I find that I need and what kind of theology I find it possible to envisage, as the person I am, living in the culture of the Europe of the late twentieth century. The gaps and conflicts between the two bring us up against the difficulties and challenges of doing theology in our time: of speaking of God. And since this essay is written, and could only be written in personal terms, it seems useful to say something about both the kind of theology that I need and that which I think possible in the intellectual situation of our day.

I start with three affirmations which are prompted by my reading of human experience. They are not specifically Christian. I believe that we are limited beings, striving to become more than we are, surrounded by mystery; that we can never understand the world, since our knowledge of it must always be limited. All answers raise fresh questions and the ultimate questions (if we can speak of them within human discourse) lie beyond human formulation, so that we can never get outside our world and see it as a whole. We have to understand our experience and how we speak of it with this situation in mind. It cannot change.

I believe that, whatever their limitations of understanding and their differences of culture, personality and of their concerns, human beings can communicate. There is a universe of discourse without which there could be no common humanity and no sharing of experience. However much we differ, however we may cut ourselves off from each other, life is impossible without communication, and communication implies the existence of a world of discourse in which we all share. And this I must accept even though it rests on an act of faith. It can only be assumed as the base of our reasoning with each other: as something that transcends all our individual exercises in reasoning.

I must believe, in the same way, in an order of values to which our experience is related, if we are to attribute significance to that experience - to regard it as having a significance in relation to other comparable experiences: a more general significance than that of an occurrence to be explained by its cultural context, the particular circumstances in which it occurred, or my own individual choice. Here again the affirmation does no more than hold on to the notion that we live in a world of shared values, whatever the differences between us: that the notion of a humanity which we all share is a valid one, even though we may be more conscious of the differences in cultures and of the values to which they give rise, for value implies comparison. Here also I find some notion of a world of shared values indispensable if I am to speak of values at all, whether ethical or aesthetic.

My third affirmation is more problematic. It is that I need a theology (and therefore a faith) which, reconciles me to life. This doesn't mean that I am to be entirely concerned with my own personal salvation, but that the theology that I need should make explicit whatever makes for life in my reading of experience and in my own participation in it. It is not to encourage a facile optimism, (I shall mention the difficulties that I find in formulating such a theology at all). But hope is impossible without reconciliation, and no theology is possible without hope.

These three affirmations express, I must recognize, humanism rather than Christianity. They express humanism in the broadest sense of the word, since they hold out a hope of human fulfilment: a prospect more cheering than Sartre's challenge to us to create our own meaning in a world in which we are condemned to be free. They affirm that a meaning is given. The hope must be grounded in faith, since we cannot look to see its fulfilment. It implies a religious dimension to our experience, since such a dimension implies that we trust where we cannot know, and in the face of experience which challenges that trust. They might or might not imply belief in a God who exists even though we might not find it possible to speak of Him. They might do no more than suggest a religious dimension of experience, which gives meaning and value to it, but without enabling me to speak of a personal God, or even about the religious dimension which I would nonetheless affirm. It is the kind of attitude which I find expressed by Stewart Sutherland (*God, Jesus and Belief*) and Iris Murdoch, (*Metaphysics as a Guide to Morals*) and, less formally, by so sensitive and widely experienced a (non-academic) person as Denis Healey.

But it is at most a theistic attitude to experience. It makes no mention of the distinctive Christian doctrines of the Fall, of sin, redemption, salvation and damnation. It makes no distinctive reference to Jesus Christ as God and man, or to the Christian story as the definitive account of human destiny.

I have been nourished by Christian tradition and find supremely important the visions of love that Christians believe it to convey: a vision which embraces both a love of life and a readiness to sacrifice present life if necessary. But I have to understand them in my own way, and this involves experiencing the devotion of Christian tradition in our critical, knowledgeable, openminded age. In particular

a. I am more inclined to question whatever cosmic order may be proclaimed than to revere, with Kant, the starry heavens above, or to be overcome, with Otto, by a sense of the numinous.

b. I have always been perplexed, like so many others, by the scandal of particularity: the need to reconcile the once-for-all revelation of God in Christ with any general account of man's relationship to God and (in the light of this) his destiny. Why this revelation at this time and in this place, and what of those who could not experience it because they did not live at that time and in that place?

c. I can't ignore the challenge to relate whatever vision we get from Christianity with what (in these days of world-wide communication) we learn about other faiths.

d. How is the notion of 'what makes for life' to be reconciled with the distinctive Christian doctrines of the Fall, of Sin, Redemption and Salvation - which implies also the reality of damnation? It was very real to men of the stature of Dante and Johnson.

These are the problems familiar to all Christians who have found themselves driven to think about the basis of their faith. They have prompted, and will continue to prompt a great deal of theological discussion. I do not, however, propose to add to it within the limits of a brief essay. I must, of course, live with these problems since I find them inescapable. But I want, rather, to refer to certain others which have concerned me personally to such a degree that I cannot refer to Christian belief without having them in mind. There are, I find, four:

a. The inescapable paradoxes of the human situation.

b. The nature of religious language.

c. The justice of God.

d. The impossibility of a portrait of Christ.

These are large questions. They are, moreover, a mixed collection; two about language, two about the subject-matter of theology. I can only say that they have concerned me and are unquestionably important. I shall do no more than indicate briefly how I see them and what implications I derive from them. I shall not discuss; I shall only say what I find.

V

The Paradoxes of the Human Situation

There are several rather different definitions of paradox in the Oxford English Dictionary: the term is itself significantly difficult to define. One is as 'a seemingly absurd though perhaps actually well-founded statement'. I am concerned with the more negative definition of it as a 'self-contradictory or essentially absurd statement', but more specifically with its assimilation to the definition of an antinomy as 'a contradiction in a law or between two laws'. I refer to paradox

30

rather than to antinomy because of the greater resonance of the former term. I follow here the example of Ronald Hepburn in his book, '*Christianity and Paradox*' (1958) and of most other theologians and philosophers. But I want to concentrate on the definition of a paradox as a pair of statements which cannot be reconciled with each other. I do not consider that we can resolve or leave on one side the paradoxes of religion in general or of Christianity in particular, but rather that theologians haven't taken them seriously enough: that they haven't addressed themselves seriously enough to the problem of living with paradoxes that aren't to be resolved. This, indeed, is the main theme of Hepburn's book - the criticism of a sympathetic agnostic.

The paradoxes themselves are familiar enough. There are, first of all, the paradoxes of theism. God acts in the world, but does not have his being in the world. He acts, yet his nature is unchanging. He is outside space and time (if 'outside' can be said to have meaning in this context) and therefore not an object of experience, yet he is believed to hear our prayers. His will is done, yet man is left to work out his own salvation. He lacks nothing, yet he wishes us to be united with him. Such paradoxes run through all the discourse in which we try to reconcile in rational terms God's omnipotence and human freedom. I have never encountered any theology that succeeds.

There follow the paradoxes of Christianity. There are the paradoxes which I encounter in the language of the Kingdom which he came to preach: the Kingdom that we must seek, but which is given; which is both new and old; which is present but still to come; which is a profound mystery, but one which we are to accept as little children. I am drawn even beyond paradox by the insistence that the Kingdom embraces all values, though it is never itself described.

There are the paradoxes which we encounter when we try to identify Jesus, who preached the Kingdom and lived a life which proclaimed its coming, though what that means remains unclear. He claims all power, but makes himself vulnerable - a sacrifice both of God to man and of man to God. He is said, indeed, to be both man and God. Both assertions are necessary, but they cannot be reconciled with each other. Human reason does not provide any possibility of a reconciliation which resolves contradiction. And the problem of finding an identity for the Christ, whom we may claim to know from unique personal experience, ends in the inexplicable doctrine of the Trinity.

There is finally, for Christians, paradox in the life that they are called upon to embrace. Through the Incarnation God has given a new value to the created world, yet we must be prepared to renounce this for the sake of the Gospel. We lose our lives, but in doing so we find them. We are to have faith in eternal life, but we can neither describe it nor predict it, for it lies outside the categories of space and time. All these are paradoxes of different kinds with which the Christian faith confronts me, and from which I ought not to be allowed to escape. They have led to the uncompromising challenges of the Athanasian Creed (of which we hear so little today), and to Tertullian's assertion that the very absurdity of the death of the Son of God made it utterly credible, and the impossibility of the Resurrection made it a fact. But although I may have to accept at the end of the day that reason isn't enough, it seems to me wrong to abandon it at the outset. If I am to act in good faith it must be because experience compels me to that abandonment.

But we aren't concerned simply with the defence of the paradoxes of religion or of Christianity, for paradox is characteristic of human life generally. It appears as soon as we look beyond the immediate problem, the finite concrete goal and think in terms of the knowledge and the fulfilment of human nature that we seek. For it is characteristic of human beings (in the West at least) to look beyond the world that they know or can know: to look for what they cannot know but to which they are drawn. We discover more and more about the universe in which we live, but we know that there will always be more to discover. ('All we can do', said Popper, 'is to grope for truth even though it be beyond our reach')[9]. The concept of finitude itself is one that we cannot define for it

32

depends on the notion of infinity which is, by definition, beyond coherent formulation. We want to assert our freedom to choose and to decide, but we have to reconcile this notion of freedom (as Kant emphasized) with that of a universe in which effect follows cause in an order determined by physical causation: an order in which we can trust. We would like our decisions to bring about a just society, but, even if we felt able to define such a society, must we not regard it as an ideal to which we cannot attain and which will not last, since all human states of affairs are mutable?

Paradox is an inescapable feature of the human condition, whether or not the individual recognizes this. To recognize this is to recognize the limitations of what we can say about it, whether in religious or in other terms. We have to learn to live with our limitations.

This doesn't mean, for me, that one should accept Tertullian's paradox, and embrace absurdity because it is divine absurdity, for what is to justify Tertullian's absurdity compared with Beckett's? It doesn't mean that one should simply accept the situation (or pay no attention to it), like Bonhoeffer's man who has come of age. Nor does it mean, for me, surrendering to a revelation which makes the paradoxes seem unimportant.

It means for me, rather finding myself confronted with Simone Weil's challenge, 'We have to elucidate the way contradictories have of being true'. I can either reject it as nonsensical - the paradox of paradoxes - and resign myself to a human situation which Sartre tells us is absurd, or I have, as Simone Weil tells us, to look beyond the limits of reason - and convince myself that it is right to do so.

VI
Language and Evidence

The question of elucidation leads on naturally to that of religious language, and what we are doing when we use it: to what Wittgenstein might have called the language-games that we play when we try to speak of religion. It is a study in which many philosophers and theologians, in English-speaking countries at least, have felt a concern. It is a concern that I myself share. I recognize that different uses of religious language overlap, but I am myself concerned with those that claim to express an evidential content: to refer to states of affairs, past, present or future, though the state of affairs may be implied indirectly rather than described directly. I am not concerned, therefore, with the language of adoration, of petition, of intercession, or of commandment. I am concerned in particular with the distinction between three kinds of statement which purport to refer to evidence: history, miracle stories and myth.

The first isn't distinctively religious at all, since it consists of statements referring to normal events which can be subjected to the examination of historians in the same way as others: that Jesus lived at a certain time and that his life ended in crucifixion. A similar account could no doubt be given of others among his contemporaries, and tested by the normal rules of historical evidence. I do not comment on how much in other religions is a matter of history; but Christianity must, of course, insist on the historicity of the life of Jesus: that he was born, lived and died on earth.

This takes me into the second kind of religious language: that of miracle, defined as events which are claimed to have taken place and which are, therefore, subject to the methods of historical verification, but which appear not to conform to the normal physical sequence of cause and effect. The events, like the Feeding of the Five Thousand, or of the Man Born Blind or (the greatest challenge) the Raising of Lazarus could all in principle be verified by historians, for the evangelists all state that they are events which occurred. But in practice the evidence which would be necessary to verify such astonishing events is no longer available; nor do we, in practice, expect such evidence to be found. We have to make do with the stories that we have. If we want certainty it has to be based on our accepting the stories as having a special status, prescribed either on Biblical authority or on the authority of the Church, (however defined). I do not think that we can ask for certainty. The understanding of such stories (like that of the larger story of Jesus) is an unending exploration, and the question from which I would start is not precisely what happened (relevant though that is) but why the miracle story was and is told? What kind of person could be at the centre of it?

The third and most complex kind of language is that of myth. Here, in contrast to historical statements or miracle stories, the notion of verification cannot apply because the knowledge that would be required to verify the myth lies beyond human experience. Myths of the Creation and of the Last Things are obvious examples. We tell myths (cosmic myths at least) in order to compensate ourselves for the limitations of our knowledge. We try to dispense with myths so far as we (consciously) can. As our knowledge develops, myths we had thought of as (more or less) literal accounts come to be superseded by explanations which can be tested and falsified (if not verified), so that testable statements come to replace myths, and the fact that they do may lead us to see all myths as dispensable in due course, as our knowledge is extended. But in practice I find (as I suspect most of us do) that things aren't as simple as that. The myths that we (or our ancestors) had regarded as true stories have lost that status, but they may speak a language which can still appeal to the imagination; they can evoke experience which I cannot define as knowledge, but which may respond to the human wish to look beyond the limits of the knowledge that the human condition imposes on us, and to learn, however unclearly, through our imagination something of what our intellects cannot apprehend. The kind of cosmic myth that continues to have power is that which gives a meaning to our world and helps us to find a place in it. It cannot be replaced by verifiable explanation, for it speaks of what lies beyond verification. I might be tempted to say that it reconciles us to the limitations of our knowledge, but its appeal depends both on whether we can apprehend its force in spite of our intellectual scepticism, and whether we can face the radical questions with which it may confront us. Who, for example, can face the implications of what myths have to say to us about the Last Judgement, Heaven and Hell? Yet these are issues with which the Christian faith confronts us.

I think that we need to distinguish between these different ways in which language is used - between history, miracle and myth - if we are to grasp something of the concerns of the New Testament writers. And this is all the more necessary given the ways in which the uses of language overlap and blend with each other. Straightforward historical narrative (a small but essential part of the whole) occurs side by side with stories of miracles (and, of course, with other uses of language to which I do not refer), and all the writers write within an implicit (not always the same) metaphysical framework. To over-simplify leads to distortion. Bultmann, in his pioneering essay, 'New Testament and Mythology'[10], made no distinction between miracle-story and myth, rejected myth more or less on principle, and set out the debate on New Testament evidence in over-simplified terms. Those who wish to interpret the content of the New Testament as 'story' can be equally misleading. There is, indeed, a story running through the New Testament, however differently it is told by individual writers. There could hardly not be, given that it is told round the life and death of an individual. But the primary object is not to tell us a story but to face us with an encounter with a person who is at one and the same time like us and unlike us. He speaks to me through the imagination, certainly, but not only through the imagination, in the way a story would do, for he claims to show me more directly the world I live in and the way in which I should shape my life.

So when we speak of religion the investigation of how language is used doesn't lead to any simple solutions, but rather to a recognition of complexities and of the need to discriminate between the language games that are being played. I don't accept Wittgenstein's dictum that on what we do not know we should be silent. We speak as we can of what concerns us (as, I think, Wittgenstein came to recognize). We speak from within our own culture, with such understanding as we have of the language we are using, recognizing its limitations and the impossibilities into which it leads us. The important thing is to recognize where we are; what we have discovered about the uses of language; what has been said to us and what we ourselves want to say.

Wittgenstein's problem in the *Tractatus* was about the impossibility of speaking of what we have no words for. Religious language seeks to get over this by the use of metaphor. Religion has to use metaphor if it is to speak at all, for it involves speaking of what can be spoken of in order to evoke what can't. Perhaps the most important task for theology at the present time is to recognize the metaphorical nature of religious language and to explore what we have tried to express in using it. It would, I think, bring home to us the diversity and richness of religious language and our own participation in that diversity and that richness. It would bring home to us also more sharply the limitations of metaphor: the truth that we are attempting the impossible. But we must try to speak until we are forced to attempt the impossible. Speech has to fall silent. The question is how much you want and should try to say before you reach that point.

In an age of cultural flux such as ours the task of theology, it seems to me, is necessarily exploratory. It involves a constant tension between a need to draw on the riches of tradition and the sense that we have to understand it afresh, though not to reduce it. (I have seen references to the need to conserve the principle of richness in theology; to be cherished in the face of reductionist belief.) And this involves a clearer understanding of the different ways in which we use language when we speak of religion. I have suggested that the task of theology is to try to understand better the metaphors of religious experience and how we can accept them.

VII
The Justice of God

Beneath the use of words are the problems of substance - the problems which have drawn men to religion or have driven them away from it. Here again I want to speak of two which have especially concerned me.

The justice of God seems to me to be the central issue to

which those who are concerned with religion, whether positively or not, most often return in contemporary debate. It is prominent enough in the Old Testament (witness the questioning in so many of the Psalms and, above all in the Book of Job). But in our time it has come to change the agenda for theology. Instead of starting out from assumptions that we are concerned with man before God - man as created being, child of God, sinner redeemed by Christ, living the Christian life as best he can, and, in the end, facing judgement - we are concerned with the question whether it makes sense to speak of God in the universe into which our lot has been cast, amid the happenings that we see in history and in our contemporary life.

I find myself thinking of the well-known questions in a series of increasing inscrutability. What, first of all, of the mismatch between virtue and its reward; of the contrast between the innocent who suffer and the wicked who flourish like a green bay-tree. We cannot say, from the evidence of history, that justice is done in the world that we know, either to the individual or in the fulfilment of some larger purpose which will somehow reconcile the sufferer to his fate. Nothing, so Ivan Karamazov insisted, can compensate the sufferer for what he has suffered. The lives of most human beings have been (as we would judge) lives of want, hardship, danger and suffering; and what material benefits our world affords are unfairly distributed amongst the human race. We can argue that what people do to each other depends on their decisions; we cannot blame God for the sufferings of war, though many have blamed him for creating a world and a human race in which such sufferings can occur, and many people are concerned over our capacity to bring about suffering on a hitherto unimagined scale.

But beyond the evil and the suffering for which, it can be argued, human beings are responsible in their dealings with each other, there is the suffering which comes about from what are called natural causes: from the physical conditions of life on our planet which make it brief and precarious, and which produce the natural catastrophes for which human beings cannot be held responsible. We are thrown into the world, as Heidegger put it, and left to make what sense we can of it - of a world which, sooner or later, will come to an end, leaving not a wrack behind. We cannot get outside the world of experience which we explore, so as to be able to see it as a whole. We have to do the best we can within our human limitations.

I may tell myself that to speak in such terms is to put the worst case for the situation, the qualities and the prospects of mankind: to ignore all the evidence of wisdom, bravery and virtue which meant so much to Johnson[11]; or, indeed, of beauty and our celebration of it. The case will always be made for cherishing what we can perceive of these precious qualities, though they may seem rarer than the ruthless and predatory selfseeking, the cowardice and deceit which seem to me so much more prominent in the way of the world. But I cannot avoid the question what such qualities show us about the world in which we live.

It is argued by those who are sceptical of metaphysics (let alone theology) that to value beauty, truth and goodness is justifiable simply because this satisfies us by enlarging our capacity for living and by appealing to our sense of order (moral and aesthetic), without telling us anything about the implications of that satisfaction, since that would be to speak of what we cannot know. Any positive notion of values has to be described in such general and undefined Lawrentian terms as 'what makes for life'. The striving persists, it is argued, through changes of culture and custom, and through changes in what we value as the good, the true and the beautiful; the striving underlies what we have to regard as the varied and imperfect human realizations of these values. I do not see what kind of metaphysic might be offered in order to relate this striving to the order of the world of experience in which we live; but to deny any such order in principle is to deny any ultimate ground to our values. We create our values, we cannot appeal to any reality other than our own choices. I would feel forced to accept Sartre's view of man as 'a being which is compelled to decide the meaning of being within itself and everywhere outside it', and possesses a freedom which is 'the foundation of values while itself without foundation'. (BN 556,38) He was himself unable to offer guidance on that freedom until he came to identify human freedom generally with the social and political freedom which he claimed to find in Marxism.

So there are two related questions. One is whether the evidence of what makes for life is more convincing than the evidence of what seems to deny life. The other is what we can affirm as regards the order of things from such evidence as we seem to have of it. What indeed, must we affirm, for what is the significance of our values if they are no more than our own choice, or the choice of the class or group with which we may share them?

We press the question of the justice of God, and the order which we may or may not discern in it harder than our ancestors did for, although there is a tradition of questioning, which can lead to the massive confrontation of the Book of Job, they were more ready to accept the life that a God, whose existence wasn't questioned, allotted to them, in the faith that all would be fulfilled in the hereafter, and the tears would be wiped from every eye, or at least from the eyes of those whom the Lord accepted in his Last Judgment. Our ancestors, whose horizons of knowledge were so limited, had to recognize the limits of their world much earlier than we do, and to design ways of transcending their ignorance, so that they could speak of their concerns and, by speaking, give themselves a ground of faith by which they could live. I have to find such a ground, recognizing that I can prove nothing; that the evidence of experience is, at best, ambiguous; that I lack Job's instinctive belief in the God whom he found that he could not question; and cannot think in terms of such a speculative metaphysic as Hegel's, which makes claims for our understanding (actual and potential) of the world which few of us today find convincing.

Simone Weil thought that evil and suffering must somehow be comprehended within a total order which embraces the whole of God's creation. Suffering, she says, is at the root of knowledge (FLN 69). But it isn't to be explained. To try to find compensation or justfication for evil is just as harmful as to try to expose the heart of the mysteries on the plane of human intelligence. But to say that the world is not worth anything, that this life is of no value, and to give evil as the proof is absurd, for if these things are worthless, what does evil take from us? 'The extreme greatness of Christianity lies in the fact that it does not seek a supernatural explanation for suffering, but a supernatural use for it', (GG68,76,73). We are not to try to explain evil, but the fact that we cannot do so does not make a meaningless chaos of our world. It is, rather, the ultimate test of our values, which we may discover when we are afflicted with evil.

There is a resemblance here to what Bonhoeffer said from a different point of view. He, too, regards explanation as impossible ('At the limits it seems to me better to be silent and to leave the insoluble unsolved'. 'The transcendence of God has nothing to do with the transcendence of epistemology' 30.4.44). Both shared a keen sense of beauty; Bonhoeffer has a more positive attitude towards the created world as good, and doesn't share Simone Weil's basic renunciation of it; but both share an insistence on what Bonhoeffer expresses as 'participation in the suffering of God in worldly life'. And that participation can only be with the help of Jesus, who shows us the supernatural use for suffering of which she speaks. Can I speak in this way?

VIII
What can I know of Jesus?

My attitude to Christianity has to be shown in what I have to say about Jesus. Whatever my views on religion in general, on whether and how one can express a religious view of life in our present culture, on the possibility of finding a closer relationship between different religions, in the end what Christianity means to me will depend on what I want to say about the individual whose life and death led somehow to the formulation of a distinctive faith. To say this is not to evaluate Christianity in comparison with any other religion, or to say anything about other faiths that might emerge in future. It is simply to insist that our Christianity, or our rejection of Christianity is determined by what we make of this individual, what we believe that he shows us about life in the world and how we are to lead it, and about what this implies as regards his own relationship to God. All this has to do with what I call the logic of Christian belief; it says nothing about the substance of it. That depends on what knowledge we have of Jesus and how we interpret it.

What counts as knowledge here? There are, I think, two ways in which the question might be answered. One is in terms of historical evidence; the other is in terms of personal experience - the kind of experience that leads us to believe that we have been shown, uniquely through that experience, all-important truth about God and man and the relationship between them. The two kinds of knowledge have, of course, always existed throughout the history of Christianity, but the distinction between them has become much clearer and more emphatic with the development of more systematic critical study of the Biblical material in modern times. We distinguish more sharply than ever before between the Jesus of history and the Christ of faith. The central figure here for most of us is Bultmann, the New Testament scholar who found little left of the Jesus of history, but then challenged us to say whether or not we accepted the Christ of faith. I put beside this challenge the judgement that R.H. Lightfoot reaches at the end of *History and Interpretation in the Gospels.* He concludes that 'the form of the earthly, no less than of the heavenly Christ is for the most part hidden from us..... For probably we are at present as little prepared for the one as for the other'. The two kinds of knowledge are interwoven.

I am not concerned here to involve myself in the state or the themes of New Testament scholarship, but only to note the implications of the conclusion that the debate can never (in this life, at least) lead to definitive results. It shares this characteristic with historical studies generally, because of the limited evidence and the changing presuppositions with which the historians approach their task; but it shares that characteristic with peculiar intensity because of the importance of what depends on the conclusions, so that it has affected the objectivity of historians. The four evangelists write their Gospels in order to state a faith and a commitment.

Critical study tells us more about the origins and reliability of the evidence, about the relationship of different parts of it to each other, about the motives of the evangelists in using their material and the ways in which they use it. But, underlying all this critical investigation is the question why should I attempt it at all, and the problems with which my reply confronts me. Whom am I talking about?

To my mind (and this is, I think, to agree with Lightfoot's conclusion) we are talking about an earthly Jesus who lived a life inspired as no other person has been inspired by a love of God and of his fellow-men which determined all that he said or did. This is, for me, the only view of Jesus that justifies the question, in terms of an answer that gives point to the claims that Christians have made for him. To see him as another and lesser figure: as a political agitator, as the last in a line of Judaic prophets, as the high priest of an individual Jewish cult makes it a matter of historiography. Here we are concerned with something that has moved into another dimension. Not that other and lesser interpretations have not been offered to us, or have not influenced those who have believed in him. Jesus has been interpreted in many ways and used to justify many interests, but in the midst of them, mingled with them, often corrupted by them, it is the Jesus who has been held to show uniquely the love that gives all, that has sustained Christian faith, however Christians have witnessed to it. This is the Jesus to whom men and women return. He has been spoken of as the icon of love.

To speak in such terms is to reveal the impossibility of doing so. The claim had to be made, but to make it (and to draw out the implications) brings me up against the impossibility of our discovering adequate evidence. We have to do (in terms of human experience) with the story of a Jewish evangelist of the first century, born into a particular culture, living within the limitations of knowledge of his time. He is concerned primarily with a mission - the proclamation of

43

the Kingdom - and reveals no interest in other human concerns, political, social, or aesthetic. The material evidence is concentrated (as we might expect) on the events of his mission and, above all, on those which led up to his crucifixion. It is presented by the New Testament editors, each in his own individual way, to show us Jesus as he thought that we should see him; to offer us a portrait that expressed his own worship.

But what kind of portrait could we expect? How adequate an account of his life, ministry, Passion and Resurrection? All historical accounts have their limitations because of the incompleteness of the evidence and the interests and prejudices of the historian, but this is an account of unique events - if, indeed, they can adequately be described as events. What kind of account could we expect of so radically new a revelation of the possibilities of man and the purposes of God as these were claimed to be? Even with the retrospection after the Resurrection, could we expect those who lived with him to tell us a complete and convincing story of a unique life, such as they claimed his to be? And how could the purposes of God be shown within the compass of the earthly life of him of whom it was claimed that he had shown them? How could we even be shown what kind of lives we ought to lead, in terms of specific choices in specific situations: situations on which his own life could throw no direct light since he never experienced them. Most situations, in any case, confront us with a balance of choices, between the good and the better, the evil and the less evil: with a perhaps agonizing choice between what we would like to do and what seems practicable. We do the best we can, perhaps, within the limits of our judgement and our courage. We fail, repent our failures and fail again. And behind all this life of compromise there lurk the absolute demands of the Gospels. I can glimpse patterns of living which seem at least to come near to fulfilling those demands, but I am all too conscious of the force of Lightfoot's assertion that we are as little prepared for the earthly as for the heavenly Christ. What can we see - what could his disciples see of either?

All this can induce a sense of intellectual vertigo. For, if we can have no adequate story, to what can I hold? Or are we faced with a story that can't be told about a way of life that can't be realized? This, I find, is what I have to live with. The debate about Christ raises these questions. Somehow or other we have this notion of a person who lives out uniquely, in his own life, the two commandments to love God and our neighbour. However it came to us, whatever has happened to the story about it, it remains an unforgettable vision, for believers and perhaps for unbelievers also: a vision with which they have to come to terms.

Lightfoot concludes that we must accept it, though we cannot say much about it. He seems to echo Schweitzer's evocation (at the end of the *Quest of the historical Jesus*) of the compelling figure who calls to us. Bonhoeffer puts it more explicitly, 'If a man like Jesus lived, then and then only has human life sense'. (21.8.44.) Kierkegaard, however, rejects the historical debate altogether. Christianity is, he insists, the absolute, 'And so it must be represented, viz. in such a way as to make it appear madness in the eyes of the sensuous man'[12]. No proof is to be had from history, and it is blasphemous to suppose otherwise, for this is to judge Christ, who is himself the Examiner. 'No knowledge can have for its object the absurdity that the eternal is the historical. All religious situations are contemporary: we are always confronted in our actions by the eternal, and therefore it is not a question of knowledge but of faith and obedience[13]. Simone Weil's attitude was less clear-cut. For her Christ is 'the point of tangency between humanity and God': she speaks of Christ as 'a symbol, a metaphor' and of God as the supreme poet. (WG 22). But there was something unique which was communicated through an earthly life, and it led Simone Weil to search for analogies elsewhere in history to Christian experience, or to some kind of anticipation of it. 'Christ must have been fully present wherever there is affliction. Otherwise where would be the pity of God?' (FLN 91).

So I am left with a Christ of whom I can conceive no adequate, or even no coherent account being possible; who is both inside and outside history; who has nothing to say to me about the beauty of life; who cannot explain the cruelty, horror and pointlessness but who yet remains someone whom I can't forget; someone indispensable. Why? Does he show me a vision without which life is both poorer and incoherent? How do I claim truth for it?

IX
The Ultimate Paradox

I said at the outset that this was a personal document. I have referred to my own concerns and have tried to show where they have led me; though what I have said about them, however summarily, does refer, directly or indirectly, to many of the problems which preoccupy contemporary theologians and others who involve themselves in the debate about religion. The four topics to which I have referred have not, of course, been my sole concerns; but they have been those which have concerned me most and they seem to me fundamental.

Where has this exploration of the four themes got me? What I have said or implied has emphasized the difficulties which arise in holding to Christian faith; it hasn't done much to identify it. To remind myself of the paradoxes of the human situation is to remind myself of the limitations of human reasoning, and therefore of rational speech about our situation and (if we wish to speak of Him) about God and our relationship with Him. To identify the different ways in which we use language when we speak of religious concerns is to remind me (among other things) of the differences between the claims to truth of statements which have, at one time or another, been regarded as literally true. This has had deep effects on our interpretation of the Christian story. To consider the problem of divine justice, and how we are to think of the things that happen in our world which we find it hard to reconcile with the notion of such justice is to remind myself that we have no point of view outside or beyond our world which can reconcile what appears to me to be the irreconcilable. I have therefore to come to terms, somehow, with phenomena which I cannot explain within the limits (actual and potential) of human knowledge; which I cannot therefore relate explicitly to a Divine purpose which I cannot know; but which I cannot leave outside it. To consider what we know of the life of Christ is to remind myself of the limitations of that knowledge. It arises not merely from the questions of adequacy and reliability which are common to all historical material, together with those of the point of view, prejudice and purpose of the author. It arises, more fundamentally I think, because of the impossibility of our having an adequate account, from material assembled and written down by fallible, limited human beings, of the Person whom Christ has been claimed to be. And this, as Lightfoot has reminded us, is not merely a matter of knowledge but one of insight and response. I cannot respond, I fear, to the ultimate demands of the Christ who is shown, however imperfectly, in the New Testament.

I might respond to this catalogue of difficulties and impossibilities by simply accepting that they are insurmountable, and that I must resign myself to the conclusion that nothing more can be said. There could be no hope of any view of my world as a whole, whether in metaphysical, in religious or specifically in Christian terms, and the search for such a view would have to be regarded as defeated at the outset, whatever may have been gained from it in the past. I would have to recognize, of course, that whatever value I might hold to would have the status only of something that human beings, in the societies in which they have lived, have evolved in order to help them to confront their situation and to live together. Questions of ultimate value would be outside the possible agenda. It would take account of Christianity, perhaps, mainly in terms of its effect on the moulding of society (for good, but also for ill), and for its effects on human relationships and human self expression: as a social and cultural phenomenon rather than as a revelation of the truth about man's place and his destiny in God's world. There would be plenty to enjoy, more, perhaps, to question or lament, but nothing more than experience in its own terms; experience whose meaning could not be further explored.

In fact I do not wish to take up this positivistic attitude: to limit the significance of experience in this way. I must thereby expose myself to the challenge that I am indulging in wishful thinking: blinding myself to the ultimate meaninglessness to which we must resign ourselves in the absence of explanations. I must recognize that I do shrink from the notion of a meaningless universe; that I do feel the need of grasping at some meaning, however obscurely perceived, in my experience. This can only be a meaning that transcends that experience: I am confronted by the ultimate paradox of speaking of what I do not know: of defending the felt need to speak of what lies beyond reason, but not beyond reality.

X
The Theme of Transcendence

The theme of transcendence has come up more than once in this essay; the possibility of speaking of it underlies the whole of the contemporary debate about religion. The protagonists of 'Christianity without religion', based on a phrase of Bonhoeffer's, seemed to suggest that Christianity was something to be discovered simply in the common life, and that any notion of transcendence was no more than a will-o'-the-wisp. They found references in Bonhoeffer which appeared to support this view, but Bonhoeffer spoke also (in the outline of the book which he wanted to write) of Christ as 'the man who lived from the transcendent'. Christians (including liberation theologians) have been accused (though they reject the accusation) of substituting political objectives for the religious transcendence of which they cannot speak. And with what have Robinson and Cupitt been concerned but the sense of the transcendent, and whether or not we can or need to speak of it as an objective reality. It floats behind Wittgenstein's references to what can and cannot be said, and the 'wordless faith' which his friend Engelmann attributed to him. 'One thing needful' says Iris Murdoch, in a book which is concerned with metaphysics and morals rather than specifically with theology, 'is a refreshed conception of transcendence'. She does not, indeed, speak directly in theological terms ('We need a theology which can continue without God'), nor do others who have expressed a similar need[14].

The appeal to the transcendent may be, and often has been regarded as a kind of cop-out from the hard realities of the world that we know. It is defined in the *Fontana Dictionary of Modern Thought* as 'the state of being beyond the reach or apprehension of experience'. I would not wish to make so clear a distinction between our experience and what may lie beyond it. I believe that we have to recognize both the limitations of our experience and the human instinct not to be satisfied to do so. The co-existence of the two is a profound paradox of the human condition. The notion of the transcendent is important because it seems to point to a meaning in our fragmentary and unclear experience as a whole: a meaning which is suggested by our interpretation of that experience, but in no more than hints and guesses. We can experience the transcendent in various fields of experience: at the limits of knowledge, when we look beyond them for an order at which we can only guess; in the world of imaginative experience, or in moral life, with the ideas that we may glimpse beyond its compromises and surrenders. In all of them humanity seems to be going beyond the limits of what we experience in our normal living: to be following a human instinct not to resign ourselves to those limits, but to strive to surpass them. Religion is rooted in the transcendent, for it becomes relevant at the point when we recognize the limits of our situation, but refuse to accept that those limits are unsurpassable, in this world or beyond it. It springs from a desire to find a completeness, or at least the possibility of a completeness which will make sense of the world that we know: of showing clues, at least, to an order, and therefore to a meaning, that we cannot discern.

There is nothing here that I could hope to prove, for what can I prove in a world which is governed by paradox, and of which I can speak only in metaphors, which can only evoke but never describe. How can I satisfy the wish to speak of ultimate situations which lie beyond my knowledge? All these refer to the transcendent. So does the Christ who, for Bonhoeffer, (and for Kierkegaard and Simone Weil also) lives from the transcendent, the Christ whose radical challenge we do not in practice accept, in a maze of questions about the justice of God which we cannot answer.

The nearest I can come to a definition is to think in terms of what affirms life in the hints that I can perceive in the human quest for goodness and beauty, a quest which is also a quest for truth. It means saying Yes to what I cannot deny, and saying it in the face of all that may seem to deny it. It means recognizing the limitations of what we can say; embracing the inescapable paradoxes within which I live my life because they point to a truth which lies beyond logic.

This can all be said in non-Christian terms; many (including Nietzsche and Lawrence) have spoken of the affirmation of life but have denied that Christianity affirms life at all. How do I understand it in Christian terms?

It must centre, somehow, on the sense of an encounter with a man who is shown to me as one through whom goodness has come into the world as in no other person, however much we may know of it in other ways and through other beliefs. It came in the person of a man who was seen as a Jewish prophet and evangelist of the first century, whose mission appeared to fail with his death on the cross, but whose disciples were somehow led to make the claim that he continued to be present with them after his death and had therefore shown them that physical death was not the end. It was not simply the memory of Socrates being present in the minds of his friends, but a continued encounter with an individual which led his followers to speak of him in unique terms, as one whom God had exalted - as one who was, indeed, the Son of God. The imagery of metaphor, the language of myth came to surround the original experience. But something unique had happened.

To speak in this way can become an attempt to protect the private visions of the individual from critical scrutiny. It can be inspired by delusion. Nevertheless, to deny the possibility of such language is to reduce the totality of our lives by a dimension which makes us truly human. To speak of it may be to invite defeat, but it is the kind of defeat which justifies human existence and does honour to mankind. It hints at verities which we cannot express. The fact that we experience it is the only evidence that we can offer of its validity, as Anselm recognised when he formulated the Ontological Argument for the existence of God: not an argument, but an affirmation and an act of worship. Without the notion of the transcendent I cannot think in terms of the fulfilment of what it is to be a human being. Without that dimension my life (and my theology) becomes unrecognizably poorer. Somehow, in a world in which more and more emphasis comes to be placed on specific knowledge, I have to be able to recognize and affirm the reality of what lies beyond (or points to) knowledge; I have to rely on values which must show something beyond themselves. All this belongs inescapably to the religious attitude, in the broadest sense of the word. It has, somehow, to be rooted in the life that we know and yet to assume that human beings will look for a fulfilment that that life cannot give, and that we have to look for such fulfilment even if we cannot speak of it. But whatever experience of the transcendent we may have is not to be separated from the life that we live in the world.

XI
The Essential Dimension

What, then, do I want to say about the transcendent? What can I, what must I say about it? For me it is the notion on which any kind of religious faith is grounded: the dimension which gives meaning to that faith. Yet what I have said about it has been mainly negative, concerning human limitations, or our inability to speak of what we do not know. I have to recognize that the vision of a fulfilment of human nature can never be realized within human life as we know it, and that we know of no other. We are in the world; we cannot stand outside it and see it as a whole. We get, at best, hints of a life that is mostly beyond us; at worst (and this has been true of most human beings) we experience a life in which defeat, pain and misery have predominated. I cannot claim that the achievement of values (in so far as they are achievable) such as a juster society and a fairer and more responsible sharing of what we have can be a substitute for fulfilment sub specie aeternitatis, for these are proximate values achieved in varying measure in a constantly changing society. They occur in a different dimension from what Christians call the Kingdom, and agnostic humanists like Forster call the beloved republic. Nor can I look forward to the achievement of wisdom through sheer longevity, as Shaw did in *Back to Methuselah.* I think, rather, of Capek's (and Janacek's) insistence, in *The Makropoulos Case,* that our lives have meaning only as mortal lives; indefinite continuance would deprive them of that meaning.

In this situation I want to speak of the transcendent not by putting it beyond apprehension, by segregating it from our day-to-day experience of life, but by starting from what we must recognize man to be: neither an idol-worshipper nor a being on the way to discover everything there is to be known, but, in Nietzsche's words, 'the weakest, cleverest being', surrounded by a universe in whose resources he can find strength. His instinct (that of Western man at least) is to look beyond his situation; to master it; to discover what there is to be known. Yet he remains surrounded by mystery, in a universe whose limits he cannot know and which (as Kant insisted) he can only perceive within the framework of time and space within which his perceptions are enclosed, haunted (if he has the sensitivity to perceive them) by intimations of meaning and perhaps of human destiny, which can never be proved.

In this situation the notion of the transcendent seems to me to be indispensable, for we do, in fact, strive to transcend what we know of our world. We ought not, however, to think in terms of transcendence as somehow separate from the world of our normal experience; it is either rooted in it or it has no roots at all. It is, I maintain, an essential dimension of human experience, without which that experience is incomplete and therefore stunted. Our contemporary problem, however, is to say or at least to hint at what lies beyond speech. That problem has always been with us; it is peculiarly acute in an age in which our criteria of what counts as knowledge are particularly stringent and our discrimination between the uses of language is perhaps more sensitive than ever before, so that we are more conscious than ever of what is description or explanation and what serves other purposes.

Most English-speaking philosophers used recently, as is well known, to hold that knowledge was of two kinds: that which was expressed in the language of reasoning (pre-eminently of logic and mathematics) and statements of fact which could in some sense be verified - though the argument about what counted as verification became increasingly involved. I prefer to think of the language in which we speak of our experience (as distinct from the logical analysis which explains its own terms) as a kind of spectrum, ranging from statements which can be subjected to verification (however problematic that notion may have become) to what I can only describe as vague hints at the horizon of that experience, stretching out into what cannot be said but (in Wittgenstein's term) only shown, or to which we can only gesture. If I want to speak of the human situation what I say has to be rooted in it but must recognize the instinct to look beyond the limitations to the point at which we cease to know, and can only try to reconcile ourselves to our ignorance, or to take up some other attitude to that ignorance.

XII
Living with the paradoxes

It is within this perspective that I have to speak of the four themes that have especially pre-occupied me, and first of all of the problem of paradox, since this seems to me characteristic of the human situation. I have quoted Simone Weil's paradoxical statement that we have to elucidate the way contradictories have of being true (GG92). She develops the thought elsewhere, and makes her own attitude clear.

There are problems that the reason cannot solve; here certain contradictions are not errors 'but doors leading to the transcendent, doors on which we must redouble our knocking, because in the end they will open' (FLN269). 'The intelligence remains absolutely faithful to itself in recognizing the existence in the soul of a faculty superior to itself, which leads thought above it. This faculty is supernatural love. The willing subordination of all the natural faculties of the soul to supernatural love is faith'. She uses, astonishingly (since there is no reason to suppose that she knew of him), the same image as Wittgenstein, who saw the task of philosophy as showing the fly the way out of the flybottle (PI.1,309). She insisted that 'We are like flies stuck at the bottom of a bottle, drawn by the light and incapable of getting to it. Yet, rather be stuck at the bottom of the bottle for all eternity than turn away one instant from the light' (FLN292).

Simone Weil speaks as an intellectual who neither asserts that the intellect can solve all the problems nor resigns herself to its limitations. She insists on a reality which transcends the intellect. It may sound like something apprehensible through mystical experience, but it is not limited to those who have such experience: it is an attitude of mind - a basis of faith which all of us, in her view, need to share. It underlies everything that she has to say. She writes, however, as one who has had the experience that enables her to perceive and to articulate insights which most of us, including myself, have not shared, but can, perhaps, only recognize when she expresses them. We can all recognize the inescapability of the paradoxes, but her experience of what this leads her to is her own; it is for us individually to consider whether and how we share it.

There are, I think, theoretically three different ways in which we might confront the world of paradox in which we live. One would be to resolve the paradoxes intellectually, which I find impossible. The second is to resolve them by bringing in a supra-rational faculty to which the reason is subordinate. This may be interpreted as mysticism inspired by love. It is Simone Weil's way. I cannot speak directly of this way (if, indeed, it is to be spoken of); I lack the experience which might enable me to do so. This brings me to the third way - the humbler way of considering how, since we cannot resolve them, we live with the paradoxes which are inherent in our experience.

I find that I have, somehow, to live with the paradoxes, since I can neither ignore them nor resolve them; and this means sometimes emphasizing one side of a paradox and overlooking the other. Thus, if I have to reach a decision, I shall emphasize my own free will, though I may try, with such sincerity as I can achieve, to justify my decision as the will of God. Similarly I shall speak sometimes of the one and sometimes of the other of the paradoxical Persons of the Trinity. I have to do this, in practice, because my activities and concerns, and the parts that I play in the situations in which I find myself are multifarious, and involve different sides of my personality and my relationships, active and passive. I cannot command a unified view either of that personality or of the universe in which I exist. The paradoxes of life are a constant reminder of this situation. In practice I lean now to one side of a paradox, now to another.

This is all very unsatisfactory for the person who wishes for a comprehensive, rational view of the world and of man's place in it, but I do not see how the conclusion is to be avoided. It means that I have to see the implications of this situation; they all have to do, one way and another, with a recognition of human limitations. We never see situations as wholes. But even the most prosaic exploration of paradox cannot stop there; the implications are too challenging for that. Either the paradoxes show us a world that is incoherent, and therefore absurd, or, as Simone Weil insisted, they point, however bafflingly, to an order that reason, however far it can take us, cannot show us. I cannot speak, as she does, of supernatural love. I can recognize that, if I consider my experience as a whole, I need both sides of each genuine paradox at different times. I must use my reason as far as it will take me, but my life as a whole is not to be described in terms that the reason can comprehend, if it is to be spoken of at all. I have to decide whether I regard this situation with disgust, with resignation, with perplexity or with awe. The last of these attitudes depends on some notion of the (indefinable) wholeness of our experience, to which I want to hold. But I have to face the question whether I am contemplating a mystery or indulging in a comforting illusion.

XIII
Religious Language and its Transcendence

The study of religious language which has taken place in our time seems to me to have made a lasting change in the ways in which we understand what we are doing when we use it. It isn't, of course, a new concern; it has no doubt existed ever since we have used religious language. Nor is it, on the other hand, a collection of specialized studies which can be isolated from the rest of our contemporary intellectual life. They are a part of it - part of the systematic enquiry which is characteristic of it. They have changed irreversibly our understanding of religious language and of what we are doing when we use it, in one or other of its forms. It is, moreover, (however much we may owe to those who have gone before us) our enquiry - our investigation, whose implications we have to recognize. The important thing, it seems to me, is that we should see the complexities of the situation and the nature of its implications. How does this bring in the notion of the transcendent?

The significance of the transcendent, I have suggested, is that it expresses a desire to say what cannot be said. In the present context this shows itself most strikingly in the use of myth. We tell ourselves stories in order to round out what we know about our place in the world and our destiny. We cease to refer to them as we replace them with empirical knowledge, but some, I have suggested, we cannot deal with in this way, since they refer to events which lie beyond the limits of the knowledge that we can hope to acquire. The use of metaphor may seem a less obvious reference to the transcendent, but it seems to me no less valid, since we are admitting, by implication, that we cannot speak of something directly and must represent it as something else (not even, as in the use of simile, as *like* something else). The image (which is recognized as such) replaces direct speech in religious language, mostly because we feel that what we want to say transcends our ability to say it. Most religious experience, I have suggested, is expressed in the language of metaphor. Compared with the complexities of myth and metaphor the problems raised by miracle stories are relatively straightforward, however insoluble they may prove to be. From one point of view they are problems of evidence, or the lack of it. From another (more fundamental) one they centre on the question why the stories should have been told at all. All three of these forms of religious language seem to me to belong to that large class of words whose meaning according to Wittgenstein, is to be found in their use (PI.I,43).

What use, then, do I wish to make of these forms of language? What use do I find that I can make of them? I have suggested that we can see what we are doing more clearly than ever before; we can see more clearly the differences between them. And there can be no going back in the search for truth of which these studies are a part, whatever the corrigible mistakes we make and the false trails down which we may stray. The study of the language in which we speak of religion is, after all, the study of what the language expresses and, ultimately, of its claim to truth.

That study may seem to have produced, so far, mainly negative results. I cannot share the unquestioning acceptance as literal truth of the stories that we have inherited. And the formulae of Christian theology are a perpetual reminder of the impossibility of theological explanation. Many of us have been forced into a kind of minimalism which makes of Christianity a kind of moral doctrine which can give no offence to men of good will. But it does so at the cost of any distinctive body of beliefs.

This seems to me profoundly inadequate. It implies that any such distinctive body of beliefs has become obsolete: the product of our ignorance and naivety, even though valuable moral insights may have been communicated through it, together with a less desirable heritage of beliefs and practices. I do not believe that we can cut ourselves off so easily from our past, or that we should wish to do so. There needs to be a tension between past and present; between what we have inherited and the use that we need to make of it; between what we receive and what we pass on.

We need a clearer understanding of the different but related language games that we play, what uses they serve and how we ourselves use them; what kinds of stories and, more broadly, what kinds of metaphor we use and how they work. These questions open up the whole complex field of the study of religious language though I want (and am competent) to say only something by way or orientation - my own.

Although our intellectual world has changed profoundly and, so far as I can see, irreversibly, our position as limited creatures living in a world which we cannot know as a whole has not. The myths - or some of them - may still speak to us, though we can only try to understand how they speak and how we are to interpret it. We use metaphors (and especially the metaphors of religion) to evoke what we cannot describe, because we are not content to limit ourselves to what we can describe.

The primary need seems to me to be to speak in good faith: to speak of what I need to speak of and to recognize as clearly as I can what I am doing when I speak: what function the words perform. I have, above all, to recognize whether I need to speak the language of religion which reconciles me to my world, and the language through which is communicated the unique Christian vision of that reconciliation. I need to see whether and to what extent the language of the past is still valid for me, and whether I need to re-interpret it, to look for a new currency, or even to decide that I enter an area in which the currency of speech loses its validity; and what, in this situation, is the meaning and relevance of transcendence. But the notion of transcendence only becomes relevant when you have examined the uses of the language that, you may think, needs to be transcended if you are to express your total experience. We can only speak profitably of transcendence when we see the nature and limits of the experience to be transcended.

XIV
Suffering and Faith

I turn now to the two questions of substance which have especially concerned me. What can I, what dare I say about what I can make of the justice of God, that greatest of all religious questions - or, rather, that complex of questions, ranging from the fates of individuals to the problem of order in a universe which our knowledge can never comprehend? Yet I have to take a stance on these unanswerable questions, for my attitude to life will depend on how I answer them. For I have no answer to Ivan Karamazov, as I have none to Voltaire on the Lisbon earthquake - none, at least within the language-game that they are playing, which depends on factual knowledge and powers of prediction that none of us possesses. I have to speak as a relatively sophisticated Western person who has led a relatively sheltered life, spared the extremities of personal suffering that have afflicted so many in our time, with no great share of the cosmic wonder which has inspired men and women to worship a Creator God, and which moved Kant to link morals and metaphysics in his affirmation of faith in the starry heavens above and the moral law within. What, then, can I say?

What I do say, as the foundation of all else, is that in practice we do not despair, even in the exploration of a world we hold to be chaotic or absurd. We cannot and do not live without hope, even if it is the hope of Nirvana - paradoxical though that may sound. We cannot resign ourselves to chaos, for the very proclamation of chaos demands order in our own thought and in the thought of anyone who may hear us; the very denial of values is impossible without some notion of value, as Simone Weil (p.42, above) has reminded us. She insists, austerely, that we can discover our values only when we are afflicted by suffering. She has no doubt that they are there to be discovered, if we are not overcome by the affliction.

It is this insistence (even if it is no more than instinctive) on the indispensability of the notions of order and value that asserts itself even in the contemplation of despair, in the portrayal of tragedy and the expression of a tragic view of life. Art, we may say, imposes its own order on the chaos that underlies tragedy. I have to face the challenge of Lear, as of the two who wait for Godot. I feel for them, I hope, as my fellow-men, but the very contemplation of their situation imposes a shape on it which is not (cannot be) chaos. This is the paradox of tragedy: a paradox with which we have been struggling ever since the days of Aristotle. We contemplate the dissolution of order and the apparent defeat of value and find the experience a rewarding one. You may say that it is salutary for us to face our human situation, and that we come to see it through the experience of tragedy, but the truth lies deeper than this. The fact that the experience of tragedy affirms order and value, even though they are shown as disrupted and overcome, reveals something fundamental in human nature: an appeal to order - even when we contemplate chaos.

In one sense, as I need not repeat, we cannot transcend experience, for we live within human limits. In another sense we cannot avoid it, for our instinct as human beings is to look beyond those limits and to make claims for an order that is beyond our knowledge, and for a sense of value that is beyond our capacity to achieve. We cherish a wish for fulfilment which we cannot see ourselves achieving. This is the situation to which I find the notion of transcendence relevant, and the way in which (in this context) I think that it must and can be spoken of.

But if the instinct towards the transcendent is no delusion in what sense is it justified? How is it fulfilled? It isn't surprising that, in our age, most of us find descriptions of fulfilment unconvincing, and that we look for justification in the very experience of suffering.

We think, like Moltmann[15] (and, I have suggested, like Simone Weil and Bonhoeffer in their different ways) in terms of the God who suffers rather than of the God who creates, rules and judges, and this has led to some penetrating exploration of the meaning of suffering. But suffering cannot be justified simply in terms of itself. Crucifixion must be followed by resurrection if we are to have hope - even a hope that we cannot express. 'Only the suffering God can help', said Bonhoeffer, but the saying, however moving and necessary, isn't enough. We cannot be left with a God who can only apologize to His creation[16]. We need Bonhoeffer's vision of a God who suffers, and at the same time is revealed in that creation.

In this situation I find that all that I have to hold to is a belief in the transcendent quality of love - the love of which St. Paul speaks in thirteenth Corinthians: the love that never ends. I cannot base that belief on an expectation that I shall see the injustices, the disasters, the end of life as we know it overcome in a way that is comprehensible within my present experience and my or anyone else's power of prediction. I can only hold on to it because of a conviction that this is the way of human fulfilment, however much may seem to make against it. And because this is so it must be reflected in what I can affirm in the universe in which I have been placed. It is not merely an expression of my own feelings; it has to do with the order of things. Whatever I make of Dante's imagery I can only echo his ultimate affirmation of the love that moves the sun and the other stars. It can, of course, only be made in faith: in response to an instinct which one cannot deny.

It can be said of such an attitude that it is based on human aspirations and longings, and of a more benign view of our place in the universe than the evidence justifies. I can only reply that without such a conviction there is no making sense of our world, whatever the unanswerable questions about God with which it leaves me, ('Though he slay me, yet will I trust in him'), even though I have no language in which I could express how that trust is justified. It can and must also be said that we all have to ask ourselves whether we live by such faith. For who are we to say, any more than Job could say (if we disregard the consolatory ending of the book, added by a later hand) how such faith is to be fulfilled? Like most of us, I suspect, I find myself living in a tension between the conviction that I must trust and a questioning as to how such trust can be justified. This is, after all, characteristic of the ambiguities of our human situation.

XV
Resurrection and Faith

The vision, the challenge are concentrated for me (and surely for all Christians) on the figure of Christ, since for them the meaning of suffering is uniquely explored in the Christian revelation. We are offered what Simone Weil called a supernatural use for suffering, rather than a supernatural explanation of it. Beneath all the debate as to how we are to interpret the diverse material in the New Testament, what kind of whole we can make of it, who Jesus was and what he communicated before his death and afterwards lies the conviction that through him we know God as we should not otherwise have known Him: known Him through the acceptance of suffering by Christ. He accepts that suffering as showing the will of God, but not (in his lifetime) how it does so. The faith of Christians, however, is that we are shown this in the Resurrection which, if it is to have the significance that Christians claim for it, has to be seen as an act of God which shows us Christ in a unique relationship to Him.

All this, it seems to me, belongs to what I have called the logic of Christian belief. But it isn't a logic whose postulates can be demonstrated, nor can its imagery ('Son', 'Father') be more than metaphorical: evocative, but hardly to be described as analogous. I can say no more than that, in the Passion and what followed, something occurred which convinced his followers (those who continued to follow him) of a unique relationship with God for which the Church has, since then, been offering forms of expression, though all such forms must be inadequate. The Christian revelation rules out from the outset any comprehensive understanding of it, for, if Jesus was all that they claimed him to be, how could we look for such an understanding? I cannot envisage either a comprehensive account of what happened or an adequate explanation of what it meant. I can say no more than that Christians inherit the belief that, through Christ, they experience a new relationship with God. Christ has become the icon of love. It shows them

God in spite of all the pain and suffering that they do not understand. How this relates to other showings of God in other religions is a matter to be explored. On the one hand Christians have to insist on the uniqueness of the Christian revelation. (There haven't been two such occurrences in human experience.) On the other hand there is, we must recognize, no limit to the ways in which God may reveal himself, if we think that there is a God who does so. We must be ready to listen to what other religions have to say about God, in his presence and his absence, while insisting that the Christian revelation has its own identity in the story of religious experience - an identity that can only be shown, not asserted.

What I have said implies that, whatever researches we may be driven to do into the origins of Christian belief and witness, in its history, and into ways of expressing it in words, it draws its strength from the acceptance of a mystery. I can only think this justified (since the truth of the mystery cannot be demonstrated) if I am convinced that it shows me something about the order of the world and of my place in it and that of my fellow human beings that I would not otherwise have known: something of value; something all-important though I can have no more than intimations of what that something is.

XVI
Christian Humanism

I said at the beginning of this essay that it was a personal document. I have emphasized throughout that I was concerned to find the kind of theology I need in order to understand in some degree where I stand. My choice of themes may be questioned by anyone who does not share my own concerns; all that I can say is that they seem to me to be recognizably important. Indeed they seem to me inescapable if one is to think theologically at all. They have, at any rate, concerned me in this way.

On the other hand I have, you may feel, said little or nothing about so many of the main traditional themes of Christian experience and Christian theology - about God as

Creator, Provider, and Judge, or about man as a fallen creature, redeemed by the grace of God shown in Christ. What I have said positively about God has, moreover, been related much more to the Son than the Father. But the themes with which theology needs to concern itself vary, since theology must address itself to the needs and concerns of the time. We may find it hard to speak with conviction of God the Creator if we are perplexed by the apparent ambiguities in his creation; or of a law-giver in a universe in which we find it difficult to discern order; or to speak of man as sinner when we are more concerned with finding a meaning in human experience and establishing human identity. I have been concerned with questions like these. They seem to me to be those with which we find ourselves confronted. We have to discern afresh the relevance of the Christian revelation to them.

In the end the way to God must lie, for me, through Christ who has become, in Christian tradition, the icon of God, who is love. He shows me, however fragmentarily through the limited and imperfect testimonies of different witnesses, the image of a man whose life was given to the love of God and of his fellow human beings. And because Christians have been brave enough to identify him with God, they claim to see, behind the vision of the man they show us, the God who is Creator and Father. Kierkegaard saw him as the absolute, Simone Weil as 'a symbol, a metaphor'; Bonhoeffer, on the other hand, insists that if Jesus had not lived our lives would (whatever the virtues of other men) have been senseless. So here again I find myself confronted with paradoxical opposites. I have to recognize the impossibility of a biographical portrait, but, at the same time, that the evidence relates to a man who lived a life on earth. I find a certain vacuity in the notion of a Christ who has no roots in life as we know it. So here again I find myself driven back into the recognition of a mystery that I cannot hope to understand. It is a miracle that we know only through the witness of the disciples. The miracle is not what happened (which we cannot know) but that it did happen. Faith in Christ is founded on a miracle and a mystery which cannot (by definition) be explained.

Such a faith must reconcile me somehow to what I must call the ambiguities of creation, and to the unanswered questions about the visible evidence of the justice and injustice of God. In Christ I am exposed to the full, the uncompromising force of love and am challenged to react to it. I have to recognize the gap between the love that challenges me and whatever love I feel and show: between the challenge and its distorting, its muting, its corruption. I may express what I have to say about all this in whatever language and imagery seems relevant to the situation, if I find it possible to speak at all. I have suggested that the language can only be the language of metaphor; what matters is what the metaphors evoke.

I said something earlier in this essay about the theology that I need, and about the assumptions which I take to underlie it: the possibility of communication, and therefore of intellectual order; the assumption that we live in a world in which, for all our differences, we share a quest for values, and the assumption that I need a theology which reconciles me to life. I have to make these assumptions without being able to prove them, but rather because I do not find it possible to live without them. I have to reconcile these general, humanistic assumptions with the particular event of the Christian revelation - with what is shown to me in a particular individual.

What I need is a kind of Christian humanism. I speak of humanism in order to imply what I have in mind as regards human limitations, human failings and human possibilities. Because we are human beings we remain surrounded by mysteries that we cannot fathom. Because we are human beings we have the need to explore the possibilities of our lives, to go beyond what we are, to live by a faith in life which inspires such exploration. But the notion of Christian humanism implies also that we see how far we fall short of the Christian vision of love and, at the same time, how much we depend on a grace of which, perhaps, we cannot speak. For although I hold to the eternal verities that give meaning to life, only the love that gives itself can be the supreme virtue - what

Bonhoeffer called the *cantus firmus* round which the polyphony of life weaves a counterpoint (20.5.44). This leads me on to the notion of a hierarchy of values, in which the demand of love becomes more insistent the more nearly you approach the Kingdom, and you must give up the lesser for the greater. But only if you think it genuinely greater.

I find myself held by this notion of Christian humanism because it seems to me the most satisfying Christian theology: the one that does most justice to life as I have experienced it, and because it speaks a language which seems to me more appropriate to our sceptical, questioning, bewildered age than one which is shaped by the traditional unquestioning emphasis on sin and redemption. (Bonhoeffer again: Jesus certainly speaks to sinners but 'he doesn't make everyone first a sinner. He called them away from their sins, not into their sins' (30.6.44). Jesus offers a love without conditions and leaves us to respond as we will to it. And the possibilities are multifarious. They may range from 'Come, Lord Jesus', through 'Depart from me for I am a sinful man, 0 Lord' to indifference or rejection. But any positive reaction springs from an act of faith for which I can offer no unquestionable evidence and which leaves me with unanswerable questions. I can do no more at best than hold to the notions of truth, value and above all, of love in the face of doubt and despair. It has, moreover, to recognize the uniqueness of Christ, however this may be expressed, and all the problems of the scandal of particularity. (Why should it be manifested at that time in that place? How is the uniqueness of Christian revelation to be reconciled with the generalities of theism?)

So I find myself, unsurprisingly, welcoming Bonhoeffer's demand that we should work out our theology afresh: that we should look again at how we are to see unchanging truth in a changing situation, how we should speak of it and how much we can say at all. (Bonhoeffer thought that we needed 'a new language, perhaps quite unreligious, but liberating and redeeming like the language of Jesus'[17]. Many of us (Christians and others) would no doubt sympathize with the demand for the reworking of theology, though we might differ in our ideas as to how it should be met.

It needs to start, for me, from values that cannot be denied: from the love that makes for life; from what we can glimpse even fitfully and dimly; from what human beings can cherish and aspire to, though we cannot imagine how the Kingdom can be achieved by human nature as we know it. I have to live with the mystery of that situation. But I can feel the need to cherish the good as the ground of our being, rather than to resign ourselves to the predominance of evil; to see the Kingdom before I seek to understand the significance of the Fall. I have to hold to such assumptions in order to function as a human being at all, however defectively and uncomprehendingly. And it is on these assumptions of order and value, however I may express them, that I have to found whatever theology can help me.

The kind of theology that is likely to be done nowadays by people who are conscious of our modern Western situation should show, I suggest, a tension between what we have inherited from the Christian tradition and the exploration in which those who seek to understand Christian experience and Christian faith must necessarily engage in a time such as ours, when the landscape of knowledge and our understanding of people is changing so rapidly. We inherit a tradition of faith, however imperfect it may be, and however imperfectly we may understand it. We inherit it through the shared tradition of experience and imagination, for in this field there is nothing decisive that we can call knowledge. We share with our forbears imaginative insights rather than demonstrable truths. We can and must speak of a faith that we share with our forefathers. We can only speak of it as we can, and what matters most we may find to be beyond speech.

XVII
Truth and Life

How can I speak of truth in this context in the face of the insoluble paradoxes with which religious language confronts us and the varied games that we are playing when we use it? At every turn I find myself recognizing that we are surrounded by mysteries; that we want to say more than can be said; that we can neither answer the questions nor content ourselves with not asking them. In the present situation Christians can have neither an explicit metaphysic nor an adequate account of the Christian revelation, and, if either were possible, we should still have the problem of reconciling the generalities of the former with the particularities of the latter. And, of course, whatever account we might give must reconcile us to the injustice, the pain and the transience of the world that we know. What truth can I claim for the Christian humanism towards which I want to look? For nothing can be proved beyond doubt, and there will always be the voice saying 'You are trying to devise something that will hide the abyss of meaninglessness from you'.

I don't want, in this situation, to play a game of beggar-my-neighbour against the atheist or the agnostic: to argue that, whatever my problems, he can offer no metaphysic as a ground to his exploration of the world and to the values to which he holds. That, after all, is his own affair, and I must leave him to deal with the questions that he has to face. He may, indeed, not wish to concern himself with them, or wish (if he thinks of himself as a man come of age) to deny that they exist. I have, rather, to say what I can think of as truth and how I can say it. This means that, since our discoveries about the world and ourselves have revealed to us the limitations of our knowledge, and since the language of religion does not overcome those limitations, I have to think in terms, not of what can be proved but of what makes for life. I have to base the notion of truth not on an epistemology which we cannot have, but on whatever interpretation of values appears to offer us some notion of human fulfilment. And, having pointed as best I can to show what this means, I must leave it to work, if it does, for the Other with whom I am trying to communicate.

What I am suggesting is that we need somehow to ground the notions of order and of value without which we cannot live, even though we may deny them, even though we have no explicit view of the world, no metaphysic to which we can relate them. They must speak for themselves, as affirming life;

or, rather, the instinct to find them, in and beyond the lives that we live, must speak for itself. I find this appropriate for several reasons. It reminds me of the unsurpassable limitations on human knowledge, while recognizing our need to discover as much as we can. It emphasizes the need to hold to the search for order and value in human life whether or not we can speak of them. It recognizes the mixture of simplicity and complexity in human experience, which should prevent us from identifying knowledge with wisdom, and giving keys to the learned which are not given to the rest of mankind. The humility which such insight may engender can also be a counter to the pessimism and cynicism to which our unsatisfied pursuit of knowledge and value might tempt us. Christian humanism claims to provide a ground, even if an inexplicit ground, which justifies our faith in human aspirations.

It has to do this in two ways, which theologians have, in the past, not found it easy to relate to each other. One is the uniqueness of what is shown to us in Christ. The other is the uniqueness of the contribution that Christian humanism can make to our experience of the wholeness of life. The first brings me back to the extraordinariness of the phenomenon of Christ - in what we know of him, leaving aside what we don't: the astonishing fact that this notion of a human being who dedicated himself without reserve to loving and serving God and his fellow-men should have sprung from the life and death of someone whom his contemporaries encountered as a Palestinian holy man of the first century, and should have given rise to the interpretation of him (in the different ways that the New Testament shows us) as having an unique relationship to God, indeed, of being himself God as well as man. Somehow or other this happened, whatever the historical details, whatever the impossibility of an adequate account of the life, death and resurrection. I have to let the life, death and resurrection speak to me as I can hear them - as Christians have always had to do.

Does such listening increase, uniquely, whatever sense I may have of the wholeness of life and of us human beings within it? It is on such a claim that the notion of Christian humanism rests. There is a long tradition of turning away from the life of the present world ('The world is very evil', said Saint Bernard of Cluny) which critics like Nietzsche have seized on in order to condemn Christianity as a rejection of life. The only answer to such a challenge, I think, is to show that the vision that we have of Christ shows the supreme value of love, which somehow transcends whatever we can discern of order and value in the life that we know, so that Dante could sum up the *Commedia* by speaking of love that moves the sun and the other stars. It is the transcendence of love in which all things are contained, and which alone can bring together humanism, with its values and its limitations, and the unique revelation that we are offered in Christ. It is (to vary the image) a question of seeing humanism in perspective, and therefore of finding a ground for it.

Such an approach has itself to be seen in perspective with the interpretations of Christianity which have emphasized, by contrast, either the corruption of mankind, which can only be redeemed by divine grace, or the human suffering for which we must look for compensation in a future life. I think that we must recognize that we need different theologies for different cultures, different situations, different needs. If we see Christ as the icon of love we have to see him from where we are, and we shall see him in different ways. This, I suggest, helps us to recognize the limitations (and, indeed, the defects) of all theologies. The important thing is that the essential vision (however it may have come to us) should not be lost: should continue to inform our experience and to challenge what we make of it.

Christian humanism is not, essentially, a complacent or comfortable view of life (though it can be made into one); there are too many problems for that. I have sometimes felt tempted to describe it as a theology of 'In spite of . . '. There are so many unanswered questions, there is so much unexplained suffering and injustice, so much choice between evils, so much evidence which seems to make against any notion that God's in his heaven and all's right with the world.

I think that, in the West, we are going through a crisis of

understanding which is also a crisis of culture, and a crisis of hope. We cannot predict the future; we can only recognize that we shall not return to the past. We may not even know for what we should hope.

> I said to my soul, be still and wait without hope
> For hope would be hope for the wrong thing[18].

What claim can Christianity make to speak truth in this situation?

The only test that I can suggest is whether or not it makes a distinctive difference in the perspective in which I see myself and my fellow human beings, in our possibilities and our achievements, our limitations and our corruptions; and whether or not it makes it more possible to speak something that we find to be a distinctive word of truth, not necessarily on what we see (which may be what non-Christians see also) but on the perspective in which we see our situation: something that is true to us as human beings and to the life in which we stand.

I said at the outset that this would be a personal document, with all the limitations that this implies. I said also that it wouldn't be a statement of personal faith with the kind of resonance that such a statement possesses. It is, rather, a brief record of an encounter with certain problems which have especially concerned me in trying to define my own faith, and with certain individuals whose thought I have found especially significant in doing so. I have been concerned with the debate on faith, rather than with themes of devotion or of action.

What I have said remains shot through and surrounded with questions, as any contribution to this debate must be. The questions remain. I cannot dismiss them. I have to recognize that the problems are insoluble, and I have to ask myself, at times of depression and scepticism, whether it even makes sense to concern oneself with insoluble problems. But the questions do not go away; and I would maintain that to ignore them, if we are aware of them, is to diminish one's stature as a human being. Conversely, I find myself maintaining that to ask the questions presupposes a faith that it does make sense to do so; that it expresses a striving that

71

makes us human beings; that we are not mocked (or do not mislead ourselves) in our striving for fulfilment. I have to hold such convictions by faith, without being able to prove them, as the way to truth and life, though we cannot see the end of it - if such a notion can have meaning. It is, in the end, faith in our human kind and therefore in the God who created us.

What I have offered in this essay may expose me in particular to two related criticisms. The first is that my own answer to Bonhoeffer's question doesn't offer a clear enough statement either of what is Christianity or who is Christ for us today. It might even lead to the criticism that such answer as I have tried to give isn't a truly Christian one. The second, related criticism is that it isn't the kind of answer that is likely to convey anything to the sceptic, for it offers neither unquestioning commitment nor conclusive reasoning.

One must speak as one can, but there is perhaps more to be said. I hope to have shown that whatever faith I have derives from a notion of a God who orders our world and from an unique revelation which has been vouchsafed to us in Christ, though I cannot speak clearly of either, or bring the two comprehensively together. But at this point I need to remind myself of the limitations of our humanity, and therefore of our understanding. The whole thrust of what I have said has been to suggest that, while we must answer whatever questions we can, in the end we are confronted with mysteries rather than questions - mysteries which surround our knowledge and our understanding, and that, in our complex and sophisticated world, we are more than ever conscious of this. We need a certain humility, rather than either overweening self-confidence or resigned scepticism: the humility which can only come of a religious outlook, which I would define as feeling able to trust although you cannot see.

It is, I suggest, the kind of humility that we need especially in an age of encounter between faiths and cultures. A sense of our limitations in the face of mystery may make us more open to respect experience to which we have no claim and interpretations of it which are not our own; more able to affirm the identity of our own faith, while recognizing those of others, which are rooted in other cultures and other experience. The language of Jesus is unique, but Christian experience is part of the experience of mankind. It is an experience which becomes harder and harder to define. We may come to see ourselves either as creatures of God, affirming a life that transcends our comprehension or as (in Nietzsche's terms), the weakest and cleverest of beings, witnesses to our own abilities but to nothing more.

Notes

1.   There have been various editions of the *Letters and Papers from Prison*. I have therefore thought it best to refer to individual letters by date and to other writings in the LPP individually.   In view of the frequency of references I have thought it convenient to refer to them in the text rather than as separate notes.

2.   *New Blackfriars*, Dec.1982. I have discussed various themes in the present essay in other papers.   It may be convenient if I list the following.

'Bonhoeffer Reconsidered'. *Theology*, Nov.1973

'Religious Language and Religious Truth'. *Theology*, Sept.1976

'Myth and Truth'. *Theology*, Jul.1980

'Paradox and Affirmation'. *Modern Churchman*, Summer 1980

'Scholarship and Interpretation'. *New Blackfriars*, Nov.1981

'A Shape of Faith'. *New Blackfriars*, Dec.1982

'Wittgenstein, Theology and Wordless Faith'. *New Blackfriars*, Oct.1989

3.   *Tractatus,* 6.522.   As with the references quoting Bonhoeffer I have given those from Simone Weil and (mostly) from Wittgenstein in the text.   They are from the English editions.

For Simone Weil; GG refers to Gravity and Grace, WG

to Waiting on God, FLN to First and Last Notebooks.

For Wittgenstein; T refers to the Tractatus, PI to the Philosophical Investigations, CV to Culture and Value.

4. E.M. Forster speaks of them in *Howards End*, Ch.V

5. Lecture on Ethics, published in the *Philosophical Review*, 1965

6. P. Engelmann, *Letters from LW with a Memoir*, 1967, pp. 135-6

7. *Being and Nothingness*, 1957, p.615

8. *Les Mots*, 1964, pp.210-11

9. *Studies in Philosophy*, ed. Findlay, 1966,p.212

10. *Kerygma and Myth,* ed. Bartsch, 1953

11. I have in mind especially the reverence which he expresses for them on approaching the island of Iona in his *Journey to the Western Islands of Scotland*

12. *Training in Christianity*, p.66

13. *Training in Christianity*, p.37

14. *Metaphysics as a Guide to Morals*, 1994, pp.469,511

15. See *The Crucified God*, passim

16. This figure of a helpless, sad and apologetic God was shown to me vividly in Wolfgang Borchert's radio play (broadcast here and in Germany after World War II) *The Man Outside (Draussen vor der Tür)*. The central figure is a soldier who can find no place in the ruined and corrupt world to which he returns - a world in which God confesses that he is ignored.

17. 'Thoughts on the Baptism of DWR', (LPP)

18. T.S. Eliot, *Four Quartets*, East Coker, III.

Postscript

Now that I have written this essay let me return for a moment to the justification for doing so. There has been, as a minimum, the need to clear my own mind as best I can about the answer that I myself would give to Bonhoeffer's question 'What is Christianity or even who is Christ for us today?'

But, whatever its limitations, I like to think that the paper may meet more than a personal need. Some of my friends, as I said at the outset, may like to see some more or less connected account of thoughts which have preoccupied me through the years, and to which we have sometimes turned in discussion.

What I have written may, however, in some modest measure, serve a wider purpose. The question has always been there but it has, I suggest, acquired a sharper edge than ever before, now that we can see more clearly both how much and how little we can know; now that we have to come to terms with the notion of a story that can't be told, but which is part of the experience of our world; now that we must recognize that we can't get outside our world so as to be able to see it as a whole; now that we have to hold to the notion of a reality that we can't describe: a reality for which we can find no adequate metaphysic. I want to insist on the insolubility of the paradoxes; the inadequacy of speech; the unanswerability of the questions, with which our experience confronts us, and yet on the grounding of faith, without which it is no more than subjective emotion.

All my interlocutors, I think, saw this situation. They differed profoundly in the implications that they drew from it. Wittgenstein and Simone Weil find radically different meanings in the image of the fly-bottle.

PART III

The Only Partly Knowable

Honor Anthony

Like James Mark I am sure that thought and faith must not be kept separate and that we have a responsibility to question our faith: I have always thought so and suspect that I always will, and as I get older hypocrisy and superficiality almost drive me out of the church at times. But the limitations and difficulties that are inherent in this process do not worry me: unlike James, I do not agonise about the Mystery but revel in it.

I was lucky to be brought up in a highly intelligent Christian family. My mother had been planning to train as a missionary and go to China until she met my father. I was actively prevented from going to Sunday school to make sure that I was not taught a simplistic or watered down faith. Later on, in my teens, I was fortunate enough to be influenced by a man who had been Principal of what I believe had been the only Christian theological college in China. In retirement he was Rector of a small Lancashire village where we had a weekend cottage during the war, and continued to preach brilliant sermons even though few of his parishioners had any idea what he was talking about. I found them intensely stimulating. When I went up as a student I found a natural home in the SCM and the process continued.

My position has been strengthened by my experiencs. As a medical researcher it became increasingly clear to me that 'proof' was hard to come by, and that you could only get relevant evidence if you were using the right tools. With anything concerning living matter you could rarely get further than showing that it was highly unlikely that the reverse was true, and you could only get as far as that using the methods that were dictated by the system. This made it increasingly ridiculous to imagine that 'science', or even reason, could disprove (or even cast real doubt on) faith, because they function in different spheres. Some eminent physicists have come to much the me conclusions. Moreover, I found that the more you appreciate the enormous complexities of the human body, the more you doubt whether our brains could appreciate more than a small fraction of the interrelations of God and the world, even if we were in a position to see the data.

But of course we are not: at the very most we have no more than a shortsighted worm's view of an elephant. With prolonged and very careful observation the worm might deduce that the four moving tree-trunks were associated in some way, but what was above would be a complete mystery.

We must wrestle with the problem of the meaning of the very limited view of God which we can see, paying scrupulous attention to all the data available, so that we can make our very best attempt to understand. But in the last resort it may not be our brains which bring us nearest. For many areas of thought and discussion words are the best channel of communication open to us but they are very limited: in prayer in particular they often actually get in the way, and between people they commonly cause misunderstanding unless there is also a will to comprehend. There are other ways of knowing people which are less open to confirmation and therefore tend to be under-regarded, but can be more important. When I see a patient, I listen to them carefully and for a long time, but my knowledge of that patient comes not only from the words that pass between us, the inflections of his voice, the expressions of his face, his other body language, the response of all these to what I have said, and my knowledge of the trials that patients like him go through, but also with most patients from some communication which seems to be more than the sum of all these. This is sometimes missing, and when it is I find it all very much more difficult.

God is a person, and so our thinking about Him, and our response to Him, must take account of the data, but must also be open to all the other ways of knowing people. To me all the paradoxes of our faith are a reminder that we can see no more of God than the worm can of the elephant, and we need to rely on other ways of knowing Him if we are to get a true picture: God is so much bigger, and more powerful, wonderful, and loving than we can conceive of. To me that is something to rejoice in, but I recognise that this only follows if one is convinced that God is a person. For myself, I have no doubt at all, but of course I could not produce evidence to prove it.

Curiously, part of what convinces me is the multiplicity

and recurring nature of the paradoxes: if there was nothing behind them they would have defeated us long ago. Another part of the conviction comes from prayer - I may not be very good at it but I am sure that it is not an activity that I indulge in alone, and I am equally certain that when 'two or three' participate it may have great power. Another part of my conviction arises from the fact that I have known a handful of people whose saintliness can almost be felt; some were extremely human and highly intelligent saints, with lots of humour and acerbity and insight as well as sympathy and empathy. And part arises from what has seemed to be episodes of vision or inspiration, sudden quantum leaps in understanding or appreciation (not only in religious matters) which seem like a gift and are difficult to explain in purely human terms.

I believe we must include these insights as well as formal data and the views of philosophers and theologians in coming to our world view. All our experience of all kinds must be included, good experiences and bad experiences. And there is a reciprocity about the good and bad experiences; at least for those of us who are aware of support in the latter. Bad experiences, lived through with support both human and divine, deepen experience and opportunity, which may also come to be regarded as evidence of the personhood of God.

I think I have been lucky in a lot of ways. It must be much more difficult to revel in the largeness and person-ness of God if you were not allowed to develop properly yourself as a child with a family that was close and loving, even if not always appreciated. And if you were subject to a lot of rhetoric and hypocritical teaching, or superficiality, that must make it much more difficult, because even our logic is much more affected by our experiences than we would like to believe. And I think that overall it is probably easier for women: most women tend to expect to accept their limitations in a way that is foreign to most men.

I rejoice in the paradoxes because the bigger God's elephant is compared to my worm, the more magnificent is the incarnation and the greater His love must be, and the more amazing that He should bother to have any communication with someone like me.

From Tradition to Discovery

A Search for Truth

Joan Crewdson

Having read James Mark's Essay on Faith I feel challenged to attempt a statement of my own beliefs and the relation they bear to traditional Christianity. As with James, what I want to say is also a comment on certain people, whose writings have influenced me. Five thinkers in particular have helped me to shape my faith and to reconsider my early beliefs. These are John Oman, Michael Polanyi, John Macmurray, Martin Buber and Dietrich Bonhoeffer. All of them hold in some sense a personalist view of reality. Christianity has been said to be a religion in search of a metaphysic and I have come to believe that the central claims of the Christian faith only make sense when considered within a metaphysical framework. James Mark himself says that we need some grounding for the notions of order and value by which we seek to live our lives and which direct our striving[1]. He does not go so far as to to offer a metaphysic which might relate this striving to the order of the world of experience in which we live (p. 39), but he does claim to find in Christian humanism a ground that justifies our faith in human aspirations and in such values as beauty, truth and goodness, which appeal to our moral and aesthetic sense and show us something about the nature of our world (p. 39-40).

I have arrived at my beliefs by a long and circuitous route, my search for truth having taken me from a childhood vicarage, through atheism, Seventh Day Adventism and various degrees of Christian fundamentalism to what might be called critical realism and the ability to believe in an uncreated, but loving Intelligence that has produced creatures like us through the method of emergent evolution. I do not believe this process is entirely blind and impersonal. I think that creatures make themselves by responding with varying degrees of appropriateness to their environment and that curiosity and initiative are at work in this self-transcending evolutionary process. Theologically speaking, I believe creation is a co-operative enterprise. God is always the ultimate Environment, saying, 'Let there be', but life emerges and grows by responding to whatever environment it experiences. Only human beings have the spiritual sensitivity to pick up the signals of transcendence that indicate a reality behind appearances. Religion is one of the main ways in which they respond to it.

I think that, at the heart of the evolutionary process, there is another factor at work in addition to chance mutation of genes and selection by the environment. Alister Hardy, in his Gifford Lectures, calls it 'behavioural selection'[2]. Creaturely curiosity and enterprise start in the animal kingdom. This encourages the development of resourcefulness and intelligence and justifies belief that creaturely behaviour can be purposive, not merely caused. No doubt life is to a large extent the product of chance and necessity, but this behavioural factor makes room for the development of fully intentional action in persons, who are agents, capable of acting freely and responsibly.

It has taken me a lifetime to arrive at my present position. Looking back, I realise that my childhood was sadly over-sheltered. I had a governess until I went to boarding school, and even managed to get through university without learning to think for myself. At the outbreak of war I still had little interest in the realities of politics and international affairs. My confirmation at school was 'routine' and I practised conventional piety until my second year at Cambridge, when I decided, with uncharacteristic honesty, to abandon the pretence of believing in a God of whom I had no experience. My first job was in industry, during which time I had an illness and a longish convalescence. In the middle of this, I had a religious experience, which lasted moments, but instantly dispelled a profound inferiority complex, that had crippled my relationships since childhood. From then on, I felt 'in relationship' at a deep level, which seemed to provide the necessary ground for relationships with people. I then began to live, day by day, relying on this mysterious inner resource which I 'knew' was God.

I left school with only two convictions of a personal nature. One came to me one day when I was watching a girl I admired and I said to myself, 'Personality is the most real thing in the world.' The other was the recognition of a void inside myself, that nobody else seemed to have. This emptiness ceased to bother me after my experience of 'God'. Looking back, I have to say the ways of God are strange, because it was not long before I got involved with Seventh Day Adventism. It was during the war and I was training to become a housing manager in London. I still experienced God as resource for each day, but it never occurred to me to link up with institutional religion. But the Adventists I met were different. It seemed to me, that for the first time, I was meeting 'real' Christians!

And so I studied their ideas and became an Adventist. I 'knew' they were right. I was given a book to read about creation, written, I believe, by an Adventist geologist. It was like a hammer breaking the rock in pieces. At the end of reading it I firmly believed that God created the world in seven days. The interesting thing is that I could believe it! I had a Cambridge Degree in Moral Sciences and a moderately trained mind, but this made no difference. It somehow made God more real and gave to the world a supernatural dimension I had not previously been aware of. For two years I kept Saturday as the Sabbath and finally decided to become an SDA missionary. This was a difficult decision I did not want to make, but felt I must. I then met some very fundamentalist, 'ordinary' Christians and after months of struggle and prayer, became convinced that the SDA view on Sabbath keeping and their obsession with prophecy and the Second Coming was not true to the main emphasis of the New Testament. I temporarily postponed becoming an SDA missionary, but finally was convinced they were wrong. This was a real miracle. I can only think it happened because my interest in truth was stronger than my conviction that the Adventists were right. My mind wasn't entirely closed.

For the next ten years, I enjoyed what seemed a rich fellowship in an independent evangelical church and attended endless services, conferences and prayer meetings. Looking back, however, I know I lived in a very narrow, fundamentalist world and I now greatly regret losing touch with old friends and cutting myself off from cultural and intellectual activities for which I had no interest. After many years in housing management I decided to switch careers and became an R.E. teacher. Then things began to move. I have always found providence problematic, but much that happened to me in the next few years seemed like divine strategy. A terrible year in a secondary modern school in London was followed by a wonderful year at Cambridge doing a post-graduate Cert. Ed. At the eleventh hour I got a place at Hughes Hall, due to a chance cancellation, though I was told that two hundred applicants had been turned down the previous January. I then had four years at a Grammar School in Wolverhampton, where I particularly enjoyed the VIth form work, though I was still a fundamentalist. When I was planning to apply for a Head of Dept. post elsewhere, my headmistress urged me to take a year off and get better qualified in theology. I pushed several doors, but the only one that opened was for a one year post-graduate Dip. Th. at Oxford, which, through no action of mine, became a three year Degree course with a scholarship.

Those three years were vital in enabling me to work all my fundamentalist convictions out of my system. At the time, I did not appreciate my good fortune in having people like David Jenkins, Eric Heaton and John Austin Baker as tutors and lecturers. But they sowed seeds in my mind, which slowly germinated. In 1969, an unexpected chance came through Sir Alister Hardy, to study for an Oxford BD, so I resigned my lectureship, believing it was a God-given chance to explore the ideas of John Oman and Michael Polanyi, whose major writings had been introduced to me by David Jenkins.

John Oman was a Scottish theologian, who, in his major work, *The Natural and the Supernatural*[3], developed a personalist metaphysic in which opposites such as matter and spirit, fact and value, the natural and the supernatural, the particular and the universal belong inseparably together. Michael Polanyi also establishes a unitary view of reality in his Gifford lectures, *Personal Knowledge*[4]. He overcomes the split between subject and object, knower and known, self and world, by showing that we are part of what we know. The part-whole relation was an important model for him, because of the unusual relation in which parts stand to the whole they jointly form. According to the logic of the part-whole relation, the whole provides the parts with a principle of unity, but is itself mysteriously *more than* the sum of the parts. This relation structures the whole of nature. For example, many particles combine to form an atom, many atoms form a molecule, many molecules form a cell, and so on. On every level of being, entities have their own reality and regulative principle, but are part of some more inclusive reality and derive their joint meaning and unity from it. Although Polanyi never applies the part-whole model to God and the world, there is some truth in the idea that God, the 'One', is the all-inclusive reality, who gives meaning to the 'Many'.

The modern term for the God-world relation is panentheism, which means that God is within everything, but is also transcendent. He participates in the world (immanence), but is separate from it (transcendence).This saves the relation from becoming pantheistic. John Macmurray, in Vol II of his Gifford Lectures, *Persons in Relation*[5], argues that transcendence and immanence are words that refer to the nature of persons as *agents* and are strictly correlative. They belong inseparably together and are the basis of all personal relationship. 'Pure immanence, like pure transcendence is meaningless' (p 223). This is true of persons as well as of the relationship between God and the world, which Macmurray insists is a personal relation. He says this in the last chapter entitled 'The Personal Universe'.

We are a society of explorers and our sense of the transcendent motivates our desire for discovery and for relationship. We experience self-transcendence whenever we achieve new powers of understanding or self expression. All creative achievement is in some sense an experience of self-transcendence. We become what we know, suffer and enjoy. To love is a self-transcending act. We find self-fulfilment through commitment to the other, to what transcends us, but is also part of us. Without commitment, there would be no knowledge of the other, no growth towards fuller being, no true communication or community. Macmurray and Martin Buber develop similar insights into the relational character of personal being. For Macmurray, the basic unit of personal being is not the individual, but two-in-relation. Buber talks of the I-Thou relation between God and the world as the ground of all relationship.[6]

Through these writers I came to see reality as personal and that a personalist metaphysic solves the problem of dualism raised by traditional philosophy, by holding opposites together in a part-whole relation. This gives us a world of both unity and diversity. Materialism reduces reality to terms of matter (physical energy) and idealism sees it in terms of ideas, (thought, mind, spirit). A purely material world offers us only uninterpreted facts, which have to be given meaning and significance by human agents. Pure meaning gives us a world of ideas and values that take shape in the mind, but are not inherent in concrete entities. This is why traditional philosophy fails to provide a metaphysics that makes sense of persons and their status as responsible agents. Persons are an embodiment of value. They are inseparably body and mind. Polanyi says, 'The mind is the meaning of the body'. It is that which give unity and identity to persons, in all their diversity. Only a personal universe can give to such diversity an all-embracing meaning and unity that can be recognised and discovered. A personalist metaphysic not only shows how such seemingly contradictory opposites as mind and matter, body and spirit belong together, but also indicates how even God and the created universe can be viewed as part of one reality. This does not make God less mysterious. It undoubtedly makes creation a greater mystery than most scientists, and even some theologians, admit.

The idea that persons are more real than anything else in the world was for me a sudden childhood insight, before I had learnt to think for myself. Polanyi came to a similar conclusion while wrestling philosophically with profound problems of personal knowing and being. His definition of reality allows us to speak of degrees of reality. He acknowledges the depth of being that makes a person more real than a cobblestone. To know a person demands a greater degree of participation, or indwelling, than to know an animal.

If human beings are the highest achievement of the evolutionary process, then it seems to make sense to take personal being as the key to the cosmos. In the course of history, we have explored exhaustively, not only the physical world, but also the world of transcendent values and meanings. We are moved by beauty, we discern the infinite and the eternal behind appearances. We worship what we experience as sacred and holy. Religion is one way in which we try to act appropriately towards the Other. We acknowledge the inexplicable mystery of the human consciousness and spirit. We marvel that beings like us can be the product of a largely biological struggle for survival.

Despite our animal origin, we have a strong and almost universal sense of being 'in God's image', and that this has something to do with God being personal (not a person). We use the word 'person' of ourselves without any real understanding of what it means, although many people have sensed the infinite potentiality of their human mind and spirit. Traditional Christianity speaks of God sharing human life in order that we might share his divinity. The word 'person' has a religious origin. It was coined by the church Fathers, who equated the Greek *prosopon* and the Latin *persona* in order to have a word that could refer to God as Father, as Son and as Spirit, without questioning God's oneness. Originally *persona* meant the actor's mask, and belonged to the vocabulary of drama. Actors are *dramatis personae*. The same actor could appear on the stage behind different masks. The term 'person', then passed into general use and is now more or less synonymous with 'human being', though it has not entirely lost its religious associations deriving from Christian doctrine. Today, when we wish to stress the sacred worth of the individual, we tend to use the word person, which is spiritually richer than the more down-to-earth human being, with its biological and psychological associations.

As persons with an animal ancestry, we face a problem of survival, which is spiritual rather than biological. In nature, survival has always depended on physical fitness, and natural selection has worked reasonably well in keeping the balance of nature. But for the human race, fitness for survival now has a spiritual character, which we ignore at our peril. We have acquired terrifying powers of destruction and are capable of ruthless greed and exploitation, which is liable to get out of control, when people cease to believe in some form of moral sanction. This happens when moral values lose their objective grounding.

Today, people are increasingly alarmed and shocked by the growth of violence, which is economic and political as well as domestic and criminal. I believe we can only survive if we recover a sense of the reality of moral virtues and ideals and allow our lives, individually, corporately and nationally, to be grounded in the transcendent values of integrity and benevolence. Unless we learn to trust and respect each other, and commit ourselves globally to a co-operative rather than a competitive way of life, I fear that the prophets of doom will have the last word.

Because of the alarming growth of violence in the world, the ideas of people like René Girard, the French anthropologist are important.[7] He argues that, in the early history of mankind, tribal groups learned to control violence within the community by uniting against a common enemy. Many of the myths and rituals of early religion were a development of this strategy, particularly rituals to do with royal sacrifice and the scapegoat. As societies became more civilised, internal violence was increasingly controlled by laws and systems of justice. The sacrificial practices of religion were given theological explanations and continued long after their origin was forgotten. Human communities have always feared the threat of chaos from social violence, and religion became the cement of society and sometimes provided standards of moral conduct going beyond the basic requirements of law.

Girard's research suggests that we are unjustifiably optimistic about our capacity to control violence without some sort of religious sanction. The instinct to oppress and to exploit is deeply embedded in human nature. Civilisation is never more than skin deep. Anarchy is a constant threat. For human beings, the stakes are very high. We have left behind our animal heritage and cannot go back to the innocent violence of nature. Greed and violence are probably the heart of what Christians mean by 'original sin'. This doctrine is linked to the doctrine of atonement, or redemption. Traditionally, this doctrine is interpreted in substitutionary terms. Christ's death was a sacrificial judgement. He paid the price of sin on our behalf. He propitiated the wrath of God and secured our forgiveness. Few people today are happy with this transactional view of atonement and prefer to understand the death of Jesus as revealing the glory and power of God's suffering love to win our hearts.

Girard was struck, when he came to study the New Testament, by the way the death and resurrection of Jesus brought to a dramatic end the cycle of reactive violence in which humanity is trapped. He saw Jesus as the innocent victim of human violence, who forgave his enemies and returned alive to offer them friendship and the friendship of God. In fact, Girard was converted to Christianity by this discovery. His theology of redemption is not new, but it is particularly appropriate today because it speaks imaginatively and clearly to those who perpetrate violence and to the victims of violence. In the cross, the vicious circle of victim and oppressor is broken. Fear is replaced by the freedom to love. We are all in some measure both victims of human violence and oppressors of others.

The message of the bible is that God chose a victim people from among the nations, who must remember that they were loved and redeemed by God, while undeserving slaves in an alien land. The prophets constantly reminded Israel that they must not be like the nations round about, but must care for the poor, the fatherless and widows and show hospitality to aliens. They must fulfil their calling to serve God and be a light to the Gentile world.

Judaism was no more succesful than Christianity has been in embodying the loving kindness of God, but in Jesus, some

Jews experienced the very presence of God. In his death on the cross, they saw God in Christ suffering as the innocent victim of human passions. Down the centuries, there has been much debate about the mystery of two 'natures' in one person. Today, we have more appropriate ways of thinking about the way God and man can be one in mutual exchange. Jesus spoke of knowing God as a son knows his father. He experienced his relationship of filial oneness with God, and their mutual love, as the way for all to come to God. I find it helpful to think of the Incarnation in terms of mutual indwelling and of an I-Thou relation, which suggests that Jesus lived in life-long communion with God and enjoyed a deep inner dialogue, different in degree from that of the greatest mystics and more sustained, though we have no proof, except the conviction of the disciples that when they met Jesus, they were in the presence of God. The resurrection seems to have been the experience which allowed the apostles to attribute to Jesus the uniqueness that Christians have always insisted on. I also feel it is important to hold onto this sense of uniqueness.

However we explain it, we tend to think of Jesus as having been so open to God, that God could live a life of revelatory love and power exactly as he would wish to live it. Jesus was God's living Word. To me, the Incarnation means a joint life of God and the historical Jesus, a life of unrestricted mutual love and participation, which reveals both God's love for the world and the perfect obedience and devotion of a human being to God. Jesus pioneered the way of salvation, as it says in the letter to the Hebrews.

This enables me to think of God as remaining fully God and Jesus as remaining fully human, but living a Spirit-filled life. Jesus never confused himself with God. It was always a relationship, but they acted as one. This was never a oneness of identity, but rather a oneness of perfect communion and agreement. I believe that, somehow, from infancy, Jesus knew a profound intimacy with God, through the Spirit, and that he demonstrated in his life, not the powers of pure deity, but the power of a human life, wholly sustained and guided by the grace of God. This would be why it says of Jesus in St. John's

Gospel, 'I can do nothing of myself. I do only those things that I see the Father doing'.

If one accepts that the life of Jesus was in some sense the life of God, or that, as it says in the New Testament, 'God was in Christ, reconciling the world to himself', then we must see in the Christ event a universal significance of a redemptive as well as of a creative character. The Cross is the place where we recognise ourselves both in the role of oppressor and victim. But if we recognise that in victimising another we victimise ourselves, the vicious circle of victim and oppressor is broken. This is Girard's point. In place of fear and violence, God in Christ put unconditional love and forgiveness. We are invited to identify with the victim and return to the world with the freedom to work at relationships in the solidarity of community. There is no longer any need to look for a scapegoat.

I used to think of creation as an act of God, achieved unilaterally, but I now see it as a creative dialogue in which creation responds to God's 'Let there be'. Even persons are the result of aeons of creaturely striving to know and relate to their environment. We have inherited our incredible and intricate sense organs, because creatures first developed them in the struggle to perceive their world. Persons are still engaged in the quest for deeper awareness of their personal 'Environment'. I believe that redemption has the same co-operative character as creation.

Redemption is a movement of recovery, made necessary because human activity has led to fragmentation and disharmony. It draws life into new patterns of wholeness and meaning. It brings reconciliation. Evolution is itself an integrative process in which new relations are formed and new and deeper coherences built up. One cannot separate the creative from the redemptive process. Polanyi's theory of personal knowledge shows that even the activity of knowing is a parable of redemption. The least significant act of perception integrates a fragmented world of sense data and gives meaning and coherence to scattered and contradictory clues. The meaning is not there in the separate elements, but is a gift plucked from experience at a more inclusive level of reality. Without realising it, our minds work on two levels of awareness, subsidiary and focal, so that, as we contemplate our world, we both discover and create meaning. Logic cannot prove the validity of the process by which we recognise patterns of meaning or by which vision comes to a focus in a new set of relations or a new and deeper coherence.

This process of integration is what Polanyi calls tacit inference. It is not a matter of formal reasoning, such as deduction or induction. It is more like intuition, which transcends formal rules of thought and relies on creative imagination, but it does not lack structure or rationality. According to Polanyi's theory of personal knowledge, there is, in all our knowing, the possibility of being mistaken. Our highest achievement is to know another person. We understand well enough that such knowledge in never final or complete. Knowing a person depends upon the relationship between us. If we take knowledge of persons as the paradigm case of knowing, we can understand why our knowledge of a personal universe cannot be exhaustive. In a personal world, everything has a meaning, or essence, that has to be experienced by personal participation. The poet knows this better than anyone.

Polanyi says, that we know more than we can tell. This is in part due to the limitations of language. We know *tacitly* far more than we can express in words. Religious experience is, of all forms of experience, the most difficult to describe. Language has given the human race immense powers of understanding and communication. But it can never be a substitute for relationship. Despite its lack of precision, the language of metaphor is still the most effective way of enabling persons to share experience. This is because, so often, words can only convey real depth and richness of meaning, when imagination has room to work, integrating opposites and resolving paradox. Paradox is an inescapable feature of personal being, particularly of the being of God. Theologians find in him a coincidence of opposites. God is said to be triune, yet one; he relates to us, yet is unchanging; he transcends time, yet is in everything; his loving purposes are sure, yet he leaves us to work out our own salvation; he is self-sufficient, yet wants our friendship; he offers us freedom, yet his love has the last word. The Christian gospel highlights other paradoxes, particularly that of losing life to gain it. But this applies to the whole evolutionary process, which depends on the biological principle of life out of death.

Life itself is a mystery, but personal being is most mysterious of all. I used to be totally mystified by the idea that Jesus should be regarded as the key to the cosmos, but if he lived out the meaning of personal existence in union with God, it no longer seems so strange to view him as the interpretative key to the created order. In the union of God and man, the universal and the particular come together. As James Mark says, If a human person is capable of living as Jesus lived, it makes sense of God's purpose to create a world of persons.

All religions worship the same God, variously envisaged. For me, this means that there needs to be a change in Christian theological thinking. We need a new starting point, acceptable, not only to Christians, but to persons everywhere. This new starting point must, I believe, be *the nature of the personal*. For Christians, it will be the nature of the personal as revealed in Jesus. But if, in his humanity and his Jewishness, he is the man God became, he represents the whole human race, and this makes the Incarnation an event of universal significance. As such, it does not belong to any particular world religion. I doubt if Jesus intended to found a new religion. The message he taught and lived was like new wine that was bound to burst the old wineskins of any religious system. His relationship with God, was, I believe, a revelation of what true humanity should be, whatever a person's religion. Religion is largely a cultural matter, but we share a common humanity in God.

I believe that Jesus provides an interpretative framework, within which all religions can find room for their ideals and cultural forms of worship. Each religion has weaknesses and strengths and falls short of its original vision. But nearly all hold some form of belief in the transcendent and seek to share in the life of God, and want to create a just society and be responsible stewards of the natural world, caring for the poor, the sick and the aged. Jesus transcends religion. He offers the world a rationality of love, that enables us to see our world and its activities in personal terms. In his person, Jesus provides us with a metaphysic, (a theory of being) that unites all those opposites, which human beings have regarded as ground for dualism, thus falsely separating what cannot be divorced in the nature of reality - God and humanity, spirit and matter, the universal and the particular, infinite and finite, and so on.

This brings me, for the moment, to the end my attempt to say how my beliefs relate to traditional Christianity. It has certainly been a personal exercise in intellectual clarification, and I would echo James Mark's words by saying, that others must judge whether it offers anything of more general interest. Like Bonhoeffer, I believe that Christianity has come to a watershed. Perhaps the Christian church ought to take Bonhoeffer's advice and, for the foreseeable future, confine its witness to living out the gospel by serving the common good in practical commitment to the poor and the victims of society. The world, he believed, has 'come of age' and needs to rediscover a Christianity that is 'without religion' (though not without God). Bonhoeffer's God seems to be inviting us to live before him, participating in his sufferings, but without airing any particular theories about him. Perhaps this should be the Church's agenda for the twenty-first century.

References;

1.   p. 68

2.   *The Living Stream,* Collins 1965

3.   CUP, 1931

4.   *Personal Knowledge: Towards a Post-critical Philosophy.* Routledge, Kegan Paul, and Chicago University Press, 1956

5.   John Macmurray: *The Form of the Personal.* Gifford Lectures.   Vol I   *The Self as Agent* 1957

          Vol II   *Persons in Relation* 1961 Faber

6.   See Martin Buber: *I and Thou.* T&T Clarke 1923 3rd edn. 1971

7. See René Girard, *Things Hidden Since the Foundation of the World*, ISBN O.8047.1403.7

See also James Alison, *Knowing Jesus* 1995, SPCK.

And Gil Bailie, *Violence Unveiled* SCM 1995. ISBN.0.8245.1464.

In Viam

Dorothy Emmet

I heard on the radio a remark that 'maturity was blessing one's origins'. I don't know about maturity but certainly in advanced old age I find myself blessing my origins. My father was a country parson and a liberal biblical scholar at a time when freedom of criticism, especially of the New Testament, could not be taken for granted, at least in this country (Germany was different). So we grew up accustomed to talking freely about religion in no special tone of voice, and thoroughly knowing our Bibles, both devotionally, and as a mine of good stories for games of Biblical charades. We also knew that the Bible was an overlay of writings from different sources and should be treated as a library rather than as a book. So when we went to school and found the Scripture teacher was trying to reconcile contradictory stories in one of the books of Samuel my sister and I (horrid little things) were ready to point out that this came from there being two manuscripts which gave conflicting accounts of the same incidents.

All this was fine, and religiously with it went a rather simple faith in God as a loving Father and a call to follow the leadership of Christ. As time went on I came to realize with regard to the latter that each one must work out his or her own 'Imitatio Christi', and with regard to the former I came to see the idea of the 'Fatherhood of God' as too simplistic. I cannot say anything very firm but will try to give some indications of the lines on which I am now trying to think.

Not only was the view of the Fatherhood of God too simple, but also the view of the historical Jesus was too moralistic, and played down the strong eschatological element in the Gospels. The latter was part of the whole Christian story, running as Man's Fall, and the involvement of the whole human race in this sin, with the ensuing demand for penalty. This was redeemed by God sending his Son and the atoning death on the Cross, bringing new life through the Resurrection. And there was the expectation of a final denoument at the Second Coming. I have put this all too summarily, giving only a broad outline. The liberal theologians of my youth tried to re-interpret it in ways which were consonant with seeing God as a loving Father and not as a judge demanding expiation and satisfaction. But I think the story made a whole which was deeply embedded in the Christian religion, and that we have now come to a time when what is called for is acknowledgement that Christianity in anything like its classical form has got to go. What came through it was a sense of the power of non-possessive, outgoing love, and this must not be lost, whatever may happen to the mythical and theological way in which it was presented.

The question is not only one of de-mythologizing but that concept of the Fatherhood of God which it was held remained when the de-mythologizing had been done. Indeed there is the whole question of the notion of Divine Personality.

That God is a Person has been a common assumption among both believers and atheists, and put like this I think that the atheists win. But is it the right assumption? A book which came to me as a revelation was C.C.J. Webb's 'God and Personality' (1919). He says that speaking of God as a person came in with the Socinian (Unitarian) controversy of the sixteenth century and was embedded in much of the language of evangelical piety. In the Doctrine of the Trinity the Divine Unity is most certainly not a person and whatever the 'personae' may be they are not persons in our sense, nor should they be thought of as like a committee of three. Webb himself says that though God is not a person there is 'personality in God', in that we establish a personal relation with Him (sic 'Him'). I am not sure what this means. Prayer does not seem like a personal conversation, but I recognize that the language of devotion is highly personal, since religion, as Webb says, is a matter of intimacy as well as ultimacy. In any case the Doctrine of the Trinity suggests something more complex and also more profound than the notion of 'a person'. Then I found that there was a tradition of philosophical theism, namely Thomism, in which God is not only not 'a person' but not 'a being'. (Of course there is no indefinite article in Latin, but the point is made by saying not 'ens' but 'esse'). My introduction to St Thomas was a seminar with Etienne Gilson, the distinguished French Thomist scholar, who was a visiting Professor at Harvard when I was there as a graduating student. There was a moment in the seminar when he said to us 'God, God you must remember is unique' (pronounced 'eunuch'). So we would say to each other 'God you must remember is eunuch'. Uniqueness is the essential point of this theism. God has no 'quiddity', no property to mark Him (sic) out as one of a kind, even a kind with only one member. St Thomas says that when Moses asked His Name he was simply told 'I am'. So God is not a being with a particular character over against other beings with their particular characters. He is Being in Itself, 'esse in se subsistens'. I am not sure what this means though I have struggled over it with the help of Gilson's book 'Being and Some Philosophers'.

I have been putting the Thomist contention that God is not a being in a very summary way. There is a considerable industry in Thomist Philosophy, but it goes on in virtual isolation from analytic philosophy, to the detriment of both. I applaud trying to present a philosophical theism in which God is not a particular personal being. The problem would not arise for polytheism where there are a number of particular gods, supernatural spiritual beings, with their own particular properties. This is logically more intelligible; the difficulty is over evidence for these spiritual beings especially as they tend to be multiplied indefinitely. The greater difficulty comes over monotheism, where this means not just that there is a High God who is 'primus inter pares' , or a Supreme Being or even 'ens realissimum', but an absolute Being with absolute properties, such as infinite, omniscient, omnipresent, omnipotent. These may be a matter of what Whitehead called paying metaphysical complements to God. Or more seriously it may be a matter of seeing that God must be unique. Could any personal Being sustain these absolute attributes?

There are substantive difficulties over the kind of consciousness such a Being might have. Take omniscience. God is prayed to as one to whom 'all hearts are open, all desires known, and from whom no secrets are hid'. And not only all secrets of all human hearts. An omniscient Being would have to know everything about everything in all the myriads upon myriads of things that exist and that have ever existed, and (there is an additional problem over this) all that ever will exist. He would have to be able to hold all this in consciousness at once. Consciousness as we know it is selective. We attend focally to some things, while holding other things in peripheral awareness. At times we shift them to focal awareness, and summon up other things from our memory. Could a personal consciousness be focally aware of everything - literally everything - at once? Would he say to someone who was praying "I cannot attend to you just now, as I am attending to Bill. I will come to you presently."? I have not found that theologians worry seriously over this. They have worried over how God knows the past and the future, but not, I think, unduly about how He can even know the whole of the present. They have tried to meet problems over omniscience concerning past and future by saying that God's knowledge is not bounded by space and time. But I think the difficulties over a completely unbounded consciousness are such that I do not see how to speak of it as a personal consciousness, even in an analogical sense. I think that the classical idea of God is incoherent.

The incoherence is partly due to the way in which there is a continuous pull towards talking of God as a person while also using expressions incompatible with this. So in spite of its difficulty I am sympathetic with the Thomist concern to speak of God as 'Being' but not 'a being'.

Part of the difficulty comes over what it then means to say that God exists. To say that something exists is now generally treated by philosophers by what is called 'existential quantification'. We can say 'There is an x such that [condition to be satisfied]' and this x can (but need not) be named. The essential need is for a description that the something satisfies. So as well as saying cabbages and kings exist we can say prime numbers exist, where prime numbers are integers having no factors, and they can be assigned names, eg 3, 5, 7 . . . We cannot apply this scheme to 'God exists' if God has no 'quiddity', no description. If we say 'There is an x such that [. .

103

. . .], and x is God', there is no describing phrase, and 'God' is, by general consent, a name and not a description. So we are thrown back on the reply to Moses, where God's name is 'I am that I am'.

Indeed this may be all that can be said, and even the personal pronoun 'I' may not be justified. At any rate it shows that this model of existential quantification is only applicable where we can say 'there is an x such that [. . . . .]'.

I call this the 'weak' sense of 'exists'. I accept it as applicable in its own terms, by which we need not feel worried about saying that prime numbers exist. But the fact that we may be worried shows, I think, that we also need a strong sense in which to exist is to be capable of acting and so making a difference to other things - 'esse est operari'. In this strong sense I would not say that prime numbers exist, while the kitten who has just jumped onto my desk certainly exists, and also, though more debatably, electrons exist.

Can we get anywhere in applying this strong sense, in saying that God exists as Being, but not a being? There may be an approach in the Thomist connection of 'esse' with 'operatio' (though perhaps not put in Thomist terms). St Thomas says God is known in the effects of his activity. So I should start to look towards a possible philosophical theism from the notion of activity. Activity is not something on its own. I see it as going on in all the innumerable things that are active, in innumerable ways, and in multiple interconnections. These activities are canalized in what we call laws of nature and within these laws more specific kinds of activity get formed. In physics these are patterns of energy, and energy is defined as a measurable capacity to do work, i.e. produce changes between one pattern and another. So we can look at what kinds of activity there are, and ask is there any kind such that it might be called divine activity? If so, I would try to see it as originative and sustaining, working creatively in and through other activities. I would not see it as the action of a transcendent Being creating a world 'ab extra' out of nothing (in this notion of the First Cause we seem to get drawn back to the notion of a Being). I see activity rather as immanent in what is going on in the world. Building on the patterns of physical energetic activity new patterns get formed, releasing new capacities. There is consciousness, starting perhaps from irritability and passing through stages from dim to clear awareness. We cannot be sure how far down some form of awareness extends. We certainly meet it in animals with their beautiful quick perceptions and with higher animals there is surely some form of intelligence. It looks as though it is only at the human level that there is a capacity to create language and deliberately to construct forms of association. As Aristotle said 'man is the political animal', and as Whitehead said 'Man is an animal intermittently liable to rationality'. It is at this level we can talk of personal qualities.

So I see myself living in a world in which new types of order emerge with new qualities, new capacities. It is a universe in process, unfinished, where there is also dissolution of order, conflict, destruction. Nevertheless it is a theatre for a plurality of creative activities.

If there is a kind of activity in all this that might be a divine activity, it would be of a fundamental creative kind. When we enter deeply into ourselves and into our relations with one another, I think we are aware of sustaining, renewing, motivating power. We are aware of it particularly in the kind of renewal which can come when we honestly look at something which has gone wrong, especially in a relation with others and when we lovingly open ourselves to the possibility of a new start.

In living in such a world, I have been surprised to find how some of the old religious language comes alive for me. For instance there is St Paul's saying 'while our outward man perishes our inward man is renewed day by day'. There of course comes a time when the perishing of the outward man takes over, and this must be accepted. There may be another stage; we do not know but we can hope.

We are living in a post-Christian world and I call myself a post-Christian rather than a Christian. I think that the gap between the theological formulations even of the liberal theologians and the view of the world that science gives us is far greater than was imagined. Although philosophy of religion is no longer relegated to meaninglessness, and logical positivism hardly exists except in the polemics of theologians, we do not find philosophers of religion who are anything like as impressive as for instance C.C.J Webb, or philisophical theologians as impressive as Austin Farrer. The Gifford Lecture kind of literature gets thinner and thinner.

A religion should be a way of life, linked with a view of the world which is intellectually tenable and imaginatively inspiring. Science is the greatest intellectual achievement of our civilisation. It is wrong to try to put it in its place by calling it reductive or materialistic. It need not be reductive if we recognize that there are kinds of order besides those described in physics, and there is no point in being materialistic when we don't really know what we mean by matter. If, more realistically, we are naturalistic, then we have to recognize that nature contains resources for all the marvellous things that come out of it, including personal life with its artistic, intellectual and spiritual capacities.

Science need not assume that this is a closed deterministic universe. But it is giving us a view of the world which is highly counter-intuitive, both on the vast scale in space and time and on the sub-microscopic scale. There is an enormous gap between this and the personalized world of most theologians. The theologian who came nearest to living imaginatively in the world shown by science was Teilhard de Chardin, and even he was living in terms of paleological rather than cosmological time. Most of us (including myself) accept the latter in theory, but cannot begin to live in it imaginatively, even if we do not recoil with Pascal; 'la silence de ces espaces éternels m'effrai'.

But even if we have not this vision, we can yet be aware of ourselves as living in a world of creative activity, that is also a sustaining activity in which we may find we can live religiously. That it is a fundamental divine activity may be an over-belief; in any case it is a matter of faith. But I think it is something we can live by, even if we cannot yet say whether it might sustain a philosophical theism. That I find myself able to speak of it in religious language, all be it symbolically, may, I realize, be due to my having had a Christian background. Nevertheless that I can do so makes me able to 'bless my origins'.

(Note. I was not able to be present when James Mark's essay was discussed. So I have responded to his invitation that we should state our own positions with regard to the Christian Faith. I am in sympathy with his wanting Christian humanism, but I find myself more radical in my view of Christian Theology. I am also in sympathy with his feelings for the mystery beyond what we know, but I am less sure that we come to insurmountable fixed limits. The limits can change and get pushed back in unexpected ways. I see paradoxes as intellectual challenges rather than as simply to be accepted, and I see religion as a way of life in the setting of an attempt to ponder on the nature of things - de rerum natura.)

My Faith

Vera Hodges

My earliest memory is of peering between the bars of my cot to watch my father saying his morning prayers. I grew up in a Christian household and prayer was real from the beginning. From my Confirmation I became a regular communicant and have never experienced any serious doubt.

There were doubts of a sort but they were doubts within the faith - what kind of churchmanship or which denomination represented the truest picture of the gospel? At Reading University I became President of the SCM. I read Philosophy. Professor W.G. de Burgh gave a course called Platonism which covered much early and mediaeval philosophy and introduced me to Plotinus, Augustine, Thomas Aquinas, Abelard and others. This course showed me that my real interest was in theology not philosophy. I talked much of this over with Bert Hodges, my tutor, Prof. de Burgh's successor, and later my husband.

Bert had drifted away from his Methodist roots and found Christianity again in an Anglo-Catholic dress. He taught me Catholic principles some of which I found hard to swallow. I think my Father had called himself a Liberal Evangelical; that seemed to mean a desire to keep to the middle of the road, to read his Bible and avoid extremes. My maternal Grandfather had been one of the founders of the Modern Churchmen's Union and my Mother had been brought up to question things. She taught me to read my Bible and try to be good, and also to question things.

Bert was drawn into the Ecumenical Movement and represented the C of E at many conferences, like the founding meeting of the World Council of Churches at Amsterdam in 1948. His Anglo-Catholicism wained; he became devoted to the Orthodox and full of respect for the doctrines of Wesley and the Reformed churches. We both settled down to a high-middle Anglicanism, and rejoiced that our two sons sang in Christ Church Cathedral Choir.

In 1940 Bert met Revd Gilbert Shaw in a train and the upshot of that was that Gilbert soon became Bert's spiritual director, and later mine. When we first met him he was working in the East End, using his skills as a former barrister on behalf of the poor and the unemployed; but soon his unemployed were in the army and his quarters bombed out of existence. He had an infectious vision of God and a firm belief that the darkness of the world could be banished only through prayer and that his first duty was to teach people to pray adequately. He died in 1967 as Warden of the Sisters of the Love of God, Fairacres, Oxford.

With Gilbert Shaw's inspiration at the back of my mind I brought up three children (a fourth died in infancy) and taught both English and Religious Studies A-level. I also worked for London University External Diploma in Religious studies, Lambeth S.Th. Diploma, and London B.D.

Bert Hodges died of Cancer after a long illness. In the year after Bert's death something happened which shook me and changed - deepened - my religious life. A cathedral canon committed suicide. What was wrong in the church that this could happen? What could I do about it? I knew of other clergymen who seemed to have gone off the rails and asked myself if it was my special job to pray for leaders of the church in some temptation. I went to see Mary Clare a former Mother Superior of the Fairacres Sisters who had worked closely with Gilbert.

She assured me that my sense that this was my work was authentic. 'From this moment,' she said, 'this is your absolute, number one, top priority.' She offered to become my spiritual director and for a few years she directed me in contemplative prayer. She expected me to find this difficult as I was about to join King's College, London, and she thought that travelling and new experiences would undermine the peace which prayer needed. However things went quite well, especially when I broke some bones in a fall and had to miss a term at King's; I spent this time studying the two masters of prayer, Lancelot Andrewes and Jeremy Taylor. Back at King's I completed an M.Th. in Church History, writing on the tension between Puritan and Laudian churchmen at the end of the Commonwealth period.

Soon after, Mother Mary Clare died. I became a lay

111

Reader, working first for the Reading Centre for Religious Education and for St Lawrence and St Mary, then for Pangbourne and associated villages. I also ran a seminar for candidate Readers of whom five have gone on to take orders. I edited and partly ghosted two books on prayer for Canon Gonville ffrench-Beytagh (formerly Dean of Johannesburg Cathedral). I felt that my skills were being thoroughly used and enjoyed that; but at the same time I was in a position to see some of the disquieting sides of the church which called for prayer.

After another fall we decided I should leave Pangbourne and join my daughter's family at Lechlade Vicarage. A year or two later I had some heart trouble and while I was in hospital the family decided that my daughter (with bad rheumatoid arthritis) ought not to be in charge of me; Wilfrid, my elder son, and his wife offered to give me a home and a downstairs room with them in Leytonstone. This has proved a happy arrangement, not least in that it brought me into contact with a local vicar, Derek Mottershead, Society of Retreat Conductors.

Once, while I was staying with Wilfrid Hodges, before I went to live in Leytonstone, I was with a group who were discussing what had brought them to that church. Fr Derek turned to me and said, 'I know why you came to St Andrew's: you came to meet me'. I was surprised, but later I saw his words as a psychic/ spiritual flash of insight into the service he was going to give me in future years.

Though I am obviously an academic type my faith is grounded in my prayer. The God I worship is the active God of the Bible. I see prayer as forging a relationship with God as one sees it in the Psalms, in Isaiah, in the Epistles etc. Prayer for me is partly personal and contemplative, but I try to keep a strict rule of praying in company with the whole Church; this means saying Morning Prayer, Evening Prayer and Compline, using the Franciscan book, Celebrating Common Prayer. Besides the Offices I say the ASB version of the Litany and build my intercession round its petitions for the love, truth and unity of the Church, and for 'the sick in body and mind. . . the

112

homeless, the hungry and the destitute. . . prisoners and refugees . . .'

My Faith rests on recognition that the Church's beliefs have been found reasonable by reasonable people. I tackle theology as a historian fascinated to learn how beliefs developed, and reaching out to see the whole picture rather than wanting to criticise or judge overmuch.

My faith also rests on some mystical experience. I don't see visions or experience anything dramatic but I do often feel that I sense God's presence strongly in my prayers. I also feel that, in God, time is transformed and simplified; past and future come together; Christ is on the cross and on the throne, passion is swallowed up in victory.

Once, I was reading something about 'surrendering' oneself to the Lord and I felt that God took the initiative and 'arrested' me; I was held still, body and mind. It was a short, simple, and quite disturbing experience; but it was a crucial signpost on my journey as it suggested to me that I needed help from someone with more spiritual understanding. I turned to Derek who offered to introduce me to the Ignatian Exercises. Ignatius Loyola's course on Christian life and prayer has been used from the 16th century for those who want to know Christ better and see their way more clearly. It provides about 70 themes for meditation and can be challenging, mentally and emotionally. We made a traditional compact: I promised to spend 1½ hours on the Exercises every day, praying for an hour and writing a short review of what happened in that hour; Derek Mottershead promised to see me once a week to watch my progress. The course took us eleven months and left me feeling a steadier and more mature Christian.

At this point Derek left Leytonstone to be Vicar of St Saviour's Eastbourne. A year later I planned to take a diocesan course on spiritual direction for which I had to be receiving direction myself; Derek offered to take me on again. The course was a disappointment to me, strong on psychotherapy but weak on spirituality; but it brought me back to Derek and for the last six years I have reported to him three times a year on how prayers and problems are going. His counsel has given inspiration and discipline to my prayers. It is hard to think of him as a father-in-God as I am old enough to be his mother, but he is like a wise and understanding son who can help me to hear what the Spirit seems to say to me.

I am well over eighty now but I am a part-time theological student working at a Ph.D. thesis on two great Anglican teachers of prayer, Gilbert Shaw and Somerset Ward. I am also attending classes at Oak Hill College on worship and on the history of the doctrine of the Trinity. As I look back over my Christian life I see much learning and much teaching; a continuing love for the C of E; a growing desire to know God better; a thanksgiving for friends he has given me; and a sense that, while I can pray, he still has work for me.

(Soon after writing this paper I became seriously ill with heart and chest trouble. I have had to give up work at Oak Hill and slim down my religious programme, but I am hoping to go on writing about prayer.)

Descartes' Evil Genius

David Hughes

"In philosophy, there are many mistakes that it is no disgrace to have made: to make a first-water, ground-floor mistake, so far from being easy takes one (one) form of philosophical genius. . . Plato, Descartes, and Leibniz all had this form of genius, besides of course others"

(J.L. Austin - *"Ifs and Cans"* 1956)

"I shall then suppose, not that God who is supremely good and the fountain of truth, but some evil genius not less powerful than deceitful, has employed his whole energies in deceiving me; I shall consider that the heavens, the earth, colours, figures, sound, and all other external things are nought but the illusions and dreams of which this genius has availed himself in order to lay traps for my credulity; I shall consider myself as having no hands, no eyes, no flesh, no blood, nor any senses, yet falsely believing myself to possess all these things; "

(René Descartes: *Discourse on Method* 1637)

My thesis is that a 'first-water, ground-floor mistake' underlies the intractability of a range of philosophical problems, with consequences which are not only of academic but also of practical importance. As the title suggests, Descartes is going to be cast as the villain but only as a tribute to the philosophical genius which enabled him to express what is a pervasive fault in philosophy with such force and clarity that it has exercised an almost hypnotic influence on subsequent thought.

The 'mistake' consisted in adopting a false standpoint in which the self is defined as a subject and as an individual in isolation. Against this 'Cartesian standpoint' an 'Alternative standpoint' defines the self as an agent and as a person in relation with other persons.[1] That, briefly, is the thesis, and the first task is to explore the background to the Cartesian standpoint.

Although the 'Cartesian standpoint' is a convenient label it, and the mistake it embodies, had its origin long before Descartes. In Plato's Allegory of the Cave, the prisoners are shackled from childhood so that they can see only shadows on the back of the cave. The shadows are cast by objects with light thrown by a fire. The shadows therefore are reality for the prisoners unless and until they can escape from their bonds and apprehend the 'true' reality which lies behind them. Already the characteristic element of Cartesian standpoint is present. The self is presented as a passive observer dependent on the input of the senses and especially on vision for material from which to construct knowledge of external reality. Its explicit formulation began, however, two thousand years later on the day in November 1619 when the young soldier René Descartes, returning from the coronation of the Emperor and detained by the setting in of winter in a Bavarian farmhouse 'remained the whole day shut up alone in a stove-heated room where I had complete leisure to occupy myself with my own thoughts.' [2] And, as he records

> "as regards all the opinions which up to this time I had embraced, I thought I could not do better than endeavour once for all to sweep them completely away, so that they might later on be replaced, either by others which were better, or by the same, when I had made them conform to the uniformity of a rational scheme"[3]

He thus set out on his long quest by 'setting aside all that in which the least doubt could be supposed to exist' in the hope of finding even one thing which is certain and indubitable: some Archimedean point on which to build his knowledge anew. As an aid in this enterprise he invokes the famous 'Evil Genius' of the second epigraph to this paper, and, as all the world knows he found his Archimedean point in the realisation that:

> ". . . . Whilst I thus wished to think all things false, it was absolutely essential that the 'I' who thought this should be somewhat, and remarking that this truth 'I think, therefore I am' was so certain and so assured that all the most extravagant suppositions brought forward by the sceptics were incapable of shaking it, I came to the conclusion that I could receive it without scruple as the first principle of the Philosophy for which I was seeking"[4]

His first move from this famous 'Cogito' is to the conclusion:

" . . . that I knew that I was a substance the whole essence or nature of which is to think"[5]

and from this to his dualism of mind and matter, the essence of the former being 'consciousness' (since Descartes' 'thinking' includes not only cognition but also feeling and willing), and of the latter 'extension'.

With this he set the agenda for centuries of debate. One of the first difficulties created by his dualistic model of the self was the problem of mind-body interaction: how could a non-spatial mind cause movement of a spatial body?   An immediate and formidable critic appeared in the form of the Princess Elizabeth of Bohemia who wrote to:

" . . . ask you to tell me how man's soul, being only a thinking substance, can determine animal spirits so as to cause voluntary action . . ."[6]

Later, having forced the great man on to the defensive she wrote, delightfully:

"From time to time the interests of my House, which I must not neglect, or the conversations and amusements that I cannot evade, beset my feeble mind so strongly with annoyances and boredom that it becomes, for a long time thereafter, useless for anything else. This will serve, I hope, as an excuse for my stupidity in being unable to understand the idea by which we must judge how the soul (unextended and immaterial) can move the body . . ."[7]

This dualistic model of the self as two distinct entities, one mental one physical, has in our time been labelled 'the dogma of the Ghost in the Machine'[8] but it is not itself the 'ground floor mistake' which is my topic but only one consequence of it.   Descartes' achievement was in part, to induce even his opponents to argue from his premises.

In one version of the story, Descartes actually shut himself in a stove and, true or not, this would serve as a striking image of the Cartesian standpoint. Reflections of it occur throughout the work of his successors, and in a modern version in which the 'Evil Genius' appears as an 'Evil Scientist', the self is represented as a brain-in-a-vat, bodiless but connected to various chemical and electrical inputs which give it the illusion that it has a body which lives and moves in the world of everyday experience.

Descartes is, however, even more thoroughgoing in that his self is not even a brain-in-a-vat; the whole of his body including the brain is part of the external world. It is the self as pure subject and David Hume takes this to its logical conclusion and dispenses with the subject itself:

"For my part, when I enter most intimately into what I call myself, 1 always stumble on some particular perception or other, of heat or cold, light or shade, love or hatred, pain or pleasure. I never can catch myself at any time without a perception, and never can observe anything but the perception. When my perceptions are remov'd for any time as by sound sleep; So long am I insensible of myself and may truly be said not to exist.

And were all my perceptions remov'd by death, and could I neither think, nor feel, nor see, nor love, nor hate after the dissolution of my body, I should be entirely annihilated, nor do I conceive what is farther requisite to make me a perfect nonentity"[9]

The fully elaborated consequences of the Cartesian standpoint finally blossom in the philosophy of Immanuel Kant. In Kant's critical philosophy the Cartesian dualism has expanded into a cosmic divide between the world of phenomena, i.e. the world as the object of sense experience and the noumenal world of the thing-in-itself which, while being the true reality behind the world of experience, is itself completely unknowable. Radical scepticism is the inevitable outcome of adopting the Cartesian standpoint: the standpoint of the self as subject viewing the world as object. It requires only elementary reasoning from this to the insight that all our perceptions of the world depend in part on our biological constitution, i.e. on the nature of our sensory equipment. Kant's analysis is, however, more radical and profound. His

119

point is not merely that the world would appear differently to, for example, a dog, a fly, or a Martian. His concern is with the very notion of a subject of experience presented with the world as object of experience; such a subject, he claims, has to take the raw 'given' of the thing-in-itself and process it in terms of forms and categories in order to make it a possible experience and these forms and categories consist of the most basic concepts such as time and space, substance, causality and so forth. It follows from this that genuinely objective knowledge is unattainable. The real world, the world of the thing-in-itself is in principle unknowable.

The self inhabits both the first, the phenomenal world of appearance and the noumenal world of reality. As part of the first it is subject, like all the natural world investigated by science, to mechanical causation by which all events are absolutely determined by preceding events. As part of the second it is a free soul able to make choices. This is an uncomfortable position and Kant's own discomfort with it is apparent.[10]

The next task is to review the consequences of the Cartesian standpoint. and in order to do this I shall make use of a metaphor suggested by Descartes himself of a city flawed as a result of ' . . making use of old walls which were built with other ends in view',[11] and briefly survey the 'post-Cartesian city'. The Mind-Body Institute has, as we have seen, given nothing but trouble from its inception, its ruins still occupied by squatters under constant threat of eviction by the scientific developers. More generally, the Evil Genius of scepticism so far from being exorcised has taken up permanent residence in the foundations. The Churches, suffering especially, survive only by extensive buttressing or by removing whole sections of the original structures; some even, under post-modernist influence, have cut away their foundations entirely and float freely on a sea of faith, immune from the most severe epistemic shocks. Descartes' original lodging has evolved into Kant's 18th century mansion at the centre of what is now the Enlightenment Quarter, but the dualism built in the Bavarian farmhouse has extended right through this stately home of philosophy. Constructed on the most rational principles it has, nevertheless a haunted wing totally inaccessable to theoretical reason. In recent years the scientists have taken up residence in it but only after completely sealing up the haunted wing and thoroughly mechanizing the rest. They have thrived better than any in Descartes' city though irritated by those who, while eager to enjoy the amenities of their modern establishment, still claim to hear spectral noises from the old noumenal wing of the house.

It is no co-incidence that the scientists should feel at home in Descartes' creation. He was a scientist. Despite a cringing introduction to the Meditations addressed to the 'wise and illustrious theologians,' in Paris he also wrote privately to Mersenne referring to

"the things that I want people mainly to notice. But I included many other things besides; and I may tell you between ourselves, that these six Meditations contain the foundations of my Physics. But please do not tell people . . ."[12]

It has been suggested that Descartes the scientist was in conflict with Descartes the devout Catholic. Having postulated a mathematicized, material, universe suited to underpin the emerging physics of the 17th century he found that it contained no room for human values: for morals or religion. He therefore had to postulate another world of mind, quite distinct from matter in which such values could have a place. But this would not do justice to the impeccable logic with which his dualism arises from his initial standpoint.

This conceptual division of reality which flows from the Cartesian standpoint has the unfortunate effect of creating unnecessary philosophical oppositions, especially those which polarize around radical scepticism, such as the opposition of science and humanities. Science has, with great success investigated Kant's phenomenal world while ignoring metaphysical questions about 'what really exists'. It also accepts as a leading principle of enquiry that all events are subject to mechanical causation i.e. that all events are determined by preceding events. This is a quite proper way to investigate physical events but scientism as a philosophy goes further by claiming that the procedures and categories of physical science will ultimately be capable of explaining all experience. Free will and all moral and religious thought is therefore illusory. If all events including our actions are fully determined there can be no choice and therefore no moral decision.

Faced with this austere, machine-like conception humane theorists feel obliged, in order to defend moral values, to claim that there must be a ghost in the machine. Some, indeed, of a post-modern persuasion, may go on to the offensive and exploit a weakness in scientism in its neglect of the force of sceptical arguments. Since, post-Kant, true reality is unknowable then all knowledge is an aspect of human culture and modern science itself is merely one form of thought, different from but not superior to medieval alchemy. In its extreme, literary form this leads to a denial that we have any access to a common external world; there is no 'ultimate signified', only a ceaselessly unstable play of signifiers. Since this position constantly undermines itself its exponents require very quick reflexes for intellectual survival!

On the one hand, we have a position (science), which retains intellectual rigour but excludes or reduces human values. On the other we have a position which in defence of human values feels obliged also to defend another world of mind or soul which is threatened by each new advance of science, or which in its aggressive form indulges in apparent intellectual irresponsibility. Both science and post-modernism are constrained to adopt a relativist stance on ethics.

The next task is to describe the Alternative standpoint in more detail and to demonstrate how it avoids this false opposition.

It is John Macmurray who provides the boldest statement to place in opposition to Descartes. His Gifford lectures (of which the 'Self as Agent' is the first volume) attempted to provide a new form of thought for philosophy. The attempt rests upon a conviction that our philosophical tradition is faulty in two respects: it is merely theoretical; and it is egocentric. It defines the self in its reflective activity, as a knowing subject; and it conceives the self as an isolated individual, withdrawn from active relation with other selves:

"Against the assumption that the self is, at least primarily a knowing subject I have maintained that its subjecthood is a derivative and negative aspect of its agency. .... Against the assumption that the self is an isolated individual, I have set the view that the self is a person and that personal existence is constituted by the relation of persons"[13]

Pursuing his first point only in Volume 1 he says

"What is here proposed is that we should substitute the 'I do' for the 'I think' as our starting point and centre of reference; and do our thinking from the standpoint of action."[14]

Now this statement, though clear in itself, is likely to provoke some deep misunderstanding and it is most important to note that he almost immediately adds:

"The proposal to start from the primacy of the practical does not mean that we should aim at a practical rather than a theoretical philosophy ... What it does mean is that we should think from the stand point of action. Philosophy is necessarily theoretical, and must aim at a theoretical strictness. It does not follow that we must theorize from the standpoint of theory."[15]

The implications of this shift of standpoint: are revolutionary. As Macmurray says:

"We have to shift the centre of gravity in our philosophical tradition, and to alter our established mode of thinking .... It is not to exchange one theory for another, but to change the basis of all theory ...."[16]

The primacy of the practical over the theoretical implies that action is prior to thought. At the conceptual level this is justified because action may be defined to include thought and the concept of thought can be derived from the concept of action but not vice versa.

"Action, then, is a full concrete activity of the self in

which all our capacities are employed; while thought is constituted by the exclusion of some of our powers and a withdrawal into an activity which is less concrete and less complete"[17]

At the empirical level it is justified because action chronologically precedes thought. Our life experience begins as a simple organism interacting with, in fact existing within, another organism. At some point this organism, already interacting, acquires consciousness. Action precedes thought. Thought emerges out of the full experience of action.

If, in the light of this, we review the ground we have covered what do we see? From Plato's Cave to Descartes stove-heated room we see an attempt to portray the primary situation of the self as that of a spectator, a subject for whom the world is perceived as object. In a modern analogy of Hampshire's, strikingly reminiscent of Plato's Cave, he speaks of '. . . the data of consciousness passing like a film before the impassive observer'[18]

Descartes, quite naturally, withdrew from all activity in order to reflect, but his 'ground-floor mistake' was to take that moment of reflection as the primary human situation. He is thus led to radically misconceive the human situation, as that of a bodiless mind which can only through a long deductive process establish the existence of objects and other persons. Instead, Macmurray offers as the primary situation, which is our most direct and immediate knowledge of the world, our experience of ourselves as agents. If we substitute this Alternative standpoint for the Cartesian standpoint the scepticism which arises from the latter cannot get a foothold.

In Hampshire's words:

"In fact I find myself from the beginning able to act upon objects around me. In this context to act is to move at will my own body. I not only perceive my body, I also control it; I not only perceive external objects, I also manipulate them. . . No knowledge is more direct and underived than this knowledge of the fact of my own intention to move or to bring about a change."[19]

There is no room for scepticism. This knowledge is the reality. Not of course complete reality but not merely second-best reality.

The Alternative standpoint reverses the traditional relation of 'true' and 'right'. Now it is the distinction right and wrong, which is primary and that of true and false which is secondary. This opens the way to a pragmatic theory of truth.[20] A fundamental objection to pragmatism is, presumably, that even if a theory 'works' it may still be mistaken about the objective situation, about the 'true reality', but as we have seen this 'true reality' is a figment created by the Cartesian standpoint. Starting from the Alternative standpoint there is no 'superior' reality to which to appeal. Actions are right if they are successful in fulfilling intentions and propositions are true in so far as they are capable of leading to right actions. All judgements of rightness must of course be provisional but will be amended, not by some appeal to 'how things really are' as perceived by a subject but by further, more comprehensive or more refined actions by an agent.

This is, in practice, the method of science and the success of science in the investigation of the physical world is the best demonstration of the validity of the pragmatic method. Science in practice implicitly adopts the Alternative standpoint but some philosophies of science such as scientism unwittingly retain the Cartesian standpoint. An experiment in the physical sciences is itself an action within human society but the physical scientist quite properly abstracts from this total situation only the data which conform to the concepts invented by his science: mass, force and the assumption of mechanical causation. This constraint is immensely fruitful and entirely legitimate. What is not legitimate however is to return to the full human situation and claim that, on the basis of his findings within these constraints, that the whole human situation can be accounted for without introducing specifically human concepts such as free-will. The trick is blatant but too often unchallenged.

The Alternative standpoint enables us to re-integrate the

worlds of matter and spirit. The material world is one which, from our most direct experience, does in fact manifest consciousness and free-will. No special philosophical problem arises from a description of the phenomenon of consciousness as an emergent property of complex formations of matter, provided that we do not a priori define matter solely in terms of the concepts of physics[21]. But the task remains of exploring the compatibility of human freedom and scientific determinism within a unitary conceptual universe[22]. The argument turns especially on the issue whether the process of the world is intentional or not and in Macmurray's words:

> "The long argument of modern philosophy, we said, has moved steadily in the direction of an atheistic conclusion; and with it the historical development of our civilization has moved towards irreligion. At the same time this has precipitated a revolutionary crisis in society, and made a break in the philosophical tradition which compels us to start afresh from a revision of its fundamental assumption, the primacy of the theoretical. We have substituted the 'I do' for the 'I think ', and made a first tentative effort: to follow out the implications of this radical modification. Very much remains obscure; but there is one result which is sufficiently clear. The argument which starts from the primacy of the practical moves steadily in the direction of a belief in God."[23]

References;
1.   The Alternative standpoint is derived mainly from:
Macmurray J. *The Self as Agent.*   Faber & Faber 1957
and secondarily from:
Hampshire S. *Thought and Action.*   Chatto & Windus 1960
2.   Wilson M.D. (ed) *The Essential Descartes.*   New American Library 1969 p 113
3.   Op. cit. p 115

4.   Op. cit. p 127

5.   Op. cit. p 128

6.   Op. cit. p 373

7.   Op. cit. p 376

8.   Ryle G. *The Concept of Mind* Penguin 1963 p 17

9.   Hume D.   *A Treatise of Human Nature* I.iv.6

10.   The Groundwork of the Metaphysic of Morals. 'There I abandon a philosophical basis of explanation and I have no other'.

11.   Wilson Op cit p 113

12.   Kenny A (ed.) (1970) Descartes: *Philosophical Letters*. Blackwell p 94

13.   Macmurray Op cit. p 11f

14.   Op.cit p 84

15.   Op.cit p 85

16.   Op.cit p 85

17.   Op cit p 86

18.   Hampshire. Op.cit p 71

19.   Op.cit p 47f

20.   This is not Macmurray's argument. What scant evidence there is suggests that he did not support pragmatism.

21.   Searle J.   '*Minds, Brains and Science*' Penguin Books 1984.

22.   Searle admits defeat on this question (Op cit Ch 6)

23.   Macmurray Op. cit. p 22

Faith for Today

Elaine Kaye

I consider myself fortunate to have been brought up within a stable family background, with parents who took matters of faith seriously; my father was a Congregational minister, my mother an artist, both from Yorkshire Nonconformist families. My sister and I were fortunate too in our education, for after my father's early death, despite the suggestions of some people, my mother considered the education of girls to be important enough to warrant considerable sacrifice.

Another factor in my earlier life was that, even in the middle years of this century, Nonconformists were in some circles regarded as second-class, ecclesiastically, culturally and socially. This has had the effect of strengthening the consciousness of my tradition's roots, and has led me to explore them, as a historian, in some depth.

Attendance at church was a regular part of life in my childhood and adolescence. When I went up to Oxford, it was my choice to attend worship at Mansfield College Chapel; this was a revelation of what worship in the Reformed tradition could be. In later life I have been able to share in it again, and, at its best, it still offers a rich and deep experience, through music, preaching and liturgy of high quality. I have of course been moved by the experience of worship in other places and in other traditions - at Taizé and Iona, in some English cathedrals and college chapels, in small village churches, in Orthodox churches in Russia, and in many Quaker meetings; as well as being bored or infuriated by some others.

Faith therefore was nurtured through worship, and surely cannot be entirely separated from it; neither can it be divorced from the life of faith communities. But because worship must involve the whole person, it must satisfy the mind as well as the heart, and engage with the challenges which life presents, both personally and on a wider scale. Faith must be subject to intellectual scrutiny, by each individual and by the community.

When I was about 13, I attended a Yorkshire village church whose minister was a gifted teacher. He gathered a few teenagers together, and taught us, among other things, the rudiments of biblical criticism, especially as applied to the gospels. This, together with lessons at school with a good and lively teacher of what was then called 'Scripture', first kindled my interest in biblical studies - as well as history - and led to intermittent reading over several years, though not to formal study until much later in life. As an undergraduate, membership of the SCM enabled me to hear challenging intellectual debates with some of the best theologians of the day, and fostered an interest in theology, and in the encounter between theology and other disciplines. One of the most stimulating of those discussions was in an SCM group on 'Christianity and history', led by Marjorie Reeves; the issues raised there have influenced my thinking ever since.

I have never thought that faith can be reached by reason alone, though up to a point it can be defended by reason. There seems to be no way of avoiding the 'leap of faith'; for Kierkegaard, this involved the 'crucifixion of the intellect'. How and why that leap is made is the challenge, for it is made in the face of enormous difficulties.

A major difficulty, insuperable for some, is the Christian claim that God is sovereign over the universe, and that his sovereignty was revealed in the life, death and resurrection of Jesus Christ. This claim is as hard to make in the last years of the twentieth century as it has ever been; how, in the light of that claim, do we come to terms with ethnic cleansing, desperate hunger, and continuing conflict in many parts of the world? While some of this suffering can plausibly be attributed to human greed, selfishness and indifference, it is more difficult to account in this way for certain diseases, or for natural disasters such as severe drought and earthquakes. Manifestly the messianic age has not yet come. It was brought home to me very strongly during a three month stay in Israel that Christians should be very careful about the kind of claims which they make for God's providence. It has been reinforced during several years of active membership of the Council of Christians and Jews, and the dialogue with Jews that that has involved. Perhaps the continuing existence of the Jewish people, who see the messianic age wholly in the future, is a necessary corrective to some unjustified Christian claims. What Jews and Christians can share is hope (which is not the same as optimism), and life within the framework of that hope. This is no 'answer' to the problem of suffering and evil, but the Judaeo-Christian tradition can offer a way of living with it. I do not forget the moment, in reading one of Don Cupitt's books, that I came across the word 'patripassianism' and learned what it meant; that, according to orthodox Christian teaching, God could not 'suffer'. It was a relief therefore to read Jurgen Moltmann's *The Crucified God,* and Paul Fiddes' *The Creative Suffering of God*, and, while realizing that the doctrine of patripassianism was first formulated in response to a defective view of God, to discover that it is possible to believe in a 'God who suffers and remains God'.

The doctrine of the atonement can be another stumbling block; notions of a ransom paid to the devil are hardly credible today, and have largely lost currency. The view that Christ's death on the Cross revealed the depth of God's love for the whole of creation is the most accessible view, and one to which I can subscribe. Linked with this is the difficult but fundamental resurrection tradition. While I maintain that the existence of Jesus Christ as a historical person in a particular place and time is important, in fact an essential element of my faith, I cannot regard the resurrection as a historical event in the same sense as any other historical event. That is to take the biblical witness in too literal a manner. It is at this point that Kierkegaard's phrase about 'the crucifixion of the intellect' speaks to me; it is not possible to explain the event called the resurrection in words, yet that some power was released, that some divine irruption occurred, I can believe. And I am prepared to claim that the life, teaching, death and what we call the resurrection has significance for the whole of humankind, and indeed the whole of creation.

I do not believe that overt faith in Christ within a Christian community is the only path to 'salvation', as against the frequent quotation of John 14:6 ('no man cometh to the Father, except through me'). A literal quotation of this phrase

132

sets one verse of one gospel over against the revelation of God in the bible as a whole; there are other ways of understanding and interpreting this verse. One of the rewards of serious biblical study, including its study in the original languages, is the realization that the literal interpretation of individual translated passages is only one of many ways of reading the text; biblical criticism has enriched and deepened the interpretation of the biblical texts. This may seem a very obvious thing to say, but the quotation of individual verses of the bible to justify certain moral stances is still very common today. The gap between theological and biblical scholarship and the Christian teaching in so many churches is a matter for great concern.

The presence in our country today of many different faith communities has created a more direct challenge to the Christian 'exclusivist' position. The only such community I have so far entered into any serious dialogue with is the Jewish community. Dialogue with other religious groups (and with open-minded atheists) is now an imperative - the kind of dialogue which presupposes that both partners to the dialogue are prepared to listen, and to be open to the possibility of change. As one who feels ashamed of the traditional Christian attitude towards and treatment of animals in the past (though there are notable individual exceptions) I have been heartened to discover that there is so much more about the humane treatment of animals in the Jewish than in the Christian tradition. This brings one to the difficult questions of 'mission' and 'evangelism'. I have been greatly helped by encountering George Fox's statement that he walked over the world recognizing that of God in all he met. This focuses on what is shared by all humanity, rather than on the superiority of one religion over another. Fortunately there is much re-thinking on this issue today, and it is one of the many current creative areas of theology.

Christian communities themselves can offer obstacles to faith. The study of the history of any century is not necessarily supportive of the claims of the Church to be 'the people of God', or 'the body of Christ', and its divisions conflict with its claim to preach a gospel of reconciliation. So the witness of the Church to faith is often ambiguous. On the other hand, it has revealed powers of renewal, it has kept alive the faith and experience of the people of the Old Testament and the account of the witnesses to the life of Jesus Christ, and, in rare moments of self-understanding, allowed itself to be judged by it; it has also produced some individuals who have revealed something of Christ in their own lives. It has had to tread a fine balance, not always successfully, between preserving the faith and at the same time allowing for the intellectual exploration of faith with the thought forms of the age. I belong to a Christian tradition which has, on the whole, allowed a reasonable freedom to its members and ministers to explore the theological frontiers, and has been more ready to formulate 'declarations' than 'creeds'; this makes it possible for people who cannot accept all the elements of a particular declaration nevertheless to identify themselves with the faith community. The group which seems best able to cope with allowing a diversity of expressions of belief, while sharing a unity deeper than the level of words, is the Society of Friends. Their practice and beliefs have long attracted me, as has their commitment to a non-violent way of life.

During the last 20 years or so, the strength of the feminist movement has posed more challenges to the Church. Some see this as a trivial issue to be ignored, others as something unscriptural to be resisted. Yet others, including myself, see it as a further challenge to break down human barriers, the first example of which was the breaking down of the wall of division between Jew and Gentile. The Christian gospel offers freedom to oppressed groups, and on a world-wide perspective, women are oppressed. A certain number of women have found the Church and the Christian tradition so irredeemably patriarchal that they have left it and called themselves post-Christian. Others take the challenge seriously, but are seeking to find resources within scripture and the Christian tradition to challenge the patriarchal structure. The use of inclusive language (for human beings) is a first step. It is significant to remember that, 50 years ago, very few women studied theology in universities; now the proportion of men to women is about equal. Distinguished women theologians, feminist in varying degrees, are making their mark, especially in the United States, and this is already having a stimulating influence on the development of theological thinking.

One of the issues which this movement has raised (and which accords with a long-standing concern of my own) is the question of guilt and the confession of sin within the liturgy. Women are more likely to need to confess shrinking from responsibility, taking refuge in trivialities, or refusal to believe in their own worth (and the Church has often unwittingly connived in this), than in pride. Yet this is rarely reflected in liturgy. As more women take a pastoral role within the Church, there may be more understanding of this issue.

What are the positive reasons for continuing to hold and practise the Christian faith? There is the continuing appeal of the figure of Christ, and indeed of many stories of the bible. They still inspire works of art and music from a far wider circle than that of the Church. Though that does not necessarily draw people into the Church, it reveals their continuing significance for humanity today. The bible (and for me, most stimulatingly, through study of the Hebrew text in company with a small group of Roman Catholic and Anglican fellow 'explorers') is an inexhaustible resource. Above all, so is the figure of Christ. Each generation's encounter with him reveals new insights. In this decade, it is the work of the anthropologist and literary scholar René Girard (particularly in *The Scapegoat* and *Things Hidden Since the Foundation of the World*) which has illuminated for me the significance of Christ in a turbulent world. Girard has proposed that Christ was unique in his refusal to re-act to any form of violence, not out of weakness but out of strength, and that he has shown humanity how to break the cycle of 'mimetic rivalry'. We have yet to understand or act on this insight.

It is right that the Church should value (but not 'idolise') its tradition, and tell its stories, but in doing so it should be prepared continually to discover new insights, to break down barriers, to realise that Christ is always ahead of us; above all keeping alive the hope without which our lives would seem without purpose.

Places of Waiting:
Faith, Story and Church

Robert Mitchell

James and I have travelled very different roads. James turned to the Christian faith in his mid-thirties, over forty years ago. I, now in my mid-thirties, have always been a church-goer, find myself most comfortable with a Quaker outlook and yet choose, with more or less commitment, to make my home in an Anglican congregation. My questions and my answers are different from his, and yet I find the fact that he is standing in a similar congregation to mine a great encouragement.

Even more than James, I must make my "confession of amateurism". However I do question James' apparent deference to the professional and the expert, for the rather Protestant reasons that it risks crediting such persons with privileged access to God and consequently undermining the value of the individual's experience and of local wisdom. Perhaps I simply wish to underline James' own conclusion that we need to recognize "the mixture of simplicity and complexity in human experience, which should prevent us from identifying knowledge with wisdom, and giving keys to the learned which are not given to the rest of mankind".

I shall first give a brief account of my own journey of faith followed by a summary of what I take to be the main points of the Essay. I shall then respond to each of those points though under slightly different headings from James'.

I.

My Faith

I have to do my theology from where I am. I must recognize that my theology will consequently differ from yours who stand elsewhere, and also that I cannot get outside my world so as to give an objective account of it. A further difficulty is that of distinguishing between theology and psychology. I am increasingly aware that what I might previously have offered as religious argument might better be presented as a psychological preference for a certain kind of solitude. The following partial account of my background is an attempt to acknowledge this.

I was born and bred a Methodist. I was not made to go to

Sunday School: going to Sunday School was simply what one did on Sundays. There has never been a time when I have not been a church-goer or when I have publicly denied the main points of the Christian creed. Privately (sometimes far more privately than I realised), my commitment fluctuated between wholehearted assent and outright denial. Rather than make the denial public, and thus be forced to give answers where I preferred to live with quiet questions, I found it more convenient to preserve the public face in order to secure a space for my solitary explorings.

Under cover of this public face, I developed during my teenage years a particular intimacy with what I chose to call "God". My faith (I cannot think of a better word) was informed by and expressed in language taken from my Christian upbringing, but it was not logically dependent on Christian premises. The faith survived, and was strengthened by, the times of denial: the question at those times was whether Christianity was the necessary or best means of expressing my faith.

The substance of my faith grew out of experiences of wonder and despair. There was conscious wonder at the mathematical, physical, natural, musical, imaginative, human world which was unfolding before me; and there were times of despair when it all seemed to collapse into a black hole or a dark night. Unpleasant though those times were, I came to see them as fundamentally important. I imagined for myself a place which lay beyond all my intellectual constructions, a place of darkness and silence where I was called to wait upon God. It was not that the place of waiting was to be reached by denying the work of the intellect. The place of waiting must shut nothing out. It could be reached only after the intellect had been pressed to its utmost limit.

I would not say I often met God there - the feeling was more one of absence, of a place where God had perhaps been, would perhaps return but where in the meantime I was required to make my offering alone...

And yet not entirely alone. There was also a sense (perhaps just something wished for) of others waiting in the

140

same darkness, some sort of community of prayer. At any rate, I came to believe, to have faith, that it was out of the waiting that "that which makes for life" would grow. The call was to move from a place of acting to a place of waiting and back again.

This still is my faith. It is not faith in a set of facts or a certain state of affairs; it is faith in the value of an activity. I do not assert that God is, simply that God might be, holding that it is more daring, demanding and fruitful to live with the possibility of God than to deny either that God is or that God is not. I do not need to assert the uniqueness nor even, directly, the historicity of Christ: in another place or time my faith could flourish within a quite different religious culture. All I can say is that for the moment this is my home.

However, I recognize better than I did the danger of delusion and the need for my private visions to be exposed to critical scrutiny. I am also now more aware of my need for the support of others to enable me both to find again the place of waiting and to live out what I hear there. Perhaps I previously took too much for granted my reliance on the Church for these things. I do, therefore, in a somewhat secondary sense, have faith in the Church, in the Christian gospel and in Jesus. The issues for me are not so much how these two kinds of faith (faith in a place of waiting, faith in a religious tradition) can be intellectually justified but rather how most wisely and fruitfully I can live out that faith.

II.
The Concerns of "An Essay on Faith"

My path has been different from James' but I find myself surprisingly close to his conclusions, particularly that, "... I have to think in terms, not of what can be proved but of what makes for life. I have to base the notion of truth not on an epistemology which we cannot have, but on whatever interpretation of values appears to offer us some notion of human fulfilment. And, having pointed as best I can to show what this means, I must leave it to work, if it does, for the Other with whom I am trying to communicate". I also

141

recognise issues of great importance in the concerns which he lists thus:

    a. the inescapable paradoxes of the human situation;

    b. the nature of religious language;

    c. the justice of God;

    d. the impossibility of a portrait of Christ.

To summarise my response to each of these headings, I find it easier than James to treat paradoxes as openings rather than as obstacles to faith, although I think some distinction between different kinds of paradox might be helpful here. With regard to language, although James acknowledges other functions of language than the descriptive function, I still think he gives a pre-eminence to the descriptive function which I would not accept and that there flows from this a major difference of approach between us. The problem of the justice of God seems to me to be very close to the heart of the religious quest; I would, however, dispute whether the position of "twentieth century man" is so very different from that of the writer(s) of the Book of Job. For reasons outlined above, problems with identifying the historical Christ do not create direct logical difficulties for me; what does trouble me is the tension between Christ as man or exemplar and Christ as metaphysical symbol.

To complete the picture, I would add two further concerns to the list. The first is about the role of the Church which James discusses very little but which I think is inseparable from questions about the tradition for which the Church is responsible. Finally, there is a concern about morals, about how all this affects the way we live. My conclusion is that a proper relationship with the "place of waiting" which I have described is an essential supplement to any system of authority if we are to live a moral life in any worthwhile sense.

III.

Paradoxes

James chooses as his working definition of paradox that of "a contradiction in a law or between two laws". He argues that theologians "haven't addressed themselves seriously enough to the problem of living with paradoxes that aren't to be resolved", implying, I think, that he himself cannot be comfortable with a faith that does not rationally accommodate unavoidable paradoxes. He lists a number of theological paradoxes covering the nature of God (acting yet unchanging etc.) and free will, the nature of the Kingdom of Heaven (present but still to come etc.), the nature of Jesus (all powerful yet vulnerable etc.) and the nature of Christian vocation (to lose life and yet find it etc.). He notes that "paradox is characteristic of human life generally" citing in particular the concept of infinity. Later, he identifies "the ultimate paradox of speaking of what I do not know; of defending the felt need to speak of what lies beyond reason, but not beyond reality". He refers to and rejects several possible attitudes to paradox. One might embrace paradox as divine absurdity, ignore it, overcome it by revelatory diktat or attempt an intellectual resolution. (The last of these would I think be impossible by definition but James intriguingly restricts himself to dismissing it as a task "which I find impossible".).

He concludes that some way of looking beyond the limits of reason has to be found. One way might be to bring in "a supra-rational faculty to which reason is subordinate. This may be interpreted as mysticism inspired by love". He declines to speak of this on the ground that he lacks the experience to do so. Instead he is left with the brute fact that paradox represents the limit of reason and yet he is compelled to recognise that something valuable lies beyond that limit. Reason has to make do with the second-best option of leaning "now to one side of a paradox now to another", defeated in its project of producing a single coherent map of the whole of experience.

The difficulties which James describes are very real. However, I am troubled by the way that "paradox" as presented by him covers a multitude of different difficulties only some of which are special to religion, and some of which may demand and may even be resolved by different responses.

A starting point is to notice that James' chosen definition of paradox is exceedingly compressed, and does not obviously cover all the examples he gives. Not every conflict between two laws can count as paradox. We are looking for a conflict between two laws which are both acceptable according to the same code for the acceptability of laws. Rules for the acceptability or coherence of laws tend to become complex. The possibility of producing a single code of coherence for everything we might want to say is, I believe, highly debatable, even if we limit ourselves to the descriptive function of saying. It seems to me that the problem of paradox in its broadest sense concerns the failure of that project of producing a single code of coherence.

There are many ways in which that failure may be encountered. At a highly abstract level, it appears that it is demonstrably impossible to produce a complete and consistent account of the rules of arithmetic (and I believe there is more arithmetic than some would allow in certain types of systematic theology). At a different (though connected) level, there is a multitude of problems arising from the enterprise of using language to map reality: the problem of purporting to take an external point of view with regard to systems in which we are unavoidably insiders; the problem that no systematic description of a limited patch of experience can take account of the total interconnectedness of the universe; the difficulty of distinguishing between the thing observed and the effect on it of being observed; the fact that the world simply is not divided up into usable linguistic units; in short, the sheer impossibility of mapping a three-dimensional world onto a two-dimensional page.

There is a further type of difficulty illustrated by some of James' examples which I think could usefully be separated from this formal discussion of paradox, and that is the tension

144

between statements of fact and statements of value, the vexed question of the relationship between "ought" and "is". This problem presents itself in two forms: the difficulty of deriving "ought" from "is" and, more importantly for present purposes, the conflict between value and experience. There is no clearly agreed boundary between statements of fact and statements of value, and, particularly in the religious context, statements of value are often presented as statements of fact. However, the assertion, for example, that "God is love" can never be justified according to the same code of coherence as an assertion about the time at which the sun will rise tomorrow. The former kind of statement expresses or depends upon a faith in value or meaning; the latter expresses or depends upon faith in order. Faith in value or meaning is specially, though not exclusively, the concern of religion. Faith in order is much more pervasive.

Faith in order must be faith in humanly expressible or at least perceptible order. Such faith is challenged whether one wrestles with numbers, words or matter - arithmetic, language and the physical universe all endlessly defeat the efforts of the greatest minds to bring them to order. What conclusions should be drawn from the experience of such wrestling? Some may extrapolate from their discovery of order to the conclusion either that God therefore must be or that God cannot or need not be. Others may argue from the failure of their attempt to impose order either that God therefore cannot be or that God must be because that is the only way to square the circle. Both types of argument are, at a logical level, illegitimate. Arguments from design or order or the lack of it can prove (show) nothing except the experience on which they are based. (Or, as James notes with reference to Anselm's ontological argument, such an argument tends to be "not an argument, but an affirmation and an act of worship".)

However, it can still be true that the experience of order, wonder and awe or paradox, failure, collapse and chaos may lead individuals to look beyond themselves to something which they cannot say or contain within their logic, something transcendent which they find to be life-giving and therefore choose to value. Whilst such experience is not to be analysed in terms of logical progression, we do perhaps need to say something about the proper, or wise, approach to it. We need an ethic of integrity for religious understanding (which may not be quite the same as the scientific ethic). First, we should never stop or expect to rest either in a system of order or a conclusion of ultimate chaos. There are no short cuts to God, and we cannot return to our previous place of waiting until the intellect has been exhausted anew. Second, another's (provisional) answer to my (provisional) conclusion of chaos or order does not invalidate my experience, although it might call me to move beyond that experience to a new place of waiting. Once again, we need to be wary of "giving keys to the learned which are not given to the rest of mankind". (Hence the significance, perhaps, of James' dismissal of the intellectual resolution of paradox not as a matter of definition but rather as that "which I find impossible") This point should also, I think, make us wary of concluding that the religious experience of our ancestors was radically different from our own; they had the experience in a different scientific and cultural setting but that should not render their wisdom invalid for us. Finally, we need to be as honest as we can about the different kinds of statement we are making, the different language games we are playing, making use of all that we have discovered about the uses of language but not assuming that, because they did not analyse it in the same way, our ancestors were not at least as good as us at exploiting those different uses.

I therefore see paradox as part of the richness of this world, where, for us as for Job, God may be sought in order and found in chaos or sought in chaos and found in order. We need to be as honest as we can about what we are doing, but not get too frustrated at the failure of one rather limiting project of coherence.

IV.

Language and Evidence

James is particularly concerned with the nature of

language, with the limits of what can be said and with the need to reach beyond those limits. I want to respond to what he says on two specific points: what we can say about God, and the functions of religious language generally.

The question "what can we say about God?" could be taken to refer to the whole field of theology or more specifically to the use which we actually make of the term "God". Taking the question in the narrower sense, I answer for myself that I do not wish to say anything about God by way of description or attribution of qualities. All I can do is comment on how the word "God" may be used to enable me to wait upon a reality which cannot be contained within words. In moral and metaphysical reasoning and perhaps in spiritual practice, "God" operates as a sort of provisional end-stop: a means of referring to that which lies beyond everything else. The word is a bit like a joker, or like the concept of infinity (which James notes to be "beyond coherent formulation") or even perhaps zero. The concept of infinity enables us to refer to the place where parallel lines meet. It thus preserves a space, prevents closure, acts like a pit-prop in our tunnelling. But it becomes extremely dangerous if we try to do arithmetic with it, to treat it as a word with definable content to be manipulated like other more concrete words. Thus it is with "God". If we try to attribute qualities to "God" and to do logic with the word, we can prove anything; far from preventing closure, we end up using "God" to blot out the darkness, to hide the abyss of meaninglessness from us. "God" becomes a means of hiding from God.

But "God" in my practice is more than just an abstract philosophical counter. The word implies not necessarily a distinct person but certainly some quality of personhood, and this makes a difference to my waiting. I wait expecting to relate. I address the darkness as Thou, as Abba. I cannot say whether what I hear is anything more than an echo of that cry. It remains my faith that such waiting is good. At the same time, I must acknowledge that the word "God" may have other less helpful implications particularly with regard to gender and all that is tied up with that. Endless wise attention

147

is needed to make the waiting real.

Moving to the more general question of the functions of religious language, James limits himself to those uses "that claim to express an evidential content", thus setting on one side "the language of adoration, of petition, of intercession or of commandment". I think James thereby gives undue primacy to the descriptive function of language. He seems to assume that that which can be encompassed within the language of description is somehow more secure, reliable and primary than that which cannot.

I want to understand language as being only partly concerned with description, verification, knowledge and information or with prediction, analysis, control and containment. Language serves other, arguably more important, purposes. There are social functions of creating and sustaining community by providing mechanisms of inclusion and exclusion, of closure and opening, of inwardness and otherness. More abstract, perhaps, but no less important are functions of questioning, challenging, breaking, pointing beyond, carrying, conjuring with possibilities and simply playing. What we are engaged in is a huge exercise in the imposition of value and meaning - a highly sophisticated communal enterprise of storytelling in which scientific validity and simple historical veracity play a smaller role than many would like to believe.

Religion, I suggest, must be understood in the context of that storytelling enterprise, an enterprise which now differs from that undertaken by our ancestors not so much because of scientific discoveries (or because of "what we have discovered about the uses of language") as because of changes in the way our stories are told, particularly those brought about by mass communication and information technology. Our science is perhaps better than theirs, but this has been achieved at the cost of forgetting the value of poetry and storytelling and consequently the need for an ethic of such things.

To limit language (and religious language in particular) to a tool for speaking of our experience, and to analyse faith whilst leaving adoration, petition etc. on one side, is almost to

148

create by definition the difficulties with which James struggles. Language is also, perhaps more importantly, a means of enabling or making space for experience. It does not need to be "about" anything, just as faith need not be faith "in" anything.

V.

Stories

The Bible stories with which I feel most comfortable are from the Old Testament, especially those of Abraham and Isaac, Jacob wrestling with the angel, Job and Jonah. These stories press as hard as is possible the question, "How, in the light of experience, can you believe in a good God?". I do not know anywhere where the paradox of the justice of God or the difficulty of having any kind of faith in meaning is more brutally confronted. None of the stories resolves the paradox. The stories end in mystery, in the insoluble tension between ought and is, and they question even the possibility of knowing what is "good". However, they do not state that mystery is the answer. They carry me as far as may be in a certain direction and leave me to walk the rest of the way on my own - which perhaps is to say that they point to what lies beyond speech.

The direction in which they carry me is towards daring to believe in meaning, in life, in love, however you wish to put it - towards living *etsi deus daretur* (which, in its implied presupposition that *deus non daretur* confronts me with an even greater challenge than to live *etsi deus non daretur*). It is not an answer that is given, but a means of living with (rather than avoiding) a huge question.

Could these stories be analysed as myth or metaphor? I certainly do not take them as history, nor for me do they come so close to claiming to be history as to raise the problems of miracle. I do not want to classify them as myth or metaphor because I do not think their function is to be descriptive in any way of anything. They are not offered, or at least I do not take them, as evidence of anything. Their value is not as an account of experience from which inferences may be drawn. They do not assert, report or represent anything; they do not demonstrate, prove, show or change the probability of anything. Rather they create a space within which I may perhaps find the experience for myself.

What I am trying to say is that to analyse language in categories of evidential content risks taking the external point of view of one who stands outside the language and looks to see where it is pointing. Storytelling, poetry and even law function as such only for those who will stand inside the language and allow themselves to be carried by it without necessarily being able to see where it is going.

Are these stories any less effective than when they were written? Two things have changed. Science has advanced and we have the story of Jesus. The advance of science has altered the point at which we encounter the paradox but it has not resolved or reduced it. Is it easier now, or harder, to have faith in the possibility of value or meaning, to know what is "good" let alone to have confidence that "all will be well"? We do perhaps find it harder now to reconcile belief in God with our scientific outlook but I suggest that this is more because we have forgotten how to live with stories than because we have discovered anything which invalidates those stories. As for Jesus, some read the gospel as superseding the Old Testament and as resolving and nullifying all its difficulties. This devalues both the gospel and the Old Testament stories. I see Jesus not as resolving the Old Testament riddles but as posing them even more sharply. All I can do is stand in relation to the stories as I think a disciple of his might have done.

Why should these stories be any more important than other great literature which confronts the same issues? Perhaps other stories may be found which are just as rich and searching, if such things can be measured, but it is not simply a question of the comparative merits of different stories in their own right. What makes these stories special is that they are so lived in - both by the Jewish people (not to mention Islam) and by the Church. There is a richness in the evolution of the stories, in the layers of commentary on them and in their influence on every aspect of our culture which makes them an inextricable part of the way we live. Any analysis of religious language will be incomplete if it focuses solely on the text of the story at the expense of the manner of its telling.

VI.

Jesus

The story of Jesus is, in a sense, just one more story, but it is obviously a very special story for two particular reasons. First, in the community within which I hear it, it is by far the most important story; second, the story as told claims, and claims to depend upon, a certain kind of historical truth.

I deliberately present those two features in that order. It is not the case that I hear what claims to be a historical story, that I consider the evidence in favour of its being historically accurate and then draw conclusions according to the weight of that evidence. Rather, I have grown up in a community where this story is taken to be fundamentally important; I have allowed that story to carry me, and have found it to be compelling and somehow inescapable; questions about its historical accuracy are only one comparatively small part of my struggle to understand why it is so compelling. Those questions have to be asked, and the answers I find will affect my understanding of the story and of the community which sustains it. However, I certainly do not expect that the accuracy of the story can somehow be independently established, nor do I find that scientific scepticism about "what happened" seriously undermines the essential validity of the story. As James observes, "the question from which I would start is not precisely what happened (relevant though that is) but why the miracle story was and is told? What kind of person could be at the centre of it?"

A crucial question is whether the story of Jesus' resurrection was fact or part of the surrounding fantasy. The question is crucial because the Church makes it so, along with Jesus' claims to be the Son of God. On these two assertions there hangs a huge amount of systematic theology. And yet my honest answer, at a purely personal level, is that it does not matter; I do not need to make factual claims on either point, and I would rather live with doubt than with the logical conclusions that some would draw from such claims. If one thinks long enough about the nature of humanness and individuality, then the distinction between one person and another begins to dissolve; if the edges of that distinction are allowed to blur a little, then the boundary between one person and the next and between the living and the dead ceases to be so important. It becomes possible to understand Jesus as a sort of "everyman", as an icon of humanness (which I find a more helpful idea than that of an icon of love), and as making his claims not on behalf of himself only but on behalf of everyone. Such an understanding reduces the difficulty of the "scandal of particularity"; it does not make his claims any less outrageous.

I have to recognise that what I have said is heretical (and also arguably an illegitimate means of ducking a paradox!). I cannot and do not propose that this is the story the Church should tell. The story is bigger than me and beyond me; it does not belong to me. I stand in relation to it like a somewhat sceptical, over-sophisticated disciple - the sort of lawyer who would have come to Jesus by night and disputed with him and more often than not gone away with a heavy heart but still come back for more the next night. This story, this Jesus, I experience as calling me, as having time for me and yet as not having me at the centre of his public purpose.

I experience the challenges which Jesus puts to me as being far more important than precisely what he was. In fact, the huge claims about what he was are one way of disabling the challenges. I simply will not accept that Jesus completed the task for us and that his sinless life and undeserved death are acceptable as the magic answer to God's impossible sums. Jesus is not the only one who has died a horrible, undeserved death for the sake of others; and I do not wish to be saved for a God who works that sort of arithmetic.

Jesus showed us a way (of looking and of being) and the call is to follow it. This brings me to my own choice of "ultimate paradox": that Jesus' way is to bring wholeness by becoming unclean himself - as a result of cleansing the lepers and enabling them to enter the town he becomes excluded from the town. This paradox might be resolved in two ways.

One is to say that Jesus had a unique calling, and that the rest of us just have to accept the gift of his healing and walk with the lepers back into the town, back to wholeness as we have always understood it. Another approach is to allow the call to question our very understanding of wholeness, just as the Old Testament stories question our understanding of the meaning of "justice" or "righteousness" or "goodness". At the heart of the matter, for Old and New Testaments the issue is the same: human wholeness lies beyond our necessary, provisional rationalisation. We are called to serve our neighbour not by eradicating insecurity from a position of security but by sharing the insecurity and recognising a different sort of wholeness in it. This call I think to be absolutely fundamental but, if not impossible, then at least utterly impractical. It is a call which I do not know how to answer. No amount of agonising about history will make that call go away for me.

VII.
Church

My faith is faith in a certain kind of value, faith in a story and faith in the Church which tells it. My faith in the Church has two aspects. The first concerns its historical role, and the second concerns its role as a community in which I live today.

Just as I cannot approach the "historical" Christ except through the story, so I cannot approach the story except through the Church which, over the years, has told it. James recognises this in several places, particularly when he objects to those who would jettison the distinctive body of beliefs which we have inherited "even though valuable moral insights may have been communicated through it, together with a less desirable heritage of beliefs and practices ... There needs to be a tension between past and present; between what we have inherited and the use we need to make of it; between what we receive and what we pass on." There is indeed great tension in the tradition we have inherited, and not just between a homogeneous past and the present. A particular point of tension for me is that between what I hear of Jesus in the gospels and that which is made of him by the fantastic

153

rationalising effort of St Paul.

Despite (or even through) that tension, it might be possible to live with the gospel as a great work of literature handed down over the ages by the Church, and even to add one's own commentary as part of the richness to be inherited by future generations. In the same way, it is possible to read and comment upon a great play without the play ever having to be acted. In both cases, though, the acting out adds an entirely different dimension which is absent from any plain reading of the literature, however learned or committed. By "acting out" the gospel story, I do not mean living according to the values of the gospel, important though that is. A life informed by a deep reading of the gospel and lived according to its values may be a very good life and I do not say that it is necessarily any less good for lack of commitment to the Church. But there is another sense of "acting out" which refers to a particular way of being involved in the specific story, something which makes a difference to how I hear (and am carried by) the story, how I tell the story and how we, as a community, live together in the story. That acting out is, of course, most obvious in the Eucharist. It is this which calls me back from the Quakers to a more sacramentally based Church, and yet in some ways this is the most tantalising part of my faith. Issues of the Christian vocation and how we should live our lives are perhaps more difficult and important. The call to play my part in the Church just seems so foolish and frustrating.

The Church with which I get so frustrated is a Church which spends far too much time talking about the story at the expense of simply telling it. Incidentally, it is also a Church that, when it does tell stories, is much happier telling the stories of Paul than the stories of Jesus. It is a Church which tries too hard to express itself scientifically and to give a complete and coherent account which closes out the paradoxes. It can achieve this only by creating a system which is not complete - a system which achieves coherence by being self-contained but cut off from the rest of reality - a system of divine justice to which I am asked to assent but which really tells me nothing at all about human wholeness (and in fact too often becomes simply a proclamation of human inadequacy). Instead of preserving a space for us to be open to the stars, it paints pretty pictures on the ceiling and calls them "God". It decides that the pictures somehow are God and that it therefore possesses God, a possession which it must now share with those outside. Its mission becomes the unhealthily circular one of simply getting bigger (a mission too often also motivated by the need to find funds to repair the boiler and, now, to pay for the vicar's pension).

The Church of my dreams is a ruined, bombed-out Church, a Church with no roof and no doors. It is a Church which has faith in the story as a means of waiting upon the darkness - of holding its people before the abyss whether the abyss prove to be one of meaninglessness or of ultimate meaning. It is a Church which shuts nothing and no-one out - in fact it invites them all in, teenagers, homeless people and all the other nuisances, not primarily because of any spiritual or material benefit that it might have to confer on them but because it needs them if its listening and its understanding of human wholeness are to grow. It is a Church which does not believe that it possesses Christ at all - in fact, it expects to find Christ out there sooner than in here. The Church's function is to feed that expectation, to be a place of waiting upon the abyss that we may better go out and wait upon that of God in every man.

My reality is, of course, a mixture of these things, just as it should be. The Church I know is a wonderfully rich community of people wrestling with God, a community which hangs together despite (sometimes almost because of) the frustrating theology. For this, on my better days, I give thanks.

VIII.
Morals

Early on, James recognises the impossibility of standing outside his own culture and intellectual assumptions, but he considers it necessary to deny that this leads either to determinism or "to the relativism that declines to speak of

155

values in an absolute sense, and regards the values upheld in a culture as relative only to that culture". He makes certain affirmations on which his discussion is founded, including the need to "hold on to the notion that we live in a world of shared values, whatever the differences between us: that the notion of a humanity which we all share is a valid one...". This affirmation, he says, is not specifically Christian. The particular contribution of Christianity is a belief in "the transcendent quality of love" which is "not merely an expression of my own feelings; it has to do with the order of things". James works towards a "Christian humanism" which recognises the limitations of being human but sees those limitations existing in a tension with the Christian vision of love. He concludes that "only the love that gives itself can be the supreme virtue ... This leads me on to the notion of a hierarchy of values, in which the demand of love becomes more insistent the more nearly you approach the Kingdom, and you must give up the lesser for the greater. But only if you think it genuinely greater."

What does my faith have to say about how we should live in a world where so many certainties seem to have dissolved and in which "we may not even know for what we should hope"? What I hear in my darkness is that there can be no return to whatever certainties we think there might once have been. The call is to live with uncertainty and with all the responsibility that that entails. We cannot derive "ought" from "is", nor can we formulate absolute values in a way that is at all useful. The call for absolute values is too often, I think, connected with a desire to distance ourselves from evil rather than to try to understand why evil is done.

The holocaust and Hiroshima are defining events of our age. Neither event was, or could be, prevented by any system of absolute values or by any structure of authority. The only way we can prevent either event happening again is, first, by acknowledging that we ourselves could perfectly easily end up being responsible for such events, and, second, by trying to develop the strength to discern and resist the tides of human conduct (individual and communal) which give rise to such events. Of course, this calls for great humility: we need provisional codes of conduct and structures of authority, and we must participate in the debate as to what they should be whilst recognising that we do not start from scratch. At the same time, we have got to be responsible for our own conclusions, even sometimes responsible for pursuing a vision of human wholeness which contradicts those codes and structures. As James suggests, we need the humility to abandon the lesser only in favour of that which is truly discerned to be greater, and grace to discern wisely.

Does the Christian story contribute anything worthwhile? It offers a great deal of wisdom, in both the Old and New Testaments, which we take to be summarised in the commandments to love God and our neighbour. It also teaches that those commandments concern orientation, not specific conduct. The harder one tries, the harder it is to know what love really requires, because there is no final definition of human wholeness, only an endlessly enriching succession of kicks in the teeth and glimpses of glory. As with hope, so love turns out to be love of the wrong thing. And yet, to continue James' quotation from Eliot, "there is yet faith, but the faith and the love and the hope are all in the waiting."

What of the Church? It has its place in society's struggle to develop a wise provisional ethic, but that place is far less influential than it was. It should continue to play its part but should not, I think, mourn its loss of influence too greatly, for that influence was perhaps bought at too great a price. As it plays its part, it must learn to speak a secular language, for arguments based on Christian premises carry little weight in a non-Christian society, and to refuse to speak the language of that society is to retreat into a self-serving ghetto. It needs faith that its story carries it to a valid vision of human wholeness: it is to that vision, rather than the source of it, that it must appeal, recognising (if the vision is valid) that it will be shared by others who have come to it by a different route.

But the Church, as a community in some sense set apart, should see its primary task as being not to influence anyone but rather to preserve a space in which all who come may be held while they wait upon "that of God" in all about them. It requires real faith, faith unsupported perhaps by evidence, to believe that such a task, such preservation of space, such waiting, is possible and worthwhile at a time when we need all the moral strength we can find if our society is not to be swallowed up in its own insecurity and greed.

Still a boundless welcome beyond streetlight
Waits with being balm to the doing day's
Ache to wake a tired heart to batflight
Moonsplash and wormglow. Still does the cool gaze
Of infinite unknowing kindly invite
To intimacy of uninspection.
Dance then, ragged soul. For your delight
This starswirl. For you the shadowdragon
Plays the deep to breathe a shouting space bright
With tears of understanding. Dance, weep, leap,
Laugh and tumble gently into night's
Deep well. There we shall softly mend you, keep
You, at last restore you to walk at ease
The new day, present, given as the trees.

A Journey into Faith

Olga Pocock

I am the only member of our group who started life as an Eastern Christian. My first religious experience was not of words but of images, of church icons of saints overarched by Christ Pantocrator, whom I saw as a small child looking down at me from the cupola in the rue Daru church in Paris. Although he was far above me, yet his eyes looked straight down into mine - the transfigured one reaching into the depths of the soul of an individual early in its formative years, informing my perception throughout my life of the mystery which transcends yet penetrates and indwells all that exists.

From this first phase of religious experience, profoundly personal but not dominated by intellectual or dogmatic notions of God, my family came to live for a while with my English grandfather, a pillar of the C. of E. externally, but a sad, cruel and narrow old tyrant in his outlook and private conduct. Against my will, I was confirmed. Convenient fainting bouts stopped me from going to church. This was my first rebellious rejection in outrage at what passed for the Christian faith.

It was not until I experienced another trauma, separation from my family in my 'teens, that my resulting distress led me eventually in my first year at college, into the university church where I came to know its vicar, Dick Milford; into the Student Christian Movement where I came to know some remarkable fellow students; and into active contact with the Franciscans with their joyous acceptance of all of life.

This account of my journey in and into faith is very personal, subjective and unintellectual . What matters, however, is the impact on me at this point and throughout my life of men and women who were to me Christ-like. The risen Christ icon and these living human beings somehow came together and began to make sense to me of my own life, leading me some years later to study for the Lambeth Diploma in Theology (which at that point in time could well have been named the Lambeth Diploma in Biblical Theology!). To understand something of the living formation of the Old Testament and to read the New Testament in Greek was a revelation - that, as far back as 4,000 years ago, human individuals had similar experiences to mine, and that the sense they made of them in the 1st century in the revelatory light of the impact upon them of the man Jesus was the sense I was making of mine. I recognised in them and above all in him the quality of life which had so deeply impressed me in people and groups at university - the capacity for joy and sorrow, the compassionate acceptance of "the sinner" and, above all, reverence for others even when confronting their unacceptable actions. Mercy and judgment went hand in hand, mercy transcending judgment in its renewing and reconciling power.

My studies of the formation and development of the early Church took place in the context of being a member of a family deeply separated within the Christian tradition by Church doctrines - my mother an Orthodox, my brother a convert to Catholicism and myself an Anglican. Already, I had experienced the consequences of divisions within the Churches. These studies corroborated my awareness that the Church and the Gospel were not synonymous, and led to my second rebellion. This time it was against traditional Church teachings about God, coinciding with the publication of "Honest to God" and the "death of God" controversy in the '60s. The doubts expressed in the writings of that period echoed my own and those of many others within the Churches, faithful yet silently questioning. I felt a deep anger against the notion of a "God out there" who judged without mercy if the Church's rules - God-given, it was alleged - were transgressed. What kind of a God was that? I did not believe in that kind of God, alleged in the Creeds to be the creator of all that is ('evil' as well as 'good'). I went through a deeply unhappy period at that time, casting myself out of the worshipping Church community until, very slowly and in long-term therapy (spiritual direction had not grasped my nettle) I came to find "God" and a new peace within myself. For me at that time, God was infinitely more than personal. The personal was within the totality of the Godhead, and God indwelt every created being and inanimate thing.

This, however, led to my third rebellion (if that is what it was) which was given substance by my work at a College of

Education when I was asked to lecture on comparative religion. I plunged into reading the sacred texts of the main world religions and discovered their perspectives on "truth", truth as they saw it. The conclusion I reached in my '50s was that there was a universal experience inherent in all human beings, individually and in community, a search, a need, for making sense of their meaning and purpose. The world religions were the formal and corporate expression of this level of search in cultures throughout the world. Each world religion represents an interpretation of ultimate reality for its adherents - "the faith" for them. But their existence also highlights that "no one has seen God at any time" in the fullness of that expression, nor has any world religion full or ultimate possession of "the truth" about existence. Jesus, the unwitting founder of Christianity, is no exception, as the gospel of St John makes clear. The Holy Spirit will, in the future, lead men and women "into all truth", but "you cannot bear [it] now." Looking back on the early doctrinal developments in Christianity, it is clear that some of the 'heresies' of the fourth century are now accepted as glimpsing more fully what pertains to 'God'. No one now questions seriously, for instance that God is capable of suffering, or that Jesus was a man who lived a fully human life and died a fully human death. The Christ, distinct from yet integral to the personhood of Jesus, is now recognized to be the interpretation his followers put upon the meaning of his life, actions and teachings, as representing how man is meant to be and what the world is meant to be. Indeed, it is a sine qua non that there are a number of interpretations of the meaning of Jesus in the New Testament.

As still within the Christian tradition though not feeling bound by Church rules, I believe that the man Jesus, living at a period of history and in a geographical area which was the thoroughfare for cultures, religions and communications in the eastern part of the Roman Empire in its decline, set off, by the impact of his personality and teaching upon communities disheartened yet not without hope, an understanding of the re-creative and liberating possibilities in suffering and oppression

162

which vivified and gave hope to his followers in the here-and-now, finding hitherto untapped resources of courage and conviction to demonstrate in their quality of life the power of agapaic love over persecution, suffering and meaninglessness.

I do not imagine, however, that agapaic love is confined to Christians. It is a universal possibility for experience. What varies is how it is interpreted in religious terms. How that love is exercised has constantly to be reviewed in the context of changes in Western and global civilization. It seems to me that, at the end of the 20th century, the influence of the Christian churches in the Western world is at a low ebb. The renewing power of God preserved in tradition needs to work upon their underlying sense of weakness and defensiveness, and give them the courage to receive and learn from the scientists, especially those who are uncovering the immensity of the universe, and from those who are uncovering the complexities of the human body and psyche.

As I see it, all human knowledge, whether of the intellect or of the imagination, or of religion, is a given; all is to be found, since it is all within the mysterious givenness of existence. No individual, no community, and no religion can claim full or superior possession of "the truth". My faith, towards the end of my life, is that of an agnostic about claims to understand or know ultimates. Increasingly, I marvel at the ordered complexities of the natural world around me of which I am a part. I am clearer for myself about what works towards the enhancement of living as a human being in relation to myself and to others. It is enshrined, for me, in the quality of relating, living and dying of the man Jesus. The "God out there" is now increasingly grasped through my increasing wonder at the givenness of every moment of my existence, the pain and the joy, what makes sense and that which appears to have no meaning. I am an infinitesimal speck within creation in its never-ending flux as it changes, dies and re-creates itself. Yet, paradoxically, I feel that I matter for the reason that I take an active part in that process into which I was brought at my birth and which will continue in, through and beyond my death.

Christian Belief and Practice: An Orthodox R.C. View

Anthony Pragnell

I
Introduction

We have been encouraged to produce papers on the philosophies that members of the Chantry Group have attempted to live by. In this present contribution, I have not made any lengthy comment on what others have said but try to explain my own belief and practice. I write as a life-long practising Roman Catholic with, as will be explained shortly, an ecumenical outlook. I find my contacts with fellow Christians immensely rewarding and I hope that some of that warmth of feeling comes through in what I write.

I am able to accept a corpus of Christian belief resting on three bases:

-revelation;

-tradition; and

-what I shall call Church teaching.

I do not feel that being a Roman Catholic makes me all that different from other Christians. My contact with them through personal friendships and through joint activity (via the Local Council of Churches, of which I have been chairman twice, and Christian Aid) confirms to me the large block of belief that we hold in common - the divinity of Our Lord; the continued validity of his teachings; the fact that he founded a Church; the recognition that, whatever the difficulties, our present divisions must be healed; the significance of our common baptism; and, a simple fact that we are prone to overlook, our common belief in the necessity and efficacy of prayer.

On this last point, we can be encouraged by what the Pope John Paul II said in 1995:

"Along the ecumenical path to unity, pride of place certainly belongs to common prayer, the prayerful union of those who gather together around Christ himself. If Christians .... meet more often and more regularly before Christ in prayer, they will be able to gain the courage to face all the painful human reality of their divisions, and they will find themselves together once more in that community of the Church which Christ constantly builds up in the Holy Spirit, in spite of all weaknesses and human limitations."

II

Revelation

"God ..... has shone in our minds to radiate the light of the knowledge of God's glory, the glory on the face of Christ. We are only the earthenware jars that hold this treasure, to make it clear that such an overwhelming power comes from God and not from us."

II Corinthians : 4:6-7

"..... what God's Son hath told me,
take for truth I do:
truth himself speaks truly,
or there's nothing true."

Ascribed to St. Thomas Aquinas, tr. G.M. Hopkins

For me, the whole New Testament story rings true and I find it impossible to think of it as in any sense a myth. I ask myself, for instance, who could invent Simeon and his "nunc dimittis" at the Presentation, or the Visitation with its Magnificat, or the encounter with Martha and Mary?

So far as the impact of scripture on the way we live is concerned, I hold that

(i)   if we are looking for specific precepts we find them through the Commandments and their filling out by the commands in Mark 12:29-31 to love God to the limit of our ability and to love our neighbour as ourself:

(ii)   we find guidance in Christ's teaching and preaching (for example in the Sermon on the Mount in Matthew, the Sermon on the Plain in Luke and the articulation of the Lord's Prayer, also in Luke); and

(iii) we find the supreme expression of selflessness and perfection of living in Christ's conduct and demeanour, culminating in his death on the cross.

III

Tradition

"There are historical characteristics of the Christian religion you just can't dismiss"

- Lord Runcie, quoted in Michael De-la-Noy's portrait of Michael Ramsey.

Despite different views about the true meaning of tradition, I myself find it a strengthening of faith if I take it to mean the continuing stream of explanation, elucidation (and dare I say it, sifting?) of belief and doctrine which, as it were, represents the accumulation of the wisdom of the Church over two thousand years and which reinforces and guides us about the lessons to be learnt from scripture.

In another sense - and here I speak more personally - I value the way in which the sequential tradition of the liturgy (God's clock, in Bruce Marshall's phrase) reflects and backs up the ongoing life of the community of Christians. I do not mean only the great feasts of Christmas, Easter and Pentecost which mirror and describe the central events which have formed our faith, but the other landmarks which punctuate the year - Lent, Advent, Corpus Christi, Peter and Paul, the Assumption, All Saints and All Souls, not to mention patronal feasts and the ferial cycle of ordinary weekdays.

IV

Church Teaching

The Good News needs to be translated into precepts and guidelines about how individuals and communities should live. How, for instance, do we translate the great exhortations about loving God and our neighbour or the proclamations of the Beatitudes into workable canons appropriate to the 1990s, for example in relation to would-be immigrants? Nearer home, how do we relate the Third Commandment to Sunday trading and our own conduct on that day?

Other aspects of contemporary life which raise moral issues for us include protection of family values (and structures), divorce law reform, the pro-life versus pro-choice debate, the purpose and content of education in a largely secular society and the conduct of the media (particularly in the matter of the protection of children).

I do not attempt to conceal that, on a number of issues where the views of Christian churches are looked for, an orthodox Catholic would find himself or herself conditioned by the magisterium of the church which enunciates and validates particular doctrines. Current examples of such issues hardly need mentioning - embryo research, euthanasia, the status of marriage and so on. I have to live (and am willing to do so) with constraints on how far I can stray in such cases from the established line.

V

Concluding Remarks: Community

What has been said above delineates the nature of the Christian faith that I hold. I would, before concluding, like to refer to another aspect of Christian life which is of importance to me. This is the aspect of "community".

It is plainly much easier to maintain and nourish belief and practice if we live in community with other Christians. This is most visibly achieved by sharing in the sacramental and preaching roles of the churches we adhere to. This is, I think, one of the central aspects of the communion of saints which we proclaim in the Creed.

Physical membership of a church also gives the opportunity to spread the Good News and to join with others in living out the Christian life.

To end by referring once again to what Pope John Paul II said last year on ecumenism, he stressed the fertile ground there was for practical co-operation between churches in social and cultural life, the defence of human dignity, promotion of peace, application of the Gospel to social life, and bringing the Christian spirit to the world of science and the arts. This co-operation should never be merely humanitarian action, for "it has its reason for being in the Lord's words: 'For I was hungry and you gave me food.' "

I have-lived for three-quarters of a century. I regard it as little short of a miracle - and certainly a matter for prayerful gratitude - that there has been so strong a thaw on the part of my church in the matter of dialogue, common worship and co-operation in action with other churches.

Deo gratias.

Credo.

Bryan Saunders

I.

Family background and early belief.

I was brought up in a solid nonconformist household. My father was a scientist who worked for ICI on dyestuffs research. He was also a stalwart supporter of the local Congregational church. For many years he was Church Secretary and used to read the notices in church on Sunday mornings in a voice that sounded as though he were announcing the Day of Judgement.

I never asked him how he reconciled his religion with his scientific work. I think I felt it would be an impertinence, and I suspect that he kept the two things in different compartments of his mind. I never could see how one could believe in the resurrection of the dead if one knew about the work of chemists and biologists. How could the molecules of which we are made be reassembled once the system has disintegrated? I remember feeling that this argument was unanswerable before I was ten. I was also conscious even then of the continuity of the animal kingdom. If there was a heaven for us to go to what happened to the cats and dogs? I know now that many people believe that they will be reunited in heaven with their beloved pets, but what about flies, tape worms and scorpions? It always seemed to me blasphemous to make religious distinctions between different members of the animal kingdom. We might *prefer* one species to another if it came to having one in the bed, but that was just a human preference, not a divine distinction.

About God I was more agnostic, but felt sure that, if there is a God, he did not interfere in the operation of natural laws in order to relieve distressed human beings. If one was unwell, a doctor was more likely to help than prayer. I think my father agreed about this, and he certainly called the doctor if we were ill, but he did not discuss these philosophical questions with us. I doubt if he was interested in them. He quite often talked about religion, but it was always about the church and its governance. He was proud of the democratic organisation of the free churches, and felt himself to be upholding and

173

participating in an important stream of English life. Although he was a cultured man, who loved the music of Beethoven and Schubert, and the songs of Hugo Wolf, he disliked anything very dramatic and could not abide opera. He told me that he had once, at the end of the 1914 war, attended a great requiem mass in Notre Dame in Paris. He said "It was a great spectacular performance, but that is all it was - no participation, no worship."

I suppose I was about sixteen when I first heard the argument that man had made God in his own image. I found it shocking. I felt it was blasphemous. I came later to realize that it could be - and was - put forward as a serious argument. I then realized that the feeling of blasphemy was the key to a puzzle. The effect of an offence against truth is paradox - a statement that appears to be both true and false. The effect of an offence against values is outrage - a statement for the making of which a person should be banished from the community. Blasphemy is the name for religious outrage. So I had to ask myself whether my belief in God was based on evidence, or had been passed down to me in the culture. I have gradually come to the conviction that it cannot be the former, since there is no evidence that supports it. But I have also come to realize that it is possible to believe in God (though not the God most Christians believe in) without evidence, and that it is possible to be religious without believing in God.

After the war, when I returned to Oxford, I found the teaching and approach of the SCM congenial. I became a confirmed member of the Church of England, because it was "official". In other words, I felt instinctively that, if religion was to be supported, it should be the recognised and established institution of the tribe that was supported.

II
Why traditional Christian belief has become difficult.

There has been a revolution in scholarship during the last three hundred years. It is often referred to as the scientific revolution, but it might be more accurate to call it the "Pragmatic Revolution", for what it has insisted on is the principle that evidence about the nature of the world must come from investigation of the world itself, rather than from creative imagination.

Most scientists probably do not think of themselves primarily as scholars, but the qualities required of them are those that have always been required of scholars; patience and persistence in the search for truth, careful attention to detail in argument, honesty and accuracy in report, respect for other workers and a cooperative approach to the subject, even under the pressure of competition.

This change in the disciplines of thought has affected religion in two different, but interlinking ways. Firstly the application of these principles to the analysis of religious texts has deeply undermined their claim to historical accuracy, and secondly advances in the understanding of the cosmos and the origins of living things have undermined long cherished tribal myths concerning creation and man's place in the world. Not only has cosmology shrunk man's place in the physical world, but Darwin's account of the rise and evolution of living things has given man a more ordinary place in the living world than his own intuition gave him.

I believe that Jesus of Nazareth was a real person of commanding genius and uniquely sympathetic personality, whose teachings had a freshness and perceptiveness that made him a natural leader among a tribe that had a religious tradition of exceptional richness and depth. I believe he was crucified by the Romans on suspicion of sedition and, after his death, a great myth was elaborated by some of his followers, principally Paul of Tarsus. This myth incorporated his teachings (as they remembered them), but also added a great deal of theology. It was perhaps the greatest of all human works of imagination. It provided a complete template for the relationship of man with his world. It offered every individual who followed it, whether weak or powerful, simple or subtle, a means to cope with his experience, whether of guilt and frustration, joy and contentment, bewilderment, enlightenment, or the awareness of approaching death. It was not just an intellectual reworking of religious tradition, but a complete basis for a tribal institution celebrating, justifying and enshrining the tribe's view of the non-tangible world of their experience - a church. Not surprisingly, its contribution to human welfare (and also unfortunately human cruelty and suffering) has been incalculable.

This remarkable structure included a number of statements, presented as historical fact, that are plainly incredible. It is not possible to believe that Jesus raised people from the dead, or that his corpse came to life after crucifixion. The whole system of living things is based on a cycle of renewal and reformation, as generation follows generation. The escape of *Homo Sapiens* from the daily fear of predators is almost unique. The idea of life after death implies an accumulation of the generations that can only have meaning in the context of a non-material world. This implies dualism, which is discussed below.

I find it impossible to believe in a God who created the heavens and the earth and looks after our welfare. There is no such pancreator, and when we die, we die - and stay dead. I do not find this distressing, but I find it necessary to assert the complementary truth that while we are alive we are alive. And we have to assert that we are fully responsible; right to the last day. Others will still wish to believe, in literal truth, "in my flesh I shall see God." They cannot be disappointed. As for me, I can imagine no heaven offering a more sublime experience than listening to Kathleen Ferrier singing those words.

This still leaves the possibilty that there is indeed a God, which is wholly transcendent - that is outside the world, and outside our experience. This is the God of the mystics: remote and crystalline, the source of all truth, beauty and justice. It (I cannot use "He" or "She" without implying a humanity that is not appropriate) is "the ground of all being"; the Principle, to use the prayer book words, "in whom we live and move and have our being", and not only we, but also everything else. Perhaps indeed the austere beauties of mathematics, of which we have so far only explored the edges, are thoughts in the mind of God. God's function is to guarantee the integrity of logic and mathematics; in other words to express in Its own Being the integrity of all existence. To exist, a thing must be itself and nothing else. That is to say, it is defined by its nature, and that nature can only be expressed in perfect language, to which we cannot attain. So (the argument goes) a God is needed to explain how anything can exist.

In one sense this is nonsense. I suspect that Wittgenstein might have said it is an example of the attempt to say what cannot be said. I would defend it on the grounds that it is not a statement at all, but a way to express an attitude to the fact of existence. Such attitudes are a matter of personal decision - they cannot be "true" or "false". They express the way a person decides to relate to his or her life experience as a whole. This kind of religion is what is known in the strict and traditional sense as mysticism. I am not a mystic, but I respect this way of life, and remain agnostic about the existence of such a God. I can certainly feel the awesome grandeur of the world displayed to us by modern physics, and easily understand why physicists should feel that they are exploring the mind of God.

James refers to the definition of transcendence in the Fontana Dictionary of Modern Thought as 'the state of being beyond the reach or apprehension of experience'. He adds "I would not wish to make so clear a distinction between our experience and what may lie beyond it." I cannot follow him in this. I think the dictionary got it right. Of course there are shadowy experiences at the limits of our understanding, but I see no excuse for blurring a clear distinction. There is the world we know (and about which we are also inexhaustibly ignorant). If there is anything beyond it, it is beyond it. As James says, "we have to recognize both the limitations of our experience and the human instinct not to be satisfied to do so." Precisely so, but instincts are just that. They tell us something about ourselves, but nothing about the world outside ourselves.

I do not feel any need to put up a lengthy defence of these

177

beliefs, because I think they are probably quite close to the beliefs of many educated people in Western Europe today. They could, I suspect, be described as "mainstream". But for this reason it is important that I address James' suggestion that for me, and many like me, "life has no meaning".

III
The importance of what we believe about man.

The most important effect of the changes in scholarship described above, is not the change in our beliefs about God, but the change in our beliefs about man.

If one has been accustomed to believe that the cosmos was created by a benevolent God, to provide a place of instruction and correction in which imperfect man might grow to perfection, and so qualify for heaven where he will praise and glorify Him for ever, then it must seem like a grievous loss to accept that, on the contrary, the cosmos is a vast indifferent system in which it just happened that, on a tiny planet orbiting a very ordinary star, the conditions for life existed, and man happened to evolve. Surprisingly, it turns out not to be a disaster, but a liberating experience.

In any case, if the evidence points to the conclusion that that is the way it is, are we not better off for knowing it? And if we only accept the **possibility** that this is the way things are, is it not prudent to work out what difference it would make to our position? For it does indeed overturn many attitudes. It causes us to stop viewing man as a strange compound creature, part animal, part angel, living in two worlds, one seen and one unseen, and trying to regain a pre-ordained state of perfection, and see him instead as an animal with unique gifts produced by the painful and messy process of evolution, struggling to improve his life without doing too much damage to the rest of the ecosystem from which he sprang, and of which he is still a part.[1] It causes us also to recognise that we alone are responsible for our actions and omissions, and all their consequences. There is no divine power ready to intervene to save us from being part of the Sixth Extinction, if that is the way our species is going.[2]

178

Despair is one possible response to such a discovery. Yet despair is in league with death, and if we see the challenges as bracing we find that the world without the old gods is no less habitable. Certainly we should not complain that it is not intelligible. The revolution in thinking since the renaissance has shown clearly that the attempt to understand the world by investigation can be richly rewarded.

It is in relation to ourselves that we seem to make progress most slowly. There may be good reason for this. There is an ancient intuition that it is dangerous to know too much about the deep springs of our own nature; it is expressed in the Greek idea of Nemesis, and in the myth of the Tree of the Knowledge of Good and Evil. **Indeed** it is dangerous when such thinking leads to conclusions that call for expression in political action. The ignorant application of mistaken ideas from genetics helped Hitler to achieve dominance for a barbaric regime over civilized people. Yet we cannot now retreat from the need to know about ourselves, nor from the prudent management of our own dangerous species. The way to curb further reversions to barbarism is to know more about the reasons for them, not to try to revert to a lost innocence. Old people may well find the challenge intimidating, but young people will not. We owe it to them to borrow their hope and share our knowledge with them.

IV
A living God and a dead cosmos.

The question I wish to address is this; if man does indeed create God in his own image, what difference does it make? I expect that the intuitive answer will be; "Such a God is not real. He has no power over us and does not merit our worship."

Any Christian who makes that reply, presumably believes that the Christian God is real. But what about the countless thousands of gods of other religions? Surely they cannot all be real, and yet they have clearly had great power in the communities where they were at home. There is no room for doubt about the power of God (however we conceive of him)

179

to change the human communities that worship him. On the other hand there is no evidence anywhere that any god actually made a star, a comet or a tree. Gods in every part of the world are human-friendly. They often embody also, in one shape or another, principles of evil, dissonance, and enmity (and James refers to these elements in Christianity) but these elements are there to represent this part of human experience, and they never triumph at the end. There are also many bestiaries in religion, but they are always anthropomorphic. There is no religion that makes **another** species the inheritor of the earth, and relegates man to an inferior servile position.

No doubt God's power over a human community depends on the fact that its members believe he is real. There is no way that can be feigned. If it is not sincere it does not work. But is it an inherent part of this concept that God is also the maker of the physical world?

The end of dualism, the end of the shadow world of souls and spirits, the end of the resurrection of the body is not the end of human spirituality. Our spirituality is part of the deep rich life of the imagination. To believe that it cannot be so, that there must be an outside agency to account for it, is to deprive man of one of his great achievements - and to relieve us of one of our great responsibilities.

Now try a thought experiment; You have been brought up in a community which does not mention a creator god, and whose churches worship a tribal deity (whose name could well be Jesus). You have been taught that your need to work for your community, to respect its laws and your fellow-citizens is a natural part of you, as natural as arms and legs. So also is the pleasure you take in your sense of belonging to it, and of the obligations which others have to you, as you do to them. You have grown up believing that the small still voice within you that tells of the most sacred and inviolable things in your life, is the ancient wisdom of your tribe; the distilled essence of its most formative experiences over many centuries. Of course you have had experiences of baffling, frustrating and apparently unfair events, when you or others for whom you care have suffered dreadful pain or loss without reason. This happens to everyone, but you have been able to accept it, as we all must, as part of life - the rough we take with the smooth. You were able to do so because you belong to a God-fearing community and accept that evil must be conquered by courage and largeness of spirit.

Now somebody says to you; "I do not know how you can live. Your life is dark and chaotic, without any purpose. How can you manage without the significance that divine purpose in creation gives to life?" Would you be likely to reply "You are right. I never thought of that." Or might you be more likely to say "I am content to be a man among men. We are the most blessed of animals, for we alone (so far) have the power of rational thought. Above all we have imagination, which enables us to travel in our minds to the furthest limits of time and space. Why should I need to invent a creator god? The only purpose such an invention could serve would be to allow me to believe that the maker of the vast indifferent cosmos is a special friend to man. Isn't that rather anthropocentric? - even a bit arrogant?"

I suggest it is silly sentimentality to suppose that we can find some higher harmony in nature itself. Nature we can only explore with diligence and respect. The order we long for must be wrested from nature **within our own environment**, as we already wrest food and water, dwelling and amenity. What right have we to describe this situation as "chaos"? We are the only species fortunate enough by chance to evolve a brain capable of symbolic language and the life of the imagination. Having this sublime good fortune, is it to be our response to demand the cosmos? In imagination we can go between the unspeaking stars and explore the infinities of space. Are we also, like children, to demand part-ownership of it? Because nature is infinite, remote and indifferent, are we to argue petulently that life is meaningless? Do we lack the modesty to accept our place in the scheme of things? Because we make our gods, are we to say they have no power? What power do we want them to have? Certainly moving mountains is not enough - we can already do that ourselves - but the power to give us more fulfilled and significant lives does not depend on moving mountains, nor even on having invented the Big Bang, but on something more profoundly human. It depends on acceptance of our nature and destiny. Part of being grown up is not expecting to have it all done for us. I have an intuition that Bonhoeffer saw this.

V

Man's place in the scheme of things. The influence of our evolution on our mental life.

Man was always a tribal animal, and the bitter conflict between tribes that formed him also formed his natural culture. The evolution of language was the evolution of a **social** characteristic. It is not surprising that the animal it created lived in groups of highly inter-dependent individuals, nor that a strong awareness of themselves and of one another was a defining character. The life of the tribe depended on the rich communication of its members, not only by formal language, but also by a vast repertiore of gesture and expression. The tribesman's world is governed by his awareness of what his fellows expect of him, and what he can expect of them. Is it surprising if he sees the world outside the tribe also in terms of duties and obligations, intentions and rewards? Is it not natural that he should see the flowing spring as having a duty to give him water and the forest to give him prey, provided he brings the gifts their guardian spirits expect of him? That this animist attitude is as problematic as it is widespread need not surprise us. The life of the tribe is highly intuitive. Each of its members know what others are thinking without effort. Their knowledge of one another is deeply instinctual; they take it for granted and do not question it (though it is one of the most remarkable and complex capacities of man).

What they find much more difficult is to relate to an outside world that cannot be known in the same way. In their efforts to understand they create an invisible world of spirits modelled on the visible world of the tribe. Our intuitive knowledge of one another has been leading us to approach the physical world in an inappropriate way for over 100,000 years.

The intellectual revolution of the last three centuries which I have described above is the latest - and largest - step in our slow ascent out of this fallacy. There are still philosophers who recommend the reinstatement of intuition in our approach to the physical world, but they are unlikely to have much influence, since the modern approach has yielded such valuable fruit.

VI
Culture, God and Language.

Should we then distrust intuition? By no means. All our culture and common life depends on it.

Life was dangerous for those early tribes and fear always present. All animals fear the agents of death; the precipice, the powerful predator, the raging sea, the forest fire. Only man fears death itself, for death is an abstract idea, only available to those with the symbols to represent it; words. Men and women are not the only animals to huddle together when afraid, but as the nature of their fear is different, so is the nature of their response. As it is their imagination that delivers them to a more ample fear, so it is in their imagination that they respond. They build together a shared reality, woven to protect them from the giddy terrifying void that opens at their feet. Into this supernatural world they pour their hopes and fears, their supplications and terrors, their love, their mourning, their remorse. The holy rock is kissed and, polished with caresses of a thousand lips, communicates from generation to generation. So it is that, by humanising simple articles and building powerful rituals, the tribe weaves a common spiritual life; the fabric of this life with its weft of generations and its warp of continuity stretches over centuries, accumulating threads of dun and bright, strong and frayed that give the tribe its deep identity. This is how religion is born, and here is the group unconscious Jung intuitively identified.[3]

Robert Mitchell, in his very thoughtful comment on James' essay, expresses his unease about the impoverishment of language by its increasingly modal use. The language of duties and obligations, intentions and rewards is the language in which the natural community communicates, the language upon which our social life is built. We neglect it at our very great peril.

Before expanding these points, I need to say something about terms. The terms used in discussing human communities are richly ambivalent. This is inevitable, and any author who tries to pin them down with neat definitions is in grave danger of confusing both his readers and himself. Nevertheless, I need to aim for precision, so I shall try to use certain phrases (rather than words) as precisely as possible. I shall use the phrase "natural culture" to mean the culture of a tribe, which I shall refer to as a "natural community". Natural culture is the set of attitudes and dispositions (mostly subconscious) which distinguish the members of a tribe, and which they express in their language, religious rites, arts and moral code. The natural culture, and the natural community it identifies and binds together, are biological entities with their own lives and life histories. They are not susceptible to conscious human control, any more than our own growth or digestion is subject to our conscious control. I draw a distinction between these natural entities and civilisation, which is a conscious artefact of human making. Civilisation is the civil order which natural communities create by making laws and building institutions.

The idea of the natural culture as an unconscious biological entity which holds the tribe together, and gives it its distinctive characteristics, is not new. I have mentioned C.G. Jung's "Group Unconscious", and it is a persistent, if slender, thread in anthropology. It is an idea we resist because man from his earliest days has thought of himself as distinct from nature, not part of it. We like to think of ourselves as rational beings, descendants of a rational god, rather than animals who happened to develop brains and imagination, as others developed claws or wings. The chief merit of this idea is that it can explain the way the political life of a tribe develops - provided that we remember that the rhythm of evolution is quite different from the rhythm of history. Where history ticks by generations, evolution ticks by millennia.

Men and women need their gods, as ants need their nests and bees their hives. Their gods are part of their natural culture. Indeed the most significant aspects of culture are language and religious ritual. Put like this, in the third person, these statements may seem platitudes. If I put them in the first person, and say we ourselves are no different, they may seem startling.

Are modern tribes no different from those primitive tribes? (I use the word "primitive" in its nice sense, to mean "the first examples"). Of course there are differences. The most obvious is the accumulation of technology - one of the benefits that language brought to man. Another is size; a tribe is now numbered in the tens or hundreds of millions. A third is the complexity and ambiguity of tribe in the modern world. People are so mobile, populations so intermingled, loyalties so ambivalent that many people would have some difficulty in saying what natural community they belong to. Many would also bridle at the mere suggestion that they belong to any natural community - they would insist that they choose which community they wish to belong to, that they transcend tribe and culture. To go forward I need to use examples.

VII
Recent history: the last 2,000 years.

I return to England, where evolution still continues, for it is not just a theory about the past. I have already argued that natural culture is not an artifact, but a biological entity with a life of its own, following its own laws, expressing its own nature. It has a vast majestic scale. The Egyptian culture of the Nile valley lasted for more than 2000 years, passing through various metamorphoses. The miraculous culture of classical Greece lasted for barely more than 400. It was "inherited" by the Roman culture, which lasted rather longer, but came also to its natural end. Must cultures, like individuals, come to maturity, blossom, wither, and die? I suspect it is so, and I do know that the present time has many similarities to the time when the Roman empire ended, and that I am not alone in having this intuition. There is the same sense of over-ripeness, of fatness and corruption, of sagging muscles and failing powers. It took about 500 years after the Norman Conquest for the English culture to come to the peak of its maturity in Tudor times and it has been declining ever since. Other European countries are in much the same condition, though England is the paradigm case.

It is astonishing how closely England in the last 1000 years fits the ancient template. Mediaeval England was a tribe on the fringe of Christendom struggling to build its coherence and identity. By the reign of Henry VIII, while it was still an absolute monarchy, it had decided it wanted no more of a corrupt and self-serving church of Rome, and preferred a home-grown high priest. It had long had a classic tribal disposition. The king gave spiritual power to the chief priest on the unspoken understanding that the chief priest gave divine authority to the king's legitimacy. In general it worked well. Just occasionally the tensions led to a priest slain at the altar (Thomas A'Beckett), or burned alive (Thomas Cranmer) *pour encourager les autres*, and it has now become a dead letter because of the withering of the spiritual power. Nevertheless the form still exists, having survived the reformation and the civil war. The struggle between the rationalists and the traditionalists was one of the issues of the civil war, but in the end, in the "glorious revolution" of 1688, it was the tribal church and the traditionalists who prevailed.

Why do I say that the Tudor age was the high point? Because this was the time when the language was most harmoniously adapted to the expression of duties and obligations, intentions and rewards. The evidence most obviously lies in the Book of Common Prayer. Modern commentators often refer to the sublime rhythms of its language. Could it be that the music of the words reflects the harmony of the thought of its writers? Since that time many observers have regretted the drift of the language towards more modal uses. Professor John Macmurray in his Gifford lectures of 1956 speaks of a "crisis of the personal". The tendencies he deplores have increased rapidly since that time.

The England of the 16th and 17th centuries was an

astonishing phenomenon. How was so small a country able to achieve so much? How was it able to breed and equip such sailors and soldiers? The explanation must lie partly in the natural culture, grown under the influence of Christian teaching and bitter war with (mostly) France. This is not the place to expand an explanation, but there is no doubt that there is a great deal to explain.[4]

Since the 17th Century there has been a slow (and latterly, rapid) decline, but there has come down to us an English church whose God broods benignly over yew-encircled churchyards and flag-bedecked cathedrals. It had a wonderful sense of pastoral continuity. It had a simple faith that supported soldiers and sailors in far and friendless places, that saw their wives and children through sickness and bereavement, that cemented civil and national society in bonds of common obligation. Who (of my generation) does not warm to part, at least, of this description? And who can provide a convincing (ie widely accepted) modern alternative vision of the English church today?

There is one more point to be drawn from this thumbnail sketch. At the time I was born, in the first quarter of the present century, England was still an unconsciously tribal nation. (I observe that the stronger the natural culture, the less its members are aware of it). People from other countries were frustrated and infuriated by the sense of 'effortless superiority' that seemed to emanate from English people, even at their most charming. The English themselves were unaware of it, until it was drawn to their attention, and then they felt it was a slightly embarrassing joke. The mission of the English to civilize the world was taken for granted, but of course never mentioned in front of foreigners. Although the decline of the language was already far advanced it still supported a great deal of purely intuitive action in government and administration. Laborious intellectual procedures invented in business schools are now needed to replace those lost intuitive channels of communication. Nevertheless, England is still a civilised country in a rapidly disintegrating world. How long will it last? Could it be that a strong natural culture is needed to provide a platform for the construction of human civilisation? European civilization (in which I include the United States) is peerless, but its natural culture is in a state of advanced decline. This is the parallel with the Roman Empire of the 1st century A.D.

It will be obvious from what I have said above that I do not share Joan Crewdson's respect for the ideas of Michael Polanyi. His project to revert to a purely intuitive approach to nature seems to me bizarre romanticism: rather like using modern technology to built a replica of a crusader castle. But when Joan writes; "The minute we return from the I-It world to the I-Thou world, we are back in the world to which persons belong, a world of mutual exchange and interaction. . . . . It is a world in which love is, to quote Bonhoeffer, the *cantus firmus*, round which the polyphony of life weaves a counterpoint. . . ." I detect a longing which I respect, and millions of us share. That I do not agree with the words I have omitted from this quotation - "not only between person and person, but between persons and the rest of nature." - does not lessen in any way my support for her plea, which is also Robert's, for more attention to the warm human functions and uses of language: for more attention to the language of duties and obligations, intentions and rewards.

It is not easy. The desiccation of our language is, I believe, the principal symptom of the decline of our culture. It would be quite unrealistic to imagine that we could reverse that decline, but we can still oppose it, and by opposing slow it. Good teaching of English in our schools can do more for our culture even than religion. The problem is to maintain a just balance and fruitful tension between the modal and human uses, and this is a moral problem. The modal use will look after itself (though the serious disciplines of scholarship will not), but the human use is continually corrupted by bad teaching, by media that encourage an ever-shorter attention span, and by the sensational treatment of serious issues. Paradoxically, the vivacious language of the street-wise youngsters is the well spring of living language, and it is at this point that the educational opportunity exists to deepen the

188

perceptions of young people, before the ad men get hold of their words and corrupt them.

VIII

Against this background, what is the good life?

In this essay I have covered much ground that is also covered by James' essay, and I have projected a view of the world very different from his. I now turn to aspects in which I expect to find we are more often in agreement.

(a)

The political and social level.

Although I cannot accept that human life is in its nature paradoxical, yet I recognise as everyone must, that life is often unjust and cruel. It may indeed be described as tragic. This is only paradoxical if one believes in a human creator, but it is unacceptable whatever one believes. Nature places no value on human individuals. They are worth the same as beetles and bacteria. Human beings have very different values and the challenge of the world we live in is to express **human** values.

There are two parts to this enterprise; first to decide what they are, and then to do it. The first part is, as Robert says, an awesome responsibility. But I see it as an essentially social enterprise and would feel there was something wrong if I found myself on a lonely mountain-top making moral decisions from first principles. The difficulty, in a declining culture, is to find ways to reach significant consensus in significant groups. The tendency is bound to be to ally oneself with smaller and smaller groups in the search for a moral environment in which one can reach acceptable compromises. The struggle to hold on to some kind of consensus at national level is surely worthwhile. Even if it is a lost cause in the long run, it is a vital value **now**. And we desperately need a consensus at the world level on a few basic principles.

It may seem at this point that I am busy sawing off the branch I am sitting on. If I believe that all our moral values come from our tribe, how can I avoid a completely relativistic position? Surely there can be no basis for any judgement about relative values between the code of one tribe and another? The answer must be that this is true: there cannot. But I observe that there is a great measure of agreement between people of all tribes about moral values . This is hardly surprising, since the function of the moral code is to enable the members of the natural community to live together and cooperate. All make loyalty to the tribe a high priority, but also require, either explicitly or by implication, respect for persons. These two together validate the principle of democracy. I need to extend this principle to argue for democracy between tribes on a world scale. This principle, I suspect, would be overwhelmingly supported by the **people** of the world - and generally rejected by their **governments.** This is the problem of peace!

Nevertheless, humanity, when it is sufficiently fearful for its future, will find a consensus. Then the problem will be how to implement it. At this point, I suspect that a journalist would start talking about 'controlling nature'. I am too conscious of the absurdity of such an enterprise to use that language. We cannot control nature, but we can manage our environment by using natural forces to modify it to a marginal extent.

If a river floods in winter and dries in summer, we may harness it to our needs by damming it, so that the winter rainfall is stored. This is a paradigm for all our interventions in natural processes. The features to note are;

that natural forces (the weight and structure of the dam) are used to manage other natural forces (the flowing water), so as to achieve a **small** modification of our environment for our convenience;

that we can only do this if we first build up a sufficient understanding of the natural processes involved;

that planned and determined effort is required (it is expensive);

and that there is a lead time (it is too late to build the dikes when the floods start).

We need to adopt a similar approach to our own cultures, which are natural forces considerably more massive than a great river. We face two huge problems: the growth of population, and reversions to primitive tribal warfare.

There can be no doubt (whatever we believe about God) that a time will come when *Homo Sapiens* will be extinct. Whether that time is twenty decades ahead or twenty million years, may depend on what we ourselves do. Coming of age is a serious business. As we look round the world today it is only too reasonable to ask "Can man abide it?" Can we abide the knowledge of our own nature? Can we find ways to manage our own political powers and processes that will place sufficient restraint on our destructive instincts to moderate the outcome of our own inevitable armageddon? One of the symptoms of the decline of European culture is the absence of any lively sense of its vulnerability. Liberal intellectuals in earnest public discussions say "I am an optimist. We have lived with weapons of mass destruction for half a century. When the possibility that they might be used has confronted us, statesmen have always managed to find a way out." As an historical statement this is true, but provides no basis for this optimism - none that justifies the lack of effective action to reform the United Nations and create an institution of world order that commands general respect as representing **all** peace-loving nations, not just the victors of the 1939-45 war. Such an institution (however embryonic it may be) is a necessary first step, but there is little prospect of it. The countries of the EU squabble among themselves (none more childishly than Britain), the US is not willing to fund the UN, and reluctant to commit its soldiers to the defence of order. These things presage a time when Europe (and possibly the US) will be ruled by people who are not Europeans. That need not concern us too much - all past empires and cultures have died - but the weapons that may be used in the conflict are such as to make the survival of the species, and many other species, problematic. We cannot stop human misery and suffering; it is not in our power. We need to accept the realities of the situation and devise sensible, robust, and minimal policies for damage limitation.

Behind these political imperatives lie philosophical and

191

moral problems. Why is the knowledge of our own nature so hard to bear? Why are the adult responsibilities that face man as he comes of age so terrifying? The answer lies in the disjunction between being and knowing. We are beginning, in a very small way (rather smaller than some biologists like to claim) to learn about the workings of our own brains. Much of what we are learning is concerned with perception; the more difficult questions about the control of behaviour are much further down the road and many may never be answered, but there is a moral question to be faced in all this work. As we put Cartesian dualism behind us and investigate the mechanism of our brains, confident that the explanation of all human behaviour lies somewhere inside our skulls, we are apparently in danger of reducing ourselves to machines. I have written elsewhere about the so-called problem of free will and I shall not repeat myself here. I sought to show two things; that we can be inside a situation (living and being), or outside it (observing and knowing), but it is logically impossible to be doing both at once, and if we are able to understand our brains as machines this should cause us, not to reduce our idea of man, but to understand how deeply rich and complex machines can be. The development of chaos theory has started to show that the "mechanical" world is not a bit like clockwork. A beautiful and complex mechanism is not less beautiful because we are starting to understand it (just a little, and in parts).

The moral question that arises from this relates to the responsibilities of those who make use of this new knowledge for the amelioration of the dysfunctions of individuals and communities. How can individuals be protected from careless or overweening interventions by their therapists, and how can a sound moral basis be found for the therapy of communities? Because our knowledge is still so slight, any attempt to treat mental dysfunction is liable to reduce the status of the human patient in practice. Some of the problems of the British health services illustrate this. And the therapy of communities is so far scarcely even contemplated. The dreadful experiences of Nazism and Fascism make us rightly cautious, but we need to look ahead, and not wait for more ignorant interventions to lead to more disasters. How can we develop a meaningful pathology of natural communities, and then a satisfactory therapy? How can this be controlled in a manner consistent with democracy?

I have pointed out that the object of life, as observed by biologists, is survival. James, I imagine, would say that mere survival is not enough. I suspect that "mere survival" is a phrase only used in comfortable degenerate cultures. If survival is problematic, I doubt if it is ever **mere** survival. Many noble men and women have found in the defeat of the forces that militate against survival reason enough for celebration and fulfilment. To survive and remain civilised is indeed the challenge we face today. The Christian tradition has a great deal to teach us about the way a culture can be strong enough to support a civil order. Our dying culture is probably beyond the reach of any therapy, but we can use the life that remains in it to build international institutions able to limit the forces of destruction in the dark times that lie ahead.

(b)
The personal level.

It may seem surprising that, despite all I have said above about religion, I can still go to church with my friends, and feel it appropriate that I should do so. Is it hypocrisy to recite the creed, believing that God is man-made? God is not man-made in the sense that cars and computers are man-made. Cultures grow their gods, as we grow our arms and legs. This is the worship of my fathers, the growth of centuries, nourished by devotion and defended by martyrs. We stand on the shoulders of our predecessors, and we partake of their labours. We cannot believe everything that they believed, but belief is only part of religion. We need to acknowledge our debt, to remember what they did, to celebrate the life we share with them. Though I belong to a dying culture, it still exists, and I still belong to it - and it will last very much longer than I shall. It is necessary to resist the neurotic tendency to "hasten the inevitable". To be faithful to the end is not just an admirable principle; it is also the best, perhaps the only, practical policy.

The Chantry Group has devoted some time to the work of Simone Weil, and we have found it time well spent. She is a romantically extravagant ascetic, after the manner of Francis of Assisi, but it is her sharp intellectual integrity that makes her work especially appealing. I once tried to explain her work and her appeal to my brother, a family doctor. He listened attentively to my (no doubt inadequate) explanation, then he said "She was mad." I have since heard that her own mother had a somewhat similar view. There is, of course, no inconsistency between the two views of her, but perhaps both are relevant when we address the problem of suffering. When Darwin proposed his theory of natural selection the argument raged around its implications for creation. Now it is an established part of biology and of ecology, and is supported by a great deal of mathematical analysis. Because it is a tool of scientific analysis, it is properly handled in a dry and rigorous way, but that does not mean that we may not also think intuitively about it. What it means, in sympathetic terms, is that all living things are statistically at subsistence level. They may enjoy an interval of ease, but the price will be a famine, an overload of predators, or a plague. Living things are in a constantly-shifting balance with those they eat, and those that eat them. How is man different? Because our brains gave us an unique advantage, we have been able to dominate all our competitors. As a result we have increased in numbers until it is the limits of the planet itself that confront us. In this situation, human suffering on a vast scale is inevitable. We have seen what can happen in Ruanda, but there may be much worse to come. There is an acute personal problem for all sensitive people in coming to terms with the facts about the world we inhabit.

The Franciscan tradition, deriving from Jesus himself, is to identitify with the poor. That was no doubt possible for people of a certain temperament in a small country where the fastest communication was by horse. How can we apply it in our world?

The communications industries have created a passing

show of oceanic size, and bubble thin superficiality. To cut oneself off from most of this is perhaps the first step to a real personal life. The next is to think carefully about our personal relationships, not only to those nearest to us, but also to the wider community. For many of us it is now less than obvious what our "wider community" is. Europe, England, Town, Church or parish, Employer organisation, Client set, Voluntary organisation, professional organisation, political party; I may belong to all these. If so, what is my natural community? In the last resort (ie in war) I would have to decide (or rather, find the decision already lying somewhere deep in my sub-conscious mind). In the meanwhile, I should not waste time on hypothetical questions, but we cannot avoid the necessity to decide how to apportion our time.

We should also remember those who have the opposite problem. The loss of culture has been especially hard on young people. If they have also never been employed they are doubly deprived of the environment needed to acquire an adult identity and motives to participate in the work of the community.

The important moral questions are not the sensational issues that grab the headlines; the life and death of foetuses, biotechnology and medical ethics, but the use of resources. The attempt to build an economic environment in which people are motivated to work hard seems to lead to ever less civilised social arrangements. Is this because the loss of culture leaves self-interest as the only motor driving economic activity? We all have to decide where we stand on these issues, and how to bring to bear such influence as we have. This may well involve us in direct action to ameliorate some of the worst cruelties of the system at the grass roots.

As a first approximation, it is only possible to love our fellow men in face-to-face situations. Having spent my working life in Whitehall, I am acutely conscious of the gulf between our daily lives as citizens and the acts of the administrators. The idea that it is possible to do more good for more people by political and administrative action is seductive, but dangerous and often false. Certainly, good administration is to be preferred to slovenly or corrupt administration. Perhaps this is mainly because it does less damage, but I am sure that the best admininstrators have modest objectives. It is not a job for fiery idealists. St Paul adjures rulers to act with "diligence"[5]. Of course the administrators are needed as long as there is a power that can impose order, and someone must do it. When disasters occur, or threaten, damage limitation is a sanctified option. Attending to what is necessary is often all that is possible.

Working on a smaller scale, within a local community, it is possible to know that help we intend to give reaches its target - or if it does not, to learn why and change our behaviour. It is here that there is most unambiguously room for genuine giving.

But why should we wish to give, to "live for others" as Bonhoeffer puts it? The answer surely lies in a phrase used both by James and by Robert - it is what "makes for life". The satisfaction that we get from knowing that we have done something to make easier someone's life, regardless of any monument or gratitude, enhances our own lives, and releases energy. For most of us this is quite an ordinary matter of living as best we can. The high romantic self-denials of the Franciscan tradition have value in reminding us that we can almost always achieve more than we suppose, and that complacency is not an option, but there is also danger in the excitement. "Who sweeps a room as for thy laws, makes that and the action fine." Even in the time of Armageddon the daily round has its value.

References

1.   On the dangers of the idea of perfectability, see Isaiah Berlin: "The Pursuit of the Ideal" in *The Proper Study of Mankind*. Henry Hardy and Roger Hausheer eds. Chatto & Windus, London 1997.

2.   See Richard Leakey: *The Sixth Extinction*. Weidenfeld & Nicholson, London 1996

3.   Eranos Jahrbuch 1934

4.   See Paul Kennedy: *The Rise and Fall of the Great Powers.* Fontana Press, London 1989.

5.   Romans 12.8

Some footnotes on Faith

Michael Smart

To do full justice to James Mark's admirable and closely reasoned essay would require a response of at least equivalent length and quality of examination which I do not feel able to produce at present. Nevertheless, the essay has spurred me to set down some general thoughts on religious understanding and commitment which I hope will contribute to a discussion which needs to be taken much further.

I write as a humanist who has also been a practising Christian, in the broad Church of England tradition, for nearly fifty years, and sees no contradiction between the two. I am a humanist in the sense that I have accepted as main guiding values in both my public and personal lives principles of human solidarity, truthfulness, responsibility and - where consistent with these - self-fulfilment and making the most of a necessarily limited, and far too short, life span. How far I have faithfully practised these values, is of course a different matter which it is not primarily for me to judge. But I have found for many years in my main activities - government service and more recently, a variety of political commitments - that the values are self-authenticating, at least among reasonably conscientious people. Applications in particular situations are naturally often a matter of vigorous argument, but there are very few if any occasions where it is necessary to bring in references to God or religion as supporting hypotheses.

Against this background, I find that commendations of a particular religious position starting at the end of 'God', as expressed in revelation or doctrine separate from authentic human observation or experience, are generally unsatisfactory or at best inconclusive. It is not at all difficult to make a case against religion on the grounds that:

-revelation is unprovable and in many, even most, cases highly improbable

-although the main religions contain many ethical assertions which secular humanists would share, these do not need any supernatural underpinning, while other assertions are unacceptably restrictive or tribal in character. (See for example the charge of Celsus against Christians in the second century, comparing them to frogs who sit in a swamp and say to one another: "To us God reveals and proclaims everything. He does not trouble himself with the rest of the world; we are the only beings with whom he has dealings.").

-religion provides symbols and rituals which can enrich the imagination and promote social cohesion. However, many other bodies can provide these without any religious reference. For example, the former Communist government of East Germany promoted a ceremony of personal dedication to good citizenship for teenagers (the 'Jugendweihe') as a secular alternative to confirmation, which has remained popular in spite of the collapse of the regime.

-finally, religious allegiances divide societies and nations, sometimes being carried to the point of violence, and can waste or distract time, energy and resources from urgently needed tasks of more obvious human benefit.

Although 'yes but' replies, sometimes quite persuasive, can be offered to all the above charges, discussion limited by positively 'God-oriented' terms is nearly always bound to end in no more definite conclusion than a wearily polite agreement to differ. However, I believe that the conversation can become more productive by beginning, much more modestly, at the end of human experience. Most people want, at least implicitly, a set of values to live by and in adopting and following them, many look for meanings which they can relate to some larger scheme of explanation. Even those who assert their right to be completely free and undetermined in their behaviour are asserting a value of a kind - in effect, 'my principle is to have no principles.' In contemporary Britain, most people would probably say that 'life itself' provides such values as are needed or which it is sensible to expect and would find psychological, sociological or cultural factors sufficient to explain them. However, many other people — largely the 'thinking (or worrying) classes' who in the past have provided many of the officers and NCOs of religious and political movements - would find such explanations incomplete because they do not adequately cover the possibility of free choice where values conflict. Moreover, within this broad group, a significant number would find it necessary to go beyond the limitations of what can be scientifically measured and proved, to an experience which could be broadly termed 'religious' involving some intimation of transcendence touching human life.

The fact that many, perhaps most, people would say that such experiences are meaningless, or that they never have them, does not alter the fact that substantial numbers of people **have** had them, finding meaningful references for life either in traditional religion or in other systems of belief. Moreover, where such experiences have been systematically studied, as in William James' classic 'Varieties of Religious Experience', they tend to show a striking degree of convergence between different historical periods and cultures. In a key passage from his conclusions (attached to this note), James identifies the main common features as a sense of a relationship to a more spiritual universe giving significance to the visible world and a consequent new zest and assurance of life.

Experiences which are superficially similar to religious experiences can be produced by drugs or mental illness and may also be associated with disturbed or sadistic personalities, who sometimes (as in Hitler's case) find the language of authoritarian religion congenial. But these can be distinguished without great difficulty from the general body of reported religious experiences, which typically produce greater inward assurance and peace, and quite often positive changes in character and conduct or commitment to some beneficial activity. (The outcome is of course often shaped by the expectations of the community to which the subject belongs). Religious experiences should not be treated as infallible guides or communications from a transcendent beyond, but simply accepted as an authentic feature of total human existence. The key question is whether the activity of religious search and questioning associated with them is a valid one, irrespective of any particular conclusions or commitments which may be derived from them. I find it heartening that this note of questioning is heard across the main traditions, in the paradoxes of the Zen masters, the Hasidic tales, the riddles of the Sufis, the Book of Job and in many of the sayings and parables of Jesus, who has a disturbing habit of answering one question by asking another.

This may seem to point to a 'supermarket' view of religion where we 'pick and choose' what suits us best from a great variety of offerings. Whether 'picking and choosing' is always objectionable may be debated, when we decide our reading, televiewing, holidays, eating out and so much else in precisely this way, but in any case several anchorages or stabilising factors are readily available. Groups in all the main religions are united in a commitment to the ethical standards set out in the UN Declaration of Human Rights (and largely implicit in their various scriptures) even if much of their activity has to be directed towards their co-religionists who have not yet been able to make this commitment. Moreover, those who are led by religious experiences or intimations to 'turn to religion' normally find it helpful to relate to a particular religious tradition. If the relationship 'takes', it can be a strong stabilising factor.

The Sea of Faith movement has done excellent work by pointing to forms of religious authority which leave their adherents in a state of infantile passivity and dependence. But an approach based on experience and free choice should remove a weight of excessive and improper authority from religious allegiance and make it possible to appreciate and enjoy distinctive religious traditions in their own right for the first time. An interesting model for future community worship is sketched out by Anthony Freeman in 'God in us' (SCM Press 1993), which combines a robust affirmation of Anglican traditions (including, refreshingly, the Book of Common Prayer) with a demand for the removal of supernatural elements, including God as usually presented. Although this may seem as paradoxical and unappealing as alcohol-free lager, a large body of Anglican lay people have for many years, even centuries, treated their worship as a set of attractive icons, to be respected and often enjoyed but not made to carry a heavier weight of authority than they can bear.

Some touching lines by John Betjeman describe how he was led to faith by 'inessentials':

......" Still for me
The steps to truth were made by sculptured stone,
Stained glass and vestments, holy-water stoups,
Incense and crossings of myself ... " (Summoned by Bells)

I would add to these, as often powerfully suggestive icons, the best of Church music and architecture, Prayer Book, Creeds and the non-historical elements in the Bible, which might more appropriately be included in a greatly expanded Apocrypha. (As in many other respects, Quaker practice is admirable in leaving copies around the meeting of the New Testament for ready reference, without over-promoting it).

I have to part company with some members or the Sea of Faith movement who describe 'icons' in this sense as 'nonsense', a term which is neither helpful nor accurate. Many people, especially those who have had unhappy experiences of authoritarian religion in early life (which I was spared), are understandably so conscious of the abuses which religious myths, symbols and credal statements have supported that they would wish to exclude them altogether, in a latter day radical Protestant iconoclasm. However, others remain affectionately attached to the icons, which continue to speak to imagination, feeling and spiritual search, and can see a baby in the murky bathwater which should be allowed to thrive. I see no advantage in reviving the iconoclastic controversy (which the Orthodox Church wisely put to rest in the ninth century, though it was later to trouble the churches of the Reformation, with regrettable effects) and would hope that the two sides could live together on the basis of an agreement to condemn and avoid the well recorded abuses. (To draw up a set of 39 Articles for the Sea of Faith movement, would be a fascinating exercise, though I would not push it very strongly!).

My approach to religion is very largely in line with that of the sympathetic but agnostic William James. It may well be asked, from both sides, what possible basis this can offer for a viable religious allegiance. An article in The Guardian in 1988 by Geoffrey Taylor, attached as Annex 2, proposed the foundation of a new body, the Friends of the Church of England, enabling its members to practise co-operation and support in acceptable ways but avoiding unauthentic personal commitments. As a potential member, I did indeed think of applying for attender status within my church, but abandoned the idea as showing insufficient confidence in the validity or my position.

This allows little if any room for evangelism, at least of the finger jabbing variety, but I do not believe that such evangelism is a suitable way of commending religious life. What can properly be done is to encourage openness to religious experience - and indeed to anything bearing on it - in the spirit of an inquirers' meeting, unburdened by any prescribed conclusions. Pursued seriously, such openness will often lead to a personal commitment, not to a set of doctrinal propositions, but to something akin to a rule of life, identified by personal search and testing and open to revision by the same process which led to it, Many who adopt such a commitment will wish to relate to a mutually supportive community - in some respects like a very loose and open religious order - which could develop shared commitments, goals and modes of religious expression or 'worship'. However, others, especially on the 'neo-Protestant' wing, may legitimately regard any kind of group relationship of a religious or 'post-religious' character unacceptable and choose to make their way without it. What matters most, is the authenticity of the personal commitment and of its enactment. Both join hands with traditional religious thinking in involving an essential element of faith, in the Pascal sense of a wager of life which does not wait for certain knowledge but learns as it goes on its continuing 'pilgrimage'.

I realise that the approach which I am commending has much in common with the beliefs and practice of the Society of Friends, who continue to provide a bright beacon and congenial meeting place for humanists of a religious turn of mind. However, many feel that distinctive Quaker customs and teachings are not for them and contemporary seekers can carry their exploration much further both into other religious traditions and secular movements addressing questions of human rights, economic and social justice, the environment and national and international political order which involve basic human values.

Let William James have the last word, in a spirit guiding an 'ecumenism' far wider than the worthy but restricted ecumenical movement: "I do indeed disbelieve that we or any other mortals can attain on a given day to absolutely incorrigible and unimprovable truth about such matters of fact as those with which religions deal. But I reject this dogmatic ideal not out of a perverse delight in intellectual instability. I am no lover of disorder and doubt as such. Rather do I fear to lose truth by this pretension to possess it already wholly . . . . Do not, I pray you, harden your minds irrevocably against the empiricism which I profess." (Varieties of Religious Experience, Lectures XIV and XV, 'The Value of Saintliness')

Annex 1

William James; *Varieties of Religious Experience.*

Lecture XX. Conclusions.

The material of our study of human nature is now spread before us; and in this parting hour, set free from the duty of description, we can draw our theoretical and practical conclusions. In my first lecture, defending the empirical method, I foretold that whatever conclusions we might come to could be reached by spiritual judgments only, appreciations of the significance for life of religion, taken "on the whole." Our conclusions cannot be as sharp as dogmatic conclusions would be, but I will formulate them, when the time comes, as sharply as I can. Summing up in the broadest possible way the characteristics of the religious life, as we have found them, it includes the following beliefs:-

1. That the visible world is part of a more spiritual universe from which it draws its chief significance;

2. That union or harmonious relation with that higher universe is our true end;

3. That prayer or inner communion with the spirit thereof - be that spirit "God," or "law" - is a process wherein work is really done, and spiritual energy flows in and produces effects, psychological or material, within the phenomenal world.

Religion includes also the following psychological characteristics :-

4. A new zest which adds itself like a gift to life, and takes the form either of lyrical enchantment or of appeal to earnestness and heroism;

5. An assurance of safety and a temper of peace, and, in relation to others, a preponderance of loving affections. In illustrating these characteristics by documents, we have been literally bathed in sentiment. In re-reading my manuscript, I am almost appalled at the amount of emotionality which I find in it. After so much of this, we can afford to be dryer and less sympathetic in the rest of the work that lies before us.

The sentimentality of many of my documents is a consequence of the fact that I sought them among the extravagances of the subject. If any of you are enemies of what our ancestors used to brand as enthusiasm, and are, nevertheless, still listening to me now, you have probably felt my selection to have been sometimes almost perverse, and have wished I might have stuck to soberer examples. I reply that I took these extremer examples as yielding the profounder information. To learn the secrets of any science, we go to expert specialists, even though they may be eccentric persons, and not to commonplace pupils. We combine what they tell us with the rest of our wisdom, and form our final judgment independently. Even so with religion. We who have pursued such radical expressions of it may now be sure that we know its secrets as authentically as anyone can know them who learns them from another; and we have next to answer, each of us for himself, the practical question: what are the dangers in this element of life? and in what proportion may it need to be restrained by other elements, to give the proper balance?

But this question suggests another one which I will answer immediately and get it out of the way, for it has more than once already vexed us. Ought it to be assumed that in all men the mixture of religion with other elements should be identical? Ought it, indeed, to be assumed that the lives of all men should show identical religious elements? In other words, is the existence of so many religious types and sects and creeds regrettable?

To these questions I answer "No" emphatically. And my reason is that I do not see how it is possible that creatures in such different positions and with such different powers as human individuals are, should have exactly the same functions and the same duties. No two of us have identical difficulties, nor should we be expected to work out identical solutions.

Annex 2.

Geoffrey Taylor: Article in The Guardian (25th April 1988)

Is there room, I wonder, for a new association to be called the Friends of the Church of England? It seems only that such a body could do useful work and would receive a fair amount of support. Whether the Church itself would welcome it is another matter. Few people are hostile to what the Church is doing, and many admire it. But even fewer are able to commit themselves in the fashion now required of them if they so much as poke their noses round the reredos. It is not a novel situation. It has grown up over the years. The divide between those who regularly attend their local church and those who fear to do so is widening. One effect of the Friends would be to narrow it.

It would be preferable not to reopen the argument about the Book of Common Prayer and the Alternative Service Book. The argument has become sterile. But it is undeniable that the adoption of the Alternative Service Book as the standard for Anglican services has forced a choice on people which they feel unable to accept.

They are obliged to make either a total commitment or none at all. They have to answer the question, "Are you a

Christian?" with either yes or no. It is no longer adequate to say, "Well, so-so. Like to think so. Difficult question. Goodness, look at the time. Must be getting along."

The General Synod must bear some responsibility for this state of affairs, though blame would be too strong a word. People cannot be blamed for genuine beliefs. Yet under the former dispensation a person could go to morning or evening service, sing a few hymns, recollect well-known and invigorating sentences, and come away feeling spiritually refreshed.

That, unfortunately, is no longer possible. Virtually every service is now a Holy Communion service. I guess there are many thousands of people who feel they would be making an act of betrayal (of themselves, that is) as well as "dissembling before the face of Almighty God", as the Prayer Book used to say, if they profaned this sacrament by pretending to be what they are not.

At the same time the latent goodwill towards the Church must be enormous, both for its social initiatives and because it trades in categories which people know to be important. How would a newspaper like this get away with the antimechanistic ideas which so regularly illumine its features columns, were it not that the ideas find such ready resonance among readers?

Yet resonance with these ideas is a far cry from the formularies decreed by the General Synod. Not everyone who strongly suspects the existence of a transcendent and immaterial world is disposed to shout, "Alleluia, Christ is risen", or exchange that embarrassing and thoroughly un-English sign of peace.

Arguments are endless, I believe, in ecclesiastical quarters, about what the role of the Church of England should be. They are almost as frequent as the doctrinal arguments from which laymen are usually happy, and probably wise, to stand aside.

Yet the Church surely has one role which it should be proud to accept. That is to provide a focus for everyone who is not content with purely mechanistic interpretations. If it did that it would re-occupy the special place in the English tapestry which it enjoyed for so long.

It is here that the Friends of the Church of England would come in. They would be in general sympathy, perhaps enthusiastic sympathy, with what the Church was trying to do. They would recognise in the Church a powerful advocate of values at one remove from those which determine the direction of political life. They would not disavow the name Christian, but they would not need to hang the cardboard albatross labelled "I am a Christian" round their necks.

To take a current example, Rupert Sheldrake has recently published his second book on his hypothesis of formative causation (The Presence of the Past, Collins, £15.). I have no idea whether he would describe himself as a Christian, and it would be fatuous to ask. Yet his hypothesis is one which both appeals to many people by its intellectual coherence, and gives that ultimate purpose to individual human behaviour on which the churches (all of them, and Judaism too) have always insisted.

If his hypothesis stands up then not only is every creature, from the crystal to the person, influenced by the form and behaviour of similar creatures distant in time and space, but every creature must have an influence, however small, on the future of its kind.

In the widest sense this is a "religious" scheme of things, in no way at variance with a Christian scheme but addressing a familiar problem from a new angle. It is the sort of idea one might expect Friends to talk about, if ever they were to meet. It is not, and could not be, among the certitudes one would expect to hear expounded from the pulpit or included in the rubric.

It should be said, though, that the Friends of the Church of England are not envisaged here as a philosophical debating society and indeed are a body of people not much given to public gatherings. Their chief purpose would be to give moral, financial, and physical support to the Church without feeling obliged to join specific acts of worship or affirm absolutes in which they do not wholly believe.

The Church does need money. Clerical salaries are ridiculously low and the maintenance of buildings, which are still of significance to the whole community, cannot for ever be a charge on the few who turn up. A Friend could covenant some of his tax benefit, as he might to any other social purpose with which he is in sympathy but not identity of view.

It is not at all certain, however, that members of the General Synod, and all the subsidiary colleges which make up the Church's voting system, would take kindly to this form of country membership. That is not only because of the distinction which they cherish between insiders and outsiders. It is also because nobody is doing them or the Church a favour by lending a sympathetic ear.

On the contrary people who don't join wholeheartedly are, in their view, cutting themselves off from a precious, an essential, experience. The Church is on the giving end, not the Friends.

That is legitimate controversy. For the purpose of this proposal, however, Synod members can be identified as nature's joiners and participators. The Friends would be the other sort - the non-joiners who are happy to pay their subs but are uncertain in their minds, do not wish to be thought sailing under false colours, and want least of all, because of their uncertainty, to attend meetings and vote.

The time may come when the Church makes fewer demands on its members' consciences (and has regard, as it once did, to aesthetics as well as ethics). At that point members and Friends will have more in common.

In the meantime relations between them would, I imagine, resemble those between bishop and archdeacon. The bishop anoints and the archdeacon takes care of the roof. I know lots of people who would gladly climb a ladder in God's name, or in the the Church's, but blanch at the thought of voicing sentiments about which, hand on heart, they are not 100 per cent sure.

To be a Pilgrim

Muriel Smith

I am grateful, as we all are, to James for his thoughtful essay. It is a challenge to write about my own thoughts and struggles.

James says he has been concerned with the debate on Faith, rather than theories of devotion or action. I have tried to follow this debate and to consider his conclusions.

In a world full of paradoxes his scholarship and tenacity lead him to the conclusion that, while we must answer what questions we can, in the event we are confronted with mysteries rather than questions. 'The vision that we have of Christ shows the supreme value of love, which transcends whatever we can discuss of order and value in the life we know'.

I should humbly like to associate myself with these conclusions.

Anselm said "I believe in order to understand". H.A Hodges, more recently, "Christianity is not extraneous to itself."

Background and Questions

I was brought up in a traditional Christian home. We attended the Anglican church as a family. My sister and I were loved and well cared for. My father brought us up on Kipling's "If", and my mother had a fund of Victorian ditties and a firm faith.

I was rather a solitary child, interested in books, music and my own thoughts. I remember that at an early age I was not especially concerned about God, but I was very troubled about infinity. I had never heard of Bertrand Russell but I would have heartily agreed with him that "logic is driving me mad". I found some relief in the thought that a fly walking round and round a curtain ring, would have no logical reason to stop. . . (What should we do without our metaphysical flies?)

Religion was largely taken for granted until I was in my teens. Then for a short time I was caught up in an evangeilcal

214

group. This did not last long, but it has left its mark on me.

By early in the 1940s I had married, lost my husband, and was living with my mother and sister, whose husband was abroad. This was in Reading. It was then that I met the Hodges family. I was invited to a small Sunday evening study group in their house, where we discussed various aspects of Christianity. For some time I just listened but gradually I started to join in - it profoundly changed my life.

These were the days when we all had to support the war effort and metaphorically 'dig for victory'. Without much enthusiasm I went to Liverpool to study Social Work. My personal choice of books however veered more towards philosophy and theology. Later I had the opportunity to study philosophy with Professor Hodges.

In vacations I attended the Summer School of Saint Alban and Saint Sergius and there had the opportunity to take part in Orthodox worship.

At this stage the question I most wanted to answer was, 'Is it possible to be a Christian and to be honest with oneself?' I came to believe that it was, and for the following reasons:

1. Christianity provides the most comprehensive answers to my questions that I have so far found. 'I have to act on the best I know'.

2. Life is enriched by the concept of the transcendent: not only in music and art but in the unseen world of the imagination.

3. Christianity gives a new dimension to life which influences our personal relations, allows for worship and gives weight to moral values.

Faith

It is fine to decide to be a pilgrim, but what did I believe? I had a rough idea of the the teaching of the church to which I belonged. Anyway to love God and to love my neighbour surely embraced everything; but what did this mean in practice?

There is an emphasis today on thinking 'from the bottom

up' rather than accepting what is good 'from the top down'. This of course, is a generalisation. The following quotation explains what I am trying to say:

"No man can reveal to you aught but that which already lies half asleep in the dawning of your knowledge.

The teacher who walks in the shadow of the temple, among his followers, gives not of his wisdom, but rather of his faith and his lovingness.

If he is indeed wise he does not bid you enter the house of his wisdom, but rather leads you to the threshold of your own mind." (Kahlil Gibran: *The Prophet*).

I decided to hold in 'suspension' some of the doctrines of the church until I had had a good look at them.

What I believe now

The following list has been made rapidly. It seems that in this way it is likely to be more accurate than if I pondered over it.

1.   Man does not stand alone in the universe, only dependant on himself, friends and family. There is a God with whom he can communicate and who can communicate with him. The ineffable God is also the loving Father.

2.   The doctrine of the Trinity, though a mystery, seems fundamental. Children need security and love and, as they grow up, a purpose in life. If they have these they are likely to be self-confident, loving and purposeful. The doctrine of the Trinity gives the same message to children and adults alike.

3.   Man is made in the image of God and is always to be respected. I do not believe this image is ever completely obliterated.

4.   Evil is very real and takes many forms. It is sometimes impossible to do the right but only to choose the lesser evil.

5.   Christians are encouraged to pray but they must also take responsibility for action. They worship together, whether in a cathedral or a mud hut.

6.   The parables told by Christ are a good guide to morality.

7.   We have the promise of an afterlife.

A modern myth

The Lord of the Rings[1] is a modern myth which has had an enormous circulation. It is a myth not an allegory. It has taught me several things without intending to do so. The three volumes cover a wide range of interests.

It images a different world, consistent of course but different. The Hobbit is small and apparently insignificant. There are great forces of evil fighting a war with the good. While the war takes place a dedicated Hobbit and his servant cross a barren wildenness unseen to destroy the magic ring which, unless destroyed, may bring destruction to the whole country. All interest is focussed on the antagonists. In the event the ring is destroyed accidentally by the evil creature who has dogged their footsteps and which they could have killed more than once but didn't.

The climax comes when the Hobbit is in combat with the evil creature which misses its step and descends with the ring which it has captured into the pit.

One may make of a myth what you will. For me it is significant that it is the small and insignificant Hobbit who gains the victory. Yet it is not entirely true because as the place of its destruction arrives the Hobbit becomes more and more reluctant to let the ring go. It is his and it gives him great power. At least this is one interpretation. He is saved only by the evil thing which he had treated with kindness.

In the Hobbit's world good intentions bring good results. In our world they do not necessarily do so. We have to persevere in hope.

1.   J.R.R. Tolkien: *The Hobbit.* 1937.

An essay on Theism

Vernon Thomas

By tradition I am a Theist, albeit a Christian one. I have taken for granted that "God is the Creator, Sustainer and End of all things", that He is present in Nature and in the life of Man; present in the Order of Nature, present in man as a seeker of Truth, Beauty and Goodness. Man is a distinctive human being. We would expect on these grounds to experience a world that is wholly favourable to our existence in it, but it is hard on the face of things to justify the ways of God to man. We experience the bright side of life and the dark side in enjoyment and tragedy. Man experiences natural catastrophes and human disaster in drought and in the flooding of the land and countless numbers of men die of hunger and thirst. These are the hard facts quoted against a benevolent creator.

Religious attempts have been made to justify Divine Providence. The book of Job is a striking epic to resolve the predicament of his own individual plight. Job is tested to the destruction of all his life supports, but defies his fate in the name of his Creator. The evidence of the disasters that fall upon him does not shake the foundation of his faith. The faith of his Fathers in him is immune from doubt and cynicism. The pure in heart see God from within. The Indian Epic of the Bhagavad Gita, now fast becoming the Indians' Bible, is a story of strife between kinsmen whose leaders are consoled by the message that their conflict is unreal and that the reality of their lives lies elsewhere. Subjective Idealism in the West echoes the Bhagavad Gita; man's knowledge is limited and incoherent. The epic of Job adumbrates the view that the Cosmic conflict of Good and Evil is being fought out in the soul of man.

C. G. Jung in our century speaks of the dark antecedent side of a struggling God confronting a world of his own making. S. Freud teaches that man's life is essentially miserable and that our only hope is to be less miserable. Life itself is unfavourable and unpromising. Jung claims that the dark sides of our lives is to be redeemed by a self conscious enlightenment. Man is an inchoate, partial whole in a condition of prevenient Grace that springs up in him and brings wholeness of life. Man is made finally to be made whole. Freud, the high moralist preaches a stern realism, almost a revolt against the unfavourable conditions of man, with no hope in a transcendant providence.

Generally speaking we experience pessimism but only exceptionally do men experience utter depression. People experience Grief and Joy even in the very worst conditions. We experience strain, tensions, frustrations, conflicts as the normal symptoms of our daily lives and we do not underestimate the pains and sufferings in the world. They give rise to anger, self-deceit and other deadly sins. We suffer from our own individual egoism in the struggle for existence and our pride and egotism of ambition. For the most part, however, we remain sane, normal human beings. We are sinners always in need of Grace. The questions of Good and Evil are endlessly baffling and cannot be put aside. They constitute the moral struggle of mankind. Weeds grow among the corn and side effects crop up in man's best endeavours "The good is positive and constructive, evil is positive and destructive" says A.N. Whitehead. The statement formally characterises the condition we find ourselves in. It is also a challenge to overcome Evil with Good, "Whatsoever things are true, whatsoever things are honourable, whatsoever things are just, whatsoever things are pure, whatsoever things are lovely, whatsoever things are of good report, if there be any virtue, if there be any praise, think on these things."[1]

We think of the individual in the wider context of a person and still wider in the context of society. The individual is a partial whole and a contingent being. Our responses as individuals are moral responses. The old word, conscience, from which the word consciousness derives, describes the moral consciousness of man. It pervades all our conscious experience. Individuals know instinctively their affinity with each other. There is a distinctive being, called a human being, defined by this biological structure and his aspirations as a self conscious being. There are as many organic needs as there are acquired ones. There are different levels of consciousness and moral consciousness in man. In the animal world there is instinctive and conscious life. I believe however that Sensation reaches down to the limits of the physical world, that matter is not inert but responsive. Matter, materialism, must account for life, thought and aspiration.

The active character of consciousness is thought as well as feeling. We live in them and through them. Our language inhabits them. The sentence we are told is the unit of thought, not just a string of words. They can be positively charged with thoughts and attitudes. Thought can be abstract and concrete. Thought can be embedded in the tangible as touch is fused with sight. We are in the world through thought and feeling. We see through our eyes, not with them. We don't discover the world through logic nor do sentences perform experiments. Experiments are active, directed conscious thoughts. Extreme forms of linguistic philosophy assert we are bound by language. But words progressively arise from experience and the need to do so. Fresh thoughts about the world and new inventions require new words. Words are not just facts or things. They are vague and facile; in their place they are dynamic. Things we see and hear are sensuous and immediate. A landscape, as an uncoded message, evokes various responses, perhaps a spontaneous sense of wonder rising to an awareness of pattern. Our perception of Nature is not bare, photographic observation, but thought fed with discrimination and intelligence. Of course we all draw our vocabularies from "The Language", from the past, but our words are relived in us. The word God, is as much an attitude as it is a thought, an appreciation or a judgement, a whole hearted response to the world. At the turn of the eighteenth century poets like Wordsworth and Coleridge grew sensitive to the plasticity and energy of thought. The Imagination was a creative process of fusion of images issuing in new creations. Wordsworth promised to take emotions into the heart of Science as he did into the heart of Nature. Nature was not an inert, soulless substance but stirred with creative energy and light. "Colour rescues the stone from oblivion".[2] Wordsworth saw the energy and light of the common man and in the least favoured of them "The Sacred instinct of curiosity"[3] drives us forward as we gain the fruits of experience and our surroundings lure us on. We are restless to know ourselves and the world and what they hold for us. We are required to grow up in our bodies and our minds.

The fertility of Descartes' conception of man is that thought is constructive and reaches forward to wider spheres of the imagination. There was, for him, a harmony of body and mind, even though he called the body a machine, a functional word like our modern word mechanism with its associated meaning of hiddeness and machination (The inner workings of the water mill and the windmill were as obscure as our bodies are opaque to consciousness). Descartes regarded the harmony as nearly perfect or fitting the original work of God. His thoughts point to our contemporary view of the psychosomatic constitution of the individual.

It has been long thought that Science is in conflict with Religion. It may now seem that the conflict is between Religion and Linguistic philosophy. The scientist of our day have penetrated deeply into the secrets of Nature and revealed its underlying microscopic character, extending backward in space and time to the beginnings of the world and to the elements of our own bodies derived from the stars. The deeper the penetration the richer the haul, not only in the utility of its information but not least for its evaluation and admiration of the creative powers of man himself. It creates in us a deeper, growing reverence for all things, great and small, a rich, complex, human sentiment towards the world.

Some linguistic philosophers in the West have exercised the via negativa power of language that creates a mystic atmosphere to the world. Perhaps the most shining example is Wittgenstein's *Tractatus,* put to music even. A study of "Mysticism East and West" by Rudolf Otto reveals many parallels and correspondences of thought among them. The richness of their self-conscious thought is often astonishing. Their deeper levels of experience are not wholly transparent to them, they are purchased by an active elaboration of thought upon themselves through age long disciplines. For them there are deeper levels of the soul of man possessing their own inherent light, the inner light of the mind. They allege an affinity between God and Man at the deepest levels of the soul. They speak of the Immanence of the Divine as well as the Transcendence of the same. An Indian explaining this to his young son speaks of how a pinch of salt in a glass of water can be tasted in every drop. The Immanent Divine in man is the place in the soul where the Transcendant visits and meets with man. Theologians in the West are apt to think that the individual loses his identity in that experience "Tat twam asi", "that thou art": the inner Divinity to the outer. The divinity in man may be the same without being equal. For them the apprehension of the Divine is more ultimate that thought, though not exterior or inaccessible to it. Besides, they're experiencing the Divine issues in a form of life. Sinking down to that deeper level through deep meditation is an occasional if recurrent experience achieved by a deliberate effort of mind issuing in refreshment of life. In principle of course, Divine Immanence is no different from the doctrine of a universal humanity where the universal is present in every particle of the individual's body.

The subjects of Otto's study are the Indian theologian Siankara and the Christian mystic Eckhard. The former lived in the eighth century, the latter in the thirteenth. Each played a significant part in his own religious sphere. The one in driving out Buddhism from the Sub-Continent, the other was the source of Luther's renewed faith. In India the individual self, denied by Buddha, was restored to Religion. In Germany there was a renewed emphasis on the individual response to God. In both, God is "That with whom personal relations are possible"[4].

Buddhism, however, has become increasingly attractive to people in the West in this century as other religions have. Islam has claimed many a convert through intermarriage in particular. As the untouchables in India, seventy million of them, turned to Buddhism under their leader Dr Ambedka because of the Caste system; so in the States, Black people feel more comfortable in Islam for much the same reason. The Literary Californian Beat generation of the Sixties explored

Eastern religions in their own writers Thoreau and Emerson, known as Transcendentalism. They took to spontaneous writing in the belief that "in order to understand the Enlightening nature of pure mind, in Essence, you must learn to answer questions with no recourse to discriminating thinking"[5]. The non-existence of the Ego or Self of the Buddhist must have appealed to them as a relief from their over burdened self conscious selves. They were in revolt against their society, "its dry bourgois life". They were men about town making sorties into the remote confines of the mountains and sea coasts. They were certainly restless. The practising Buddhists, of course, live in the conventional world of objects as all men do but contemplate a metaphysical world wholly without inherent existence. Self hood is made up of Desires to be disengaged from, for entry into the Emptiness of the "Big Mind". Matter has no inherent existence, the category of substance does not hold. Buddhism is a strong challenge to ethical discipline and it is most relevant to see, that for it, ethical discipline precedes all higher apprehensions. Morality, we may say is the precondition and gate way to salvation. Convinced Humanists see life in this way as a struggle for a high morality and openness of mind.

The word God has stood for a dimension of human awareness and still occupies a wholly significant place among us. That God is not an object does not deny him objectivity. The mystic has long spoken of God as "No Thing", but as a presence to man. Theologians may be shy of God as Immanent. But what really worries them is what Karl Barth called, Immanentism. Church Worship displays an altar; a Bible; has sacred objects for the presence of God to its worshippers; and has a liturgy of prayer and praise. Such things address people from outside themselves and call for response, individual and collective. The Church has always addressed people as individuals in Baptism and confirmation and sought to form a Community of faithful believers. "The Kingdom of God is within you", as well as among you. These were 'believing times' when the name of God was upon peoples lips and the blessing of God felt in their hearts.

Distance has crept in. God is neither "up there" nor "down there", He is often a notion to fill the gaps in our thoughts about the world. He is still a topic of conversation and heated argument. We still have thoughts about Him but He is always ahead of us. We cannot consciously bear the fullness of the face of God, but the burning bush in the wilderness never seems ever to be consumed. After walking the streets of Prague with a retired Professor of Philosophy during the winter of 1969, a year after the country had been taken over by the Communists, on our last evening I asked him what he thought about reiterations of Nietsche's declaration that God was dead. His answer was immediate "As long as man is alive God will not die".

The two most prominent continental Theologians of the twentieth century are Karl Barth[6] and Dietrich Bonhoeffer. They both look back to an exceptional figure, namely Soren Kierkegaard, a Dane, and further back to Luther, and ultimately to the Augustinian tradition. Both Luther and Kierkegaard[7] faced a crisis in their religious lives. It was a crisis of their very existence, calling for a once and for all decision. It was Kierkegaards conviction that the moral life of man provided no grounds for redemption. Man is by nature alienated from God. Man is always in crisis of the angst of separation from God, the condition of psychological dread. All are in the same predicament. Since the original fall of man all are mortally flawed. Only by the intervention of Grace can he be reconciled. Natural man stands in need of regeneration and the dethronement of his natural Ego or Self. It must take place at a definite moment of conscious decision. Life thereafter must be a continued, faithful commitment to the decision. In Kierkegaard's case however it was a decision of allegiance to Jesus of Nazareth, the Jesus of the Gospels, not to the Christ of the Epistles. His personal allegiance was to the God-Man. He had revolted fiercely against Hegel's metaphysics. For Hegel man emerged to ever higher planes of being, a higher level of consciousness, under the influence of the World Spirit. In turn mankind bestows the fruits of his earthly experience upon the World Spirit in the form of a new consciousness. For Kierkegaard the individual had no place in this scheme of things. There is however a strain of this thought in Christian Theology, namely that the Ascension of Christ was the ascension of His humanity into the Godhead.

Barth played down the idea of personal crises, but emphasised the Transcendence of God in the Church, the Sacraments and the Bible - the whole Bible. The hidden God continues to be manifested in Christ, through the Church, the Sacraments and the divine Scripture. They were not to be taken on their face value, they contained the means of Grace. Natural man was alienated from God. It was God's approach to man not man's approach to God that brought reconciliation.

The point of contact of God and man was the Incarnation continued in the Church, the Sacraments and the Bible. By the visitation of the Holy Spirit "The Word of God" was revealed in the Church through the Sacraments and the Written word. Christ is "The Word of God", operating in the Old and New Testaments, not discovered but revealed by the Holy Spirit. The initiative of our reconciliation lies with God. This is not Barth's last word, but it is his necessary first word. In a spirited and vigorous mood, his trend is forward. Nevertheless, he leaves us to the initiative and transcendence of God operating through the Church, the Sacraments and the written word of God.

Bonhoeffer[8] was wholly confronted by the drift of Europe to the secular and asked the stark question, what form can Christ take in a wholly secular world, a world where the witness of the Church was of no account and the horizons of life structured to the here and now. He seems to have concluded that the Christian believer should make his way in the world as befits him, as teacher, as banker, as worker, continuing to feed on the Grace offered to him by ministration of the Church. Presumably their lives would witness to Christ or perhaps they would remain an inspired remnant to rekindle the flames of the Church to life again. Barth thought he was pessimistic.

The present state of the Church in a secular world reminds one of the early church who "outthought and outlived" the pagan world. There's no doubt however, that the eventual triumph of the Christian Church in the West as the educator of the people of Europe came about by adopting and exploiting the rich heritage of the past. If man has come of age, his heritage was that of Christendom. It has been true for a long time that the world no longer revolves around the axis of the Sabbatical Church, but is still penetrated with Christian values, in its law, its governance, and Education. But such institutions are now open to debate and evaluation on grounds of reason without the over arching influence of the Church. The Secular Society in which man has come of age, no longer directly under the Church, is of a highly heterogeneous make up, pluralist and of various amorphous activities and beliefs. Yet Christian moral values are still a force in the land. Can we trust our morality and ethos to a churchless world, which is not the same as a Godless world? Contrary to Kierkegaard's view of the scope of morality I tend to believe it is the growing point of human life. Orthodox church members tend to believe that the Christian religion depends upon the historical continuity of the Church and possibly the only way in which God operates in the world. This view seriously, if not fatally, limits the outlook of the Christian. Theism commits God to the world. The recently retired Cardinal Suenens of Belgium speaks of the Holy Spirit as the principle of Surprise in the Church. A.N. Whitehead speaks of God as the principle of novelty in the world. Christianity has to confront the world. Christian Doctrine does not change, says Cardinal Newman, but deepens. I believe that Christian Doctrine will deepen its own view on the world in the direction of other living religions. Theism requires this. Karl Barth asserted that you can compare Religions but not Revelations. True, they have their histories. Many of the outstanding scholars among Eastern religions particularly among Buddhists, question how far their teaching reach among those already orientated to them. East and West are still relative Strangers.

C.G. Jung has also warned against such a drift, a warning not least directed to his own followers. It is not clear how far you can separate a Religion from its cultural surrounding. Hindu friends of mine say that Hinduism finds a place for Christianity in its own doctrines. We are all struck with the compassion of the Buddhist as we are by St Francis of Assisi. We know Moslems for their piety and devotion. As men and women we can have fellowship with them and see eye to eye with them in matters of common life. There are too, I have noticed, certain cultural traits underlying these religions remaining strong against religious officialdom. Moral values are widely shared amongst all living religions. Institutional religions can be oppressive and militant. They can be tribal and nationalistic. Bishop John Robinson in his study of Hinduism found the phrase "The Incarnation" of Church Doctrine to be too exclusive and proposed the dropping of the definite article, "The". Incarnation, he found, is a common place belief in India. There are visitations of Gods to earth that affect peoples lives. As Christ was the "God-Man" he was also a "Man of God", and there is strong evidence in the Gospels that he was the "Adopted" Son of God. Einstein[9] speaking of Gandhi, says of this historic man "Generations to come will hardly believe that such a one as this, in flesh and blood, walked the earth". People have felt the same about the historical Jesus.

"Knowing is a process of exploration."[10] Knowing in itself is a value, but there is more to life than knowing. Life is creative and constructive for each generation. God is always "equi-distant to all men at all times". There is reality to process that transcends us. We see changes without seeing their meaning, we only feel their impact upon us. "The systematic thought of ancient writers is now nearly worthless, but their detached insights are priceless"[11]. Aristotle in his great work on Ethics turns to the poet and the dramatist for confirmation. J.S. Mill's fine Essay on Liberty elicits the high moral sentiments of his own society.

Michelangelo's lofty portrait of man, "Nor did God show Himself elsewhere more clearly than in Human form Sublime, and since they image Him, Him alone I love" strikes a new note of renascent man echoed by our own William

Shakespeare, "What a piece of work is Man". We cannot but see the profound creativity and dignity of the phenomenon of man; self-evident, though not self-explanatory. As early as the Book of Genesis the first word was spoken by the Judaic mythopoeic declaration that man is made in the 'Image of God', to be re-iterated and amplified in the New Testament. Here is a paradigm of religious belief confirmed by our astonishment and admiration for the creative powers of man; a sufficient ground for our belief in the Transcendent. And the exalted view of man does justice to our highest human aspirations. The Image of God in man is a 'projection' of Himself in us to be worked upon. St Augustine is spoken of as God intoxicated: Wordsworth was impassioned by Nature: St Francis by the needs of the poor and the charm of lowly creatures. Compassion for all creatures is a mark of the same passion. Such marks of passion often at the cost of personal pain and suffering identifies with the passion of Christ. God imparts to us an image of His Freedom bodied forth in us in moral passion and wholehearted devotion. God imparts to us His powers of creativeness and vision. We can single out men like Plato, Newton, Madame Curie, Einstein for their intellectual passion, not to be put down simply to brain power. We can single out individuals like Kagawa who lost his eyesight in the service of the poor in the slums of Tokyo, or Wilberforce for his long, patient campaign on behalf of the slaves or Schweitzer of Lambaréné for his life commitment to the sick. These were men and women for others. They all, and others like them, exemplify and articulate the image of God in man.

We celebrate individuals and cherish their memories for their courage, inspiration, achievements and pioneering spirits. We derive the same supports from people we know personally and look up to them for the good qualities they display in their lives.   In every society admiration is celebrated for founding Fathers. These are men and women whose lives have been of critical value for the insights they have brought to us and stand out as men for all seasons. Men inspire men whatsoever their sources of inspirations; we are responsive to exceptional individuals, they are our sign posts in the journey of life and the task of Soul making. These cross all frontiers of creed and clime. We are naturally drawn to our own traditions, but the one world we now inhabit brings fresh news and good tidings from afar and long ago that we welcome and rejoice in.

Kierkegaard's uncomprising emphasis on the individual could appear socially and religiously offensive. But his humility could be expressed in the words of a sermon I heard preached in St. Mary's, Oxford, by a member of the French Resistance during the war, that has a touch of existentialism about it, "Humility is to be on one's face before God and on one's feet before man". Kierkegaard championed the individual. Abraham was the singular Father of the Faith. He admired Socrates for his uncompromising stand before the court at Athens. He hated the "Mass" which included the National Church of his day, for its compromises and its Bishops who acted as remote administrators. He championed the individual for his convictions, but in doing so he undervalued the place of fellowship, that religion can be shared and the individual confirmed and strengthened. But "Individuality" is not the same as individualism. Individualism, like collectivism, is an ideology, a distorting abstraction. We are, as individuals, incomplete, partial wholes in an incomplete world, a world of travail "Waiting the adoption of the sons of God".

"The last Enemy is Death", says the Book of Revelation. The second law of Thermodynamics speaks of our planet running down when the sun ceases to shine upon it. Life on earth ends in a cold death. That is what mankind can expect in terms of Physics. There are debates on the expanding and contracting Universe from the mighty atom to a mightily extended space. Aristotle saw the meaning of the acorn in the full grown flowering oak tree. The beginnings of things were interpreted in terms of the promise of things. The genetic approach is defective. The Universe itself has a history to be seen from a higher vantage point. Karl Barth in his latter writings brings the End, the 'eschaton', more into the centre of his thinking. The life of the Believer is reconciled here but

231

redeemed in the End. The Christian enjoys eternal life here and now, the eternal is a realisation and a destiny. All living Religions contemplate a world hereafter. I am mindful to leave our eternal destiny to God, 'our Creator, Sustainer and End'. God is the name we give to the Transcendent.

References

1. St Paul's Epistle to the Philippians, IV.8
2. A.N.Whitehead
3. Einstein
4. J.C.Webb: *Philosophy of Religion*
5. *Big Sky Mind: Buddhism and the beat generation.* Ed. Carole Tonhiason. Thomsons
6. H.R.Mackintosh: *Types of Modern Theology* Nisbet
7. Ibid.
8. John A Phillips: *The Form of Christ in the World* Collins
9. Dr R.V. Kao: *Sevegram* Sevegram Ashram Publications.
10. A.N.Whitehead: Essay on Immortality in *The Library of Living Philosophers* Ed. P.A.Schilp. Evanston and Chicago.
11. Ibid.

Credo quia non possibile

Eberhard George Wedell

The second part of James Mark's Essay on Faith identifies the position from which he writes: "I must operate with the intellectual assumptions which I have evolved ..... in encounter with the culture in which I live and in exchange with my contemporaries."[1] This applies to all the contributors to the volume, although each of us is likely to vary the mix of the three elements and, indeed, each of us benefits from a unique set of influences, which no one else can share.

I
The role of Nurture

Childhood and family experience is, clearly, important. But in some ways the articulation of values and commitments of early adulthood begin to show what we have made of our inheritance. It is a time when edges are not yet blurred by experience and compromise, and when the developmental horizon is as yet pretty infinite. There is no immediate rush to beat the clock, though impatience with external constraints makes up for that in creating a sense of urgency.

My own religious development so far falls into three stages. The culture in which I grew up was the first. Circumstances conspired to make it more embattled than that in which most contributors to this Symposium were formed. Growing up in our household involved an external conflict on two fronts: the struggle of the Confessional Church against the totalitarian claims of the Nazi regime; and the concurrent attempts by the same regime to eliminate families with Jewish connections from professional and public life. The consequence of these pressures was that I absorbed the commitment to the Judeao-Christian tradition, as it were, with my mother's milk. There was no room in those years for the luxury of laodicean relativism[2]. In so far as my family was protected from the murderous attacks of the storm troopers, this was attributed to divine intervention. The Compline petition "Keep me as the apple of an eye: hide me under the shadow of thy wings" was as real to us as to the Psalmist.[3] In the existential situation of the Church's struggle against the Nazi regime, there was no room for a qualified definition of the miracle of faith.

This conviction that "the Lord He is God, be the nations never so unquiet" has remained with me over the years. It has conditioned much of my thinking about the relationship between the Christian faith and the socio-economic order, both national and international. In that sense I have always found it relatively easier to come to terms with the first and the third persons of the Trinity than with the person of Jesus, the Christ. James Mark identifies the theological issues relating to Jesus lucidly in part VIII of his paper; and Bryan Saunders deals with them existentially on pages 6-8 of his. It is the specificity of Jesus and his life on earth that makes him at the same time the key and the stumbling block for me as the man on the Clapham omnibus. I have lived with the Gospel narratives all my life, and what they tell me about Jesus is the mainspring of my hope. I am content to remain agnostic about the claims made for the precise manner of his birth and his resurrection. These seem to me to be incomparably less important than the way he lived his short life (see also the extracts from Leslie Houlden's article on the Resurrection below). Without his 'template' (vide Bryan Saunders) I would be of men and women the most miserable.

The concept of the action of the Holy Spirit in bringing about among a fractious humanity an element of mutual respect and convergence is one which from time to time I have experienced. Coupled with a natural conservatism this has allowed me to continue to enjoy the fellowship of the Christian community in spite of my own, by now, laodicean relationship to the creeds and to some of the more extreme demands of organised religion.

In the light of these personal reflections I return to my experience of a household in the frontline of religious and political persecution and the excerpts from Dietrich Bonhoeffer's Letters and Papers from Prison in James Mark's paper.[4] I can perhaps from my own experience throw a little light on the setting within which Dietrich developed the concept of "a world come of age". Dietrich Bonhoeffer was my senior by 21 years; he belonged to the generation of my parents. They must have thought him sufficiently mature a cousin by 1927 to ask him to be one of my godparents. By 1934, at the age of only twenty-eight he was exposed to the full blast of the Nazi persecution of the Church and all other civilising elements in the country. This being so his formulation of the concept of a "world come of age" seems in retrospect the more remarkable. Withdrawal into a religious redoubt would have been a more natural reaction. It was the inclination of many of his contemporaries, even those who stood firm in resistance to the regime. The recognition of the movement towards human autonomy "the discovery of the laws according to which man can live in the world of learning, political and social affairs, ethics, the arts and religion, so that man has learned to come to terms with himself in all important questions without having to avail himself of the working hypothesis - God" (8.6.44) was certainly the way in which National Socialist concepts were developed. It is remarkable that Dietrich Bonhoeffer recognised this as being part of a wider process of secularisation, and accepted it as such. "The God who lets us live in the world without the working hypothesis of God is the God before whom we stand." (16.7.44)[5].

The publication of these insights of course lay a decade or more ahead of the experiences I have recounted. My last encounter with Dietrich Bonhoeffer occurred in St. Leonard's-on-Sea in the July of 1939 when he stopped off in England on his return journey from the United States to Germany to see, among others, his close friend George Bell, Bishop of Chichester.[6]

II

The intellectual challenges

The links via the Student Christian Movement to the nascent Ecumenical Movement formed the second stage of my Christian development. Here there was a vigorous climate not so much induced by external constraints as by the determination to deal with the intellectual challenges posed for Christians by the pressures of modern society. The most articulate critic at that time of the liberal attitudes taken up by Christians to social and economic problems was Reinhold Niebuhr. Dorothy Emmet has recently provided a perceptive account of his influence during the war years.[7] As president of the SCM in the LSE during the Mission to London in 1946 I was thrown into this universe of discourse at the deep end, and only prevented from drowning by Ted Wickham,[8] the missioner and a life-long friend from that time on.

As a young civil servant in the Ministry of Education in the 1950's I learnt to value this immersion, since it provided a much-needed antidote to my rather woolly notions about setting the world to rights. Dorothy Emmet quotes a passage from Niebuhr which spoke to that condition: "Humanity always faces a double task. The one is to reduce the anarchy of the world to some kind of immediately sufferable order and unity; and the other is to get these tentative and insecure unities and achievements under the criticism of the ultimate ideal." [9] Much as my head needed to develop careful analytical method, a motive force for disinterested public service was also required. As Dag Hammerskjold discovered "The 'great' commitment all too easily obscures the 'little' one. But without the humility and warmth which you have to develop in your relations to the few with whom you are personally involved, you will never be able to do anything for the many. Without them you will live in a world of abstractions, when your solipsism, your greed for power and your death wish lack the one opponent which is stronger than they are ....It is better for the health of the soul to make one man good than 'to sacrifice oneself for mankind'. For a mature man these are not alternatives, but two aspects of self-realisation, which mutually support each other ....." [10]

III

A community of friends

That sobering recognition came to sustain me in hard times, together with the support of friends. The coalescence of a group of friends and the liberating effect of middle age has, in retrospect constituted the third stage of my religious development.

The Chantry at Sevenoaks, from which after forty years without one, our group now derives its name, did, in the event, exercise some influence on our development. It was the home of Beatrice Hankey who had collected around herself a group of Edwardian contemporaries anxious to pursue the Christian way of life. She modelled their discipline on Tennyson's Idylls of the King.[11] They came to be known as the Blue Pilgrims. After the second world war these images no longer appealed to the imagination of the young Pilgrims, including Rosemarie and myself. The work of Charles Williams on the same theme and in particular his collection of poems entitled The Region of the Summer Stars,[12] emerging as it did from the neo-orthodoxy expressed by T S Eliot, C S Lewis, J R R Tolkien, Dorothy Sayers and others, attracted our early interest in the 1950's.

For those linked with St Anne's House in Soho, run at that time as a Centre for Christian Discourse, this use of poetry, drama and literature to reinterpret the Christian faith was important. It is not irrelevant that Patrick McLaughlin, the spiritus rector of St.Anne's, was one of Beatrice Hankey's Blue Pilgrims. Although we have never used 'The Founding of the Company' as a defining text, it does, stripped of its more extravagant Arthurian images, uncannily trace the evolution of these friendships. The first stanza describes how "a few found themselves in common":

About this time there grew, throughout Logres,
a new company, as (earlier) in Tabennisi
or (later) on Monte Cassino or in Cappadocia
a few found themselves in common; but this, less-
being purposed only to profess a certain pointing.
It spread first from the household of the king's poet;
it was known by no name, least his own,
who hardly himself knew how it was grown
or whether among the readers or among the grooms
it took source from doctrine or toil but among his own
it was first nobly spoken as a token of love

238

between themselves, and between themselves and their lord.
Grounded in the Acts of the Throne and the pacts of the
  themes,
it lived only by conceded recollection,
having no decision, no vote or admission,
but for the single note that any soul
took of its own election of the Way; the whole
shaped no flame nor titular claim to place.

The second stanza describes the role of the new company:
Grounded so in the Acts and pacts of the Empire,
doctrine and image - from rose-lordly Caucasia
to the sentences sealing the soul through the whole of Logres
by the mouth qf London-in-Longres: from the strong base
of maids, porters, mechanics, to the glowing face
of Dindrane (called Blanchfleur) and the cells of the brain
qf the king's college and council - were the wise
  companions.
The king's poet's household opened on the world
in a gay scene devised before the world
and prized by (however darkened) the very heathen.
They measured the angle of creation; in three degrees
along the hazel they mounted the mathematics of the soul,
no wisdom separate but for convenience of naming
and the claiming by the intellectual art of its part
in the common union. So at the first station,
were those who lived by a frankness of honourable
  exchange,
labour in the kingdom, devotion in the Church, the need
each had of other this was the measurement and motion
of process - the seed of all civil policy. . . . .

Charles Williams articulated the dynamics of friendship. His insistence on the freedom of individuals "being purposed only to profess a certain pointing" is crucial to the polity of friends. They "live only by conceded recollection ..... having no decision, no note or admission but for the single note that any soul took of its own election of the way". In this type of relationship dogmatic agreement ceases to be necessary because reciprocal commitment and trust replace it.

IV
Commitment and Conformity

The problem of the Church throughout the centuries has been precisely the tension between commitment and conformity. The expansion of Christianity beyond the primary group has led to the creation of credal tests and other measures of conformity designed to serve non-theological purposes.

The emphasis on conformity in matters of dogmatic theology has, throughout history, tended to be determined as much by political as by theological considerations. If it had not been for the perceived need to rally the largest possible number of supporters to an ecclesiasticopolitical objective; and to identify who is "one of us" and who is not, doctrinal disputes would have played a much less important part in the history of Christendom.

If one takes the early debate between those, like St. Paul, who argued that in Christ there is neither Jew nor Gentile; and the particularists, who insisted that only circumcised and practising Jews could become Christians; then the political character of the debate becomes evident. Similarly the break between the Eastern and the Western Church in 1054 over the filioque clause was a power struggle between Rome and Byzantium. The echoes reverberate to the present day in the incompatibility of Roman Catholic Croats with Orthodox Serbians in the former Yugoslavia. The non-theological causes of the Reformation have been identified by R H Tawney and others.[13] They have drawn attention to the failure of a secularised ecclesiastical establishment to respond to the spiritual needs of the increasingly literate and individualised populations of the 16th century. Nothing less than the personal relationship of the individual citizen to his or her God was at stake.

And so on, to the present day. The trouble with The Sea of Faith movement brought about by the writings of Don Cupitt is that it has thought it necessary to exact a specific

240

criterion of conformity. So it has substituted one dogma for another. If the movement were content to affirm that matters of religious belief are a matter of individual perception; and not to insist that "the concept of God is an exclusively human construct"; it could be a more constructive force in the Church today. As it is one has the impression that those who attend its conferences are largely the people who, half a century ago, attended the Swanwick conferences of the Student Christian Movement, and set much store by conformity to precise denominational formulae. The failure to resolve the problem of the cohesion of the Christian community without the imposition of dogmatic affirmations, may well come to be recognised as the key issue as the Church enters the third millennium.

Leslie Houlden is among those who have tried to unblock the dogmatic logjam. In a recent article in Theology he writes "The claim is frequently made that Christian faith stands or falls by the belief that Jesus rose from the tomb on the third day.[14] It comes from the pulpits at Easter and it comes in official pronouncements about the irreducible bases of Chistianity. The claim is often made with defiant conviction but, often seemingly by rote, as if to say how could anyone possibly suppose the contrary? It seems to be incontrovertible. Whatever else is up for debate and negotiation, this is not. There is at least one reason why this is a pity. It is the reason of a prudential and, more importantly, pastoral kind; though firm adherents of the claim will not be impressed by it. While modern western Christianity probably includes a majority of Christians of the latter type, others of more liberal or light-and-shade kinds have drifted off incredulous or discouraged, there are still many who doggedly wish to be counted in but who find traditional faith, including claims such as that I began with, impossible to accept. In the nature of the case they are often amongst the most thoughtful Christians, for thought breeds dissatisfaction with slogan-like take-it-or-leave-it statements." And Houlden illustrates the way in which the Gospel accounts of the Resurrection do not on the whole regard it as the most important part of the story they are trying to tell. "It seems that what fired these witnesses was a variety of aspects of the 'Jesus event'. It touched each differently according to formation, character and need, and, yes, prejudice. The effect of Jesus has been ever so and defies straight-jacketing. It cannot be so narrowly prescribed as the claim made for the Resurrection suggests. The wind blows where it will?"[15]

The dilemma of the need to assert credal conformity even in the face of sound biblical scholarship is dealt with in a more general way in the recent biography of Robert Runcie, the former Archbishop of Canterbury. "It is manifestly absurd to go around saying things that you don't actually fully understand or aren't quite sure that you believe, at any rate as expressed in that kind of terminology. It's intellectually dishonest and it doesn't in the end allow you and what you are preaching to be integrated. Some bishops spout about believing in this, that or the other, and you know perfectly well that they don't. You don't need to challenge [Robert Runcie] about beliefs; he challenges himself the whole time. He has a pragmatic, cobbled-up structure for dealing with a multi-layered community. Push any bit of it too hard and the ceiling leaks but when you don't push it too hard, it actually succeeds in keeping the rain out".[16] This somewhat flippant description by Humphrey Carpenter of the dogmatic problems experienced by some of the present generation of bishops illustrates the urgent need to tackle the issue of credal statements and their role in the Christian community. Nowadays the effect of many years of apologetic exegesis of the credal texts has been to reduce their value as tests of belonging. And yet it is supposed that the saying of the words of the creeds remains a test of orthodoxy.

What is the alternative? It is arguable that, the political reasons for credal tests having disappeared almost entirely, they could now be dropped without replacement. Those who want to be counted among the Christians are few enough, and the worldly benefits to be gained by rallying to the Christian cause are sufficiently minimal, to discourage all but those determined to follow the Christian way. The Church could therefore welcome them, encourage them to take a full part in the Church's life and not, as Geoffrey Taylor proposes in the extract from The Guardian quoted by Michael Smart merely as "Friends of" a particular church.[17] The blessings and the demands of life in the Christian Community; the ebb and flow of the Church's year; the self-authenticating revelation of God in the Bible to which Anthony Pragnell draws attention;[18] are bound to engage people who wish to be counted in. The concern of Christians for the socio-economic order of society makes demands which further distinguish those whose engagement is serious from the rest. If such a revival of the equivalent to the former catechumenate were to be agreed (although in this case there would be no discrimination against the catechumens), questions would be raised about the safeguarding of tradition. This responsibility of the episcopate could now perhaps be shared more widely with the community of Christians at large. It is an experience of our days that Christians from widely differing theological and ecclesiological traditions are able to join together in matters concerning their witness in the community at large. A kaleidoscope of individual perceptions of the Christian experience is contained between the covers of this volume. This has not prevented the friendships which have held us together for many years. Bonhoeffer's verses about Christians and unbelievers express this coinherence:

"Men go to God when they are sore bestead,
Pray to him for succour, for his peace, for bread,
For mercy for them sick, sinning or dead:
All men do so, Christian and unbelieving.

Men go to God when he is sore bestead,
Find him poor and scorned, without shelter or bread,
Whelmed under weight of the wicked, the weak, the
*   dead:*
Christians stand by God in his hour of grieving.

God goeth to every man when sore bestead,
Feedeth body and spirit with his bread,
For Christians, heathens alike he hangeth dead:
And both alike forgiving."[19]

Notes and References

1) James Mark, p. 17

2) See Renate Rocholl and E G Wedell *Vom Segen des Glaubens*, Dusseldorf, Archiv der Evangelischen Kirche im Rheinland 1995, chapter IV (at present available only in German).

3) Psalm XVII, verse 8.

4) See James Mark pp. 21 - 23

5) Bryan Saunders discusses the consequences of this recognition of the state of the world pp. 189-191, and very pertinently asks "Can man abide it?"

6) See Edwin Robertson *Unshakeable Friend*, London, CCBI 1995, chapter 3.

7) Dorothy Emmet *Philosophers and Friends*. London, Macmillan 1996, pp. 56-61,

8) At that time the Head of the Sheffield Industrial Mission and the chief theoretician of the concept of mission to an industrialised society. Later he was made Bishop of Middleton in the Manchester Diocese.

9) R Niebuhr, *An Interpretation of Christian Ethics*, New York and London, Harpers 1935, (quoted in Dorothy Emmet, op. cit. p 60).

10) Dag Hammerskjold *Markings*, London Faber & Faber 1964, pp 116 - 117.

1 1) See Charles E Raven & Rachel F Heath *One called Help*, London Hodder and Stoughton 1937, chapter 3.

12) Charles Williams 'The Founding of the Company' in

The Region of the Summer Stars, London, New York, Toronto, Geoffrey Cumberlege, Oxford University Press 1950, pp 36-37. See also Humphrey Carpenter *The Inklings: C S Lewis, J R R Tolkien, Charles Williams and their Friends,* London, Allen & Unwin 1978.

13) R H Tawney, *Religion and the Rise of Capitalism* (Holland Memorial Lectures 1922 first published 1926) Pelican Books, 1948.

14) Leslie Houlden *'The Resurrection and Christianity'* in *Theology*, Vol XCIX, No 789, May-June 1996, London, SPCK, pp 198-205.

15) ibid.

16) Humphrey Carpenter *Robert Runcie: The Reluctant Archbishop*, London, Hodder and Stoughton, 1996, p.160.

17) See Michael Smart, , Annex 2.

18) See Anthony Pragnell, p. 168.

19) Dietrich Bonhoeffer *Letters and Papers from Prison:* London, S C M Press, 1952.

Learning to create Human Values

Rosemarie Wedell

In this paper I am attempting to account for the learning process I have undergone and am still undergoing, and the changes that have taken place in my thinking and feeling as a result of it.

Three major encounters were/are influential in this process:

1) my encounter with the other world-faiths and world-views about which I have been teaching during the past twenty years.

2) my attempts to understand the impact of modern science on our understanding of the universe and of the human species, particularly in the sphere of brain-biology. Three books I am still struggling with are:

Daryl Reanny, a brain biologist: *"The Death of Forever - A New Future for Human Consciousness"*,

his last book *"The Music of Mind* - An Adventure into Consciousness"*, and

Richard Leakey's: *"The Sixth Extinction"*.

3) my encounter with the Feminist Movement and Theology.

These encounters and readings have convinced me of the need for a new, some would prefer a revised value-system in our European world-region. This need has arisen from the fact that we Europeans have lived and are still living in a state of dualism and tension after almost two thousand years; ie: the dualism between the spirit and the body, between religion and science, and between supernatural Reality and the phenomenal environment of our earth and universe.

The Sea of Faith Network, to which I belong, has given itself the task of "exploring and promoting religious faith as a human creation". It is trying to replace Christian credal statements with new metaphors and new symbols, and new concepts which can meet the needs of our time, and contribute towards bridging the gaps that have characterised our faith-system and world view. The Network also participates in the challenging and difficult task of deconstructing the elaborate metaphysical constructs which have dominated European philosophical thinking.

Don Cupitt, by his courageous development of the notion of "Non-Realism" since the 1980s, of human history as a "stream of language-formed events" of his idea of the "outsidelessness" of human existence and its state of "ecstatic immanence" has also contributed to the profound shifts in my consciousness.

My encounters with members of other faith systems and world views in this country and in India and China have made me realise that they are as much concerned with the discovery of meaning and value for human life and behaviour as we are. David Hart's book "One Faith? - Non-Realism and the world of Faiths" contains valuable ideas and information on this matter. So does Keith Ward's book "A Vision to Pursue".

As my friends in the global network of the Interfaith Movement and I look towards the 21st century, we envisage that the emerging European Christian Humanism will be matched and complemented by the humanism of other faith-communities and human societies. I say Christian Humanism because our European obedience and commitment to holiness and goodness are inspired by and derived from our own great Teacher, Jesus of Nazareth, and based on his humanity, the example of his life and teaching. Judaism and Islam, Hinduism and Buddhism, Confucianism, Taoism and Shintoism have produced their own human face and type, their own unique brand of humanism derived and based on the lives and teachings of their own great religious geniuses and examples. We shall learn to recognise our common humanity in each other more and more, and rejoice in the diversity and profundity of the evolutionary paths by which the human species, world-wide, is reaching human adulthood and maturity.

Reassessing our Christian History.

Jesus' first friends and followers who were Jews, saw in him The Anointed One, The Messiah who their people were expecting to deliver them from the power of Roman

249

domination. Their Resurrection-experience added another dimension to their perception of him which had its roots also in the Judaism of the inter-Testamental centuries.

Later Paul took the story and the teaching of Jesus into the Gentile world and adapted the Jewish Messiah-figure to fit into the Greco-Roman world with its notions of divine Saviour-figures and their cults.

During the twenty-first century the combined influence and effort of the world-faiths will we hope contribute to the creation of a world-society where the conditions of peace, justice and order between and within human societies can prevail.

My ongoing study of the history of the European world-region reveals that, at the time when Judo-Christian Monotheism was brought to our backward northern European regions, the Humanist Tradition arrived with it, though generally ignored and rejected by the official church.

The latter had its roots in the writings of the philosophers, dramatists and scientists of an earlier and more advanced European civilisation, the Greco-Roman one, which was culturally and religiously pluralistic and sophisticated. Its influence on northern Europeans, though largely hidden until the Renaissance, exerted itself nevertheless from the beginning of the Christianisation of northern Europe.

With the Renaissance, roughly 1450-1500, a period of rehabilitation of that earlier civilisation took place. Plato and Aristotle, who had introduced the concept of Metaphysics into Greek culture, were now "baptised" into a new Christian Humanism of which Erasmus of Rotterdam and others were outstanding representatives. A result of this new Humanism was regular contact with Islamic and Jewish scholarship and mysticism.

One of the most important long-term effects of the Renaissance on European culture was the rediscovery of the delight which the ancient Greeks and Romans had found in the human body and its depiction in sculpture and the arts. The Greeks had invented the concept of sport and the

250

Olympic Games.

The Italian artist Michelangelo, more than any other, painted and sculpted the naked human body, depicting God reclining on a cloud, whilst creating Adam and Eve naked in "His image". It is a splendid painting in the Sistine Chapel in Rome. My father had a large reproduction of it in his study.

Michelangelo's paintings and sculptures set in motion the very gradual, very reluctant freeing of the Christian imagination from its bondage to the Church's teaching about the sinfulness, perversity and inferiority of the human body compared to Man's immortal soul.

During the Reformation in the 16th century, Luther's insistence that the individual Christian must live his/her life by Faith alone, Sola Fide, and in accordance with his/her conscience, led him to translate the Bible into the vernacular. A scholar and professor of Theology at Wittenberg university, he made use of Erasmus' earlier translation of the New Testament into its original Greek from the Latin Vulgate and the translation, by Hebrew scholars of the Old Testament into its original Hebrew. Luther's translation of the Bible into German was, therefore, based on the original texts.

He set a precedent for other scholars and friends of the Reformation to translate the Bible into their native languages all over northern Europe.

During the first Scientific Revolution in the 17th century, Copernicus, Kepler, Galileo and Newton began to open up the universe to European men and women.

With the Enlightenment in the 18th century, another big step was made in the emancipation of European culture and civilisation. Europe was weary of the 30 years' war of ideological struggle. Instead, the new religious and scientific insights and changes of the Reformation and Scientific Revolution were brought together in a new synthesis, a mutual clarification which produced a new perception of the human being as enlightened, reasonable and rational, and capable of creating a new and better human society from the previous church-dominated one. I see in The Enlightenment a true forerunner of our present state of Post-Structuralism.

Further scientific discoveries in what became known as the Social Sciences of Sociology, Psychology, Biology and Economics were to follow in the 19th century. Their knowledge and insights brought about "fractures in human consciousness" to use a phrase by Daryl Reanny. These fractures, or, to use another phrase "alterations" in the Christian European consciousness were and are still contributing to the ongoing disintegration of the unified, static and absolutist psycho-intellectual vision of the pre-Reformation and pre-scientific European minds and imagination. We know from Don Cupitt's books, not only scientists have contributed to these fundamental changes. Outstanding philosophers of the 19th century, who he has done much to make us aware of in his books, played their part in changing and enlarging human understanding and knowledge in Europe.

The emergence of the Social Sciences in the 19th century was followed, in our own century, by further explosions in the realms of Physics, Mathematics, in Chemistry, Biochemistry, Medicine, and above all, Brain Biology, followed by the preoccupations with Language and Linguistics for the past decades.

I read European Christian history as having passed and developed through preparatory stages, as a steady movement towards closing the rifts in our faith system and culture, as an evolution in human consciousness and awakening which is beginning to reach its apotheosis in this and the 21st century. This is not a new idea. Paul introduced it into the New Testament in Galatians when he suggested that the Old Testament was the Tutor to, and preparatory to the insights and revelations of the New Testament.

During the enlightenment period this idea was developed further by one of the great German Enlightenment-figures - Ephraim Lessing. In his book "The Education of the Human Race" 1780, he sets out to show that the human species has evolved and developed through different stages and reached the state of enlightenment and adulthood or autonomy during this present age of Enlightenment. Alas, humanity was not ready then, but required more time and experience to learn and to grow up.

The contribution of the Bible to my own ethical development.

I am greatly indebted to the ethical and inspirational teachings in the Old and New Testaments, and see in our present situation the beginnings of the fulfilment of some of the more remarkable visions of the religious geniuses in the two Testaments.

As I look at the old Genesis warning in Chapter 2 v5 "your eyes will be opened and you will be like gods knowing good and evil", I must admit that, during the course of this century our eyes have, indeed, been opened to the presence of good and evil in the human heart and psyche as never before. Does this lead to a greater readiness to accept responsibility for what is happening, or to cowardly fear and doubt?

I have always enjoyed reading Joel's prophecy about the outpouring of God's spirit upon all flesh, Joel 2 vv 28/9. . . . "I will pour out my spirit even upon slaves and slave-girls". Is it too far-fetched to see, not only in our developed western world, signs of this happening through the Television and Cable media accessible and available now to everybody, providing information and instruction, good and bad?

I recall the ethical teachings of Amos and Hosea calling the people to apply God's laws to the political, economic and social ordering of their society. Their teachings contained the seeds of the modern concept of the Welfare State, strengthening the will to make human societies more just, more equal and more caring.

Isaiah's vision of a future when peace, justice and order will be established in all the world , Chapter 2 v 4, is cut in stone, and stands in the courtyard of the UN buildings next to a statue depicting the beating of the sword into a ploughshare. Surely, the founders of the UN believed this ancient hope and vision was to be realised in the not too distant future.

253

The UN, the European Union, the Commonwealth, the OSCE, the still-faltering attempts at creating a "Commonwealth of Independent States" from the former Soviet Union are the beginnings of the working out of these visions.

Jesus' call to his friends to be "the salt of the earth" and "the leaven" in the body of human society bring his ethical teaching right down to our personal level. He also said: "If the salt loses its savour, it is only fit to be thrown away". His ethical teachings represent a treasure-trove of insights and directives for us to learn from and be guided by.

Lastly, Paul's vision in Romans 8 vv 22-25 is another such teaching which is profoundly relevant for today. Our present self-perception is deeply affected by our new understanding of Ecology, the workings of natural processes, and by the realisation that the human species forms an indissoluble link in the eco-system of our planet Earth and its other inhabitants.

Many have recognised by now that the position of lording it over the Earth, enjoined upon us by the world-view of Genesis 1 vv 27-29 must be abandoned totally if we are to avoid the sixth extinction of which Richard Leakey warns us in his book "The Sixth Extinction". Dietrich Bonhoeffer encouraged his fellow-Christians in the forties with his vision of "Man has come of age" and the need for a "religionless Christianity", to accept the fact profound changes were facing them. If we are going to meet the challenges and the opportunities that are awaiting us in the 21st century, we must indeed have courage and accept the responsibilities which our human autonomy and adulthood lays on us.

Christianity, at its best, has taught that the ethical teachings of the Bible have to be worked out and expressed in the context of human history. "The Kingdom of God" is to be realised in the here and now. This is not an unrealistic, pious hope, but our human task and privilege.

The importance of other teachers and teaching in my life.

This brings me to the life and teaching of the Buddha to whom I owe a great debt. He lived about 500 BC and was, like Jesus, an itinerant teacher moving about Northeast India. He encouraged his followers and listeners to "put on Buddhahood" or "Buddha-nature" which, according to his teaching, is the rightful calling of all human beings, since human beings represent the highest form of consciousness in the Universe with the potential to achieve holiness and goodness. At the same time he taught them to see themselves as "psycho-physical organisms", with five sense faculties, and mind as the sixth faculty, without possessing a permanent or immortal self. Buddha, having himself tried every available method and teaching Hinduism provides for the seeker after holiness, had come to the conclusion that there are no certainties either beyond this earthly existence or in human relationships which can deliver us from the suffering, the loneliness and misfortunes of human life, except total commitment to the practice of meditation, self-scrutiny and self-reliance. These will lead to the attainment of Buddhahood and the state of Nirvana, a state of liberation from all "fetters" and all "clinging" in this life.

The fruits of such a life are revealed through compassion towards all living beings and through wisdom. Human beings are responsible for their own enlightenment and for the well-being of the world; nobody else is. There is no concept of sin, but: greed, anger and delusion, envy, malice and hatred are the chief fetters, and ignorance and doubt the two worst states of mind.

Although Buddhists have been tempted to divinise Buddha as Christians have divinised Christ, Buddha has remained The Teacher par excellence, calling men and women to put on Buddhahood by their own effort and commitment. The Buddhist learner lives in the community of monks and nuns because learning the life of Meditation requires regular help from an experienced teacher. To enter a Buddhist monastery is seen as a specific learning experience which can be terminated or lead to a lifelong commitment to membership of the Buddhist-Sangha. Celibacy, in the Buddhist life, is not necessarily a lifelong commitment; monks and nuns can leave the community without stigma attached to it.

The Japanese Buddhist writer Daisaku Ikeda has written a fascinating book: "Life an Enigma - A Precious Jewel". The three jewels of Buddhism are: The Buddha, the Dhamma (Teaching), and the Sangha (the Buddhist community of monks and nuns). Ikeda also wrote, jointly with Arnold Toynbee, the British Humanist, the book: "Choose Life" which is a call to the civilised world to wake up to its true responsibilities. There is another splendid Zen-Buddhist saying: "Every prayer is a 'light sitting in the light'".

A very different and quite unexpected influence exerted itself on my thinking and feeling when I was studying the particular nature-symbolism in Japanese Shintoism.

It explains, to my mind, the remarkable vitality, energy and ability with which the Japanese have adapted themselves to the changes imposed on them after World War II.

Until that war, the Japanese islands had never been invaded and occupied. Due to an unfortunate impulse to ape European imperialism, Japan began to enforce her own form of colonialism, beginning with the invasions of Korea and China, ending so disastrously for her in World War II.

The symbol which expresses the spirit of classical Japanese culture is found in the opening section of "The Records of Ancient Matter" compiled in CE 712. The symbol is "The Sprouting Reed-Shoot". It reads:

"When the land was young resembling floating oil and drifting like a jellyfish, there sprouted forth something like Reed-Shoots".

The land is Japan. The mysterious vitality of Nature is expressed in the image of the sprouting reed-shoot, which became the living symbol of the reproductive powers of life for the Japanese.

This symbol influenced their understanding of history

256

also. They perceived three aspects of history: First "To become" and "that which becomes and appears, appears by itself", second "that which appears" will continue by "next-next", and third, "that which continues" will gather "momentum" from unseen forces. The Japanese view of life and history was developed from the image of the Sprouting Reed-Shoot and summed up in the saying: "Next-Next, continuously becoming by momentum". In the beginning, these unseen forces were perceived as the Excellent Reed-Shoot Male gods which, eventually, were succeeded by a pair of male and female procreative deities: "Male deity who invites" and "Female deity who invites" and together they created the human species.

In later writings these unseen forces were conceived as two cosmic principles governing history, representing good and evil.

Because the image of the energetic Sprouting Reed-Shoot is always inspiring hope, Shinto has remained confident of the ultimate victory of good over evil. Evil will succeed in asserting itself from time to time, but the good will always prevail. Good and evil follow each other as life follows death, and day night. This confidence in the Japanese psyche, based on the symbol of the Sprouting Reed-Shoot which, though bending under the lashing and whipping of winds and storms, even being broken by them, yet always recovers, and, standing upright, is a symbol of life and survival which the Japanese express as: "Next-Next continuously becoming by momentum". It helps to explain Japan's amazing recovery and success after the most devastating experiences of the war: Hiroshima and Nagasaki, the American occupation, and the setting up of a democratic form of government. There have been other religious teachings which have shaped the Japanese mind - Zen-Buddhism and Christianity also. It is, however, their psycho-mystical attitude to and awareness of Nature as exemplified by the irrepressible Sprouting Reed-Shoot which comes through to me as I encounter the Japanese presence in the western world, not only in business, but also in music and the arts, where they demonstrate their amazing mastery of, and willingness to identify with different aspects of European culture.

The Gender issue in Christianity

I was born in 1920, and belong to a generation who, generally, did not have difficulties in their Christian thinking about "Gender".

Judaism, Christianity and Islam are naturally gender-minded and gender-orientated in as much as their faith stories and myths represent God as father and creator of man and woman. In the earlier of the two creation-stories in Genesis 2, woman is made from a rib taken from man with God clothing the flesh round it. The later story in Genesis 1 hints at a possible equality of status between the two, but throughout the Old Testament this hint/suggestion is never developed and given prominence. It is possible that the writer of Chapter 1, part of the priestly source-material of the Old Testament, experienced the place and function of the goddess in the Mesopotamian creation-story and worship during the Exile and spent some time reflecting on the matter, sufficiently to suggest in his creation-story that God valued man and woman alike.

In the New Testament we have Jesus' attitude to and treatment of woman and some of his sayings to go by. His acceptance of their friendship and status give out light and hope. Paul in Galatians 2, expresses a profound insight into the potential of the man-woman relationship in a state of adulthood when both have "put on Christ" or "put on Buddhahood".

Where in the Church-fathers and in later Christian theology do we find further reflections on and developments of this theme?

It is through my daughter, a thoroughgoing Feminist, and through marriage that I learned to think more deeply and personally about this important issue of Feminism.

Feminist scholars have gone into the ancient past and studied the mythologies of the Greeks and the Egyptians and of India. They discovered the cults of and stories about the mother-goddess and the virgin-goddess. Both of these, their cults and their stories have exercised an influence on the Christian cult of Mary, virgin-mother of God which was developed by, or baptised into the church during the first three hundred years when both the Greek and Egyptian religions were still flourishing in the Greco-Roman empire.

The goddess in India is thought of as the "Shakti" of the god, his female part. In China, the "Yin and the Yang", the male and the female, are seen as complementary opposites.

The absence of a properly defined concept and tradition about the essential nature of the man-woman relationship in our Judeo-Christian culture has done much harm. In as far as there has been, in European literature, Christian or otherwise, an emphasis on woman as a source of inspiration to man in his quest for knightly adventure and deeds of valour, it derived from the cult of Mary. Christian nuns, likewise, derived their justification for their choice of living from the church's teaching about Mary, virgin-mother of God.

In contrast, the lot of woman as daughter of Eve, according to Genesis 2 v 23, has a depressing ring to it, and has, as we all know, led to abuses of women in marriage and in society. Here I want to mention that the idea and practice of Lesbian and Homosexual relationships was an accepted alternative option in the Greco-Roman world. Even the aggressive, strident aspects of some Lesbian groups today have their counterparts in the stories of the Amazons and their independent lifestyle in ancient Greek and Near Eastern recordings. Likewise, more ancient civilisations than our own like India and China have tolerated and tolerate alternative lifestyles besides the heterosexual one which has always been and will always remain the norm for human sexuality. The emerging practice of Lesbian and Gay relationships in the present-day societies of modern Europe and North America should not be viewed with fear and horror as dangerous aberrations, (I recommend a reading here from Romans Chpt. 1 vv 24-32). Instead we should see them as aspects of human sexuality and self-expression which contribute to the rich variety and diverse strands in human relationships and culture.

During the second half of this century, "Feminism" and its tasks have emerged as a force to be reckoned with.

Christian Feminism has produced some outstanding theologians in The States, in Britain and on the Continent. However, they are still working within the framework of Gender. Their thorough research into Biblical and Church-history has unearthed women and their stories from centuries of oblivion, but for Non-realists, gender-language in religion has become irrelevant. Many others also can no longer accept that the concept of God can be expressed in, or defined by gender.

In the 21st century, our daughters and sons and their offspring will continue the task of creating mature relationships which will enable both partners to achieve their personal potential in marriage and family life. They will be learning to provide rôle-models for parenting, and by setting an example to their children by their own acceptance and practice of their responsibilities for the health and welfare of human society, they will encourage their children to practise the duties of citizenship and contribute to making Democracy work in the global context of today and tomorrow.

Learning never ends

As I look back over the past 50 years and the changes they have brought about within me, I can only wonder at such profound alterations in my consciousness.

I am the fourth generation child of a Lutheran vicarage, and proud of it. When I came to England in 1939, I left behind a terrible and brutal modern version of ideological authoritarianism. Here, I became aware of Protestant variations within Christianity and their estrangements which, however, began to be put right with the setting up of the World Council of Churches in 1948.

From the late fifties onwards, I have learned to accept the universal nature of religious and cultural pluralism.

Lately, I have begun to grapple with the insights and contributions which the scientific mind and imagination are bringing to bear on the creation of human values.

I am learning to see myself as a psycho-physical organism among countless sentient and human organisms, living in the biosphere and as part of the ecosystem of this beautiful planet Earth, with the potential for psycho-mystical awareness in my relationships with nature, the universe and my fellow human beings.

My children and grandchildren will find it easier to live in their brains and get to know how it works than I can, since I have been used to living with my immortal soul and attending to it, thanks to the centuries-old teaching of the church and of Plato and Aristotle. I cannot and do not want to deny that their teaching and its influence on the European psyche, imagination and intellect has produced wonderful and remarkable constructs and imaginative flights of fancy in philosophy, religion and the arts, particularly music. They have enriched and ennobled European men and women. I am always deeply moved by Beethoven's wonderful scoring of the duets in "Fidelio" with Florian and Leonore expressing their most thrilling and ecstatic feeling of loving mutuality. Likewise, in the marvellous quartet at the end of his 9th symphony, Beethoven achieved a most sublime and blissful rapture in the male and female voices expressing their commitment to the Joy that resides in the Peace and Harmony between all human beings.

The Declaration of Intent of the Sea of Faith Network says: "A Network for exploring and promoting religious faith as a human creation". Today, I want to omit the phrase "religious faith", and say instead: "A Network for exploring and promoting the human potential for creating human values".

I am encouraged by our own great teacher, Jesus of Nazareth, who told his friends: "You cannot put new wine into old wine-skins". (Matthew 9 vv 16-17). He said this very early on in his ministry and was not thanked for it. Jesus will, above all be trusted and loved for the contribution he made to the fact and experience of suffering, innocent suffering freely accepted and endured. Inspired by Isaiah's Servant-songs, Jesus showed us how suffering can become the redemptive and liberating agent in the overcoming of hatred and evil in the world. and by so doing he inspires and empowers men and women everywhere to do likewise.

I believe, as Hindus do, that human beings have different psycho-mystical needs and aptitudes, and that the major religious options within Hinduism: Theism, Polytheism, Pantheism, Monism and Atheism can supply these needs according to individual requirement and choice without the chooser being rejected by his/her fellow religionists whose choices are different.

Christianity developed a variety of denominational practices and emphases within the overall framework of Monotheism. But, until 1948 they were separated and in a state of Schism with each other. Hinduism allows its adherents total freedom of choice of option within an overall cultural framework and tradition.

Where do all these explorations and experiences leave me? In a state of wonder about the range of the human imagination and its rational mind, world-wide. In a state of thankfulness that human beings have evolved and are still evolving towards greater "complexity consciousness" and personal autonomy, accompanied by a greater willingness to take on responsibility for their natural, social economic and political environment.

This feeling of relief and thankfulness to be adult, at last, and to have reached the state of full autonomy is shared by all in the Sea of Faith Network, not too late, we hope, to save our beautiful planet earth from the Sixth Extinction.

Imagination and God

Shirley Wren-Lewis

Reading the 12 credos I was struck by the common Christian background revealed by 9 of the Chantry Group who contributed. James is silent about the ethos from which he "turned to Christianity in my mid thirties" and two do not mention their early beliefs.

My own difference from this common religious background illuminated for me the reason why I have found it difficult to be more than a long-time intermittent observer rather than participant in the group. I describe here my lack of belief in terms of biography in order to avoid the fundamental lack of interest I now feel in religious debate. Michael Smart's description of discussions in "'God-oriented' terms" as "bound to end in . . . a wearily polite agreement to differ"[1] chimed with my own experience.

My father was a freethinker who early taught me to question theism. "If God made us, who made God?" Father's question was an unanswerable conundrum to the 6 year old I was then, standing on the hearthrug, getting ready for bed. It led to the thought that God wasn't true and thus, I knew, would have an immediate effect on my life.

I had imagined little goblins poking through the bannisters above the dark stairs on my way to bed. The only way I had found to banish this fear was by thinking of the Holman Hunt "Light of the World" picture I had seen reproduced on the walls of my uncle's Methodist Sunday school. The remembrance of the picture's warm glow had banished the imaginary black imps from my nighttime journey. I feared that if God and Jesus did not exist, as my father implied, the glowing picture wouldn't banish demons anymore.

However, further independent thought led me to an empowering notion. Whether God existed or not didn't make any difference; I could still imagine the picture, and the quiet glowing figure could still drive away dark demons. And so it proved as I stumbled up the stairs to bed. Of course I said nothing to anybody about my momentous discovery of the reality of the human imagination; it was too precious and too private.

Later I began to project my own imaginative myth-making propensities onto the changing stability and space of the countryside, when we lived there briefly before the war. Just as the child Coleridge found refuge from a bullying school in the night sky seen from a sky-light, so I found the surrounding countryside held a magic, an otherness, which could sooth away domestic discord.

Teenage years were war years; my father, like many fathers, was absent. I became the class atheist; a rebellious left-wing anti-monarchist pacifist. When I was sixteen a school acquaintance introduced me to John Wren-Lewis because she thought he might remedy my atheistical state. Through him I came into the aegis of a local newly arrived clergyman and his wife. He had brought division to a local thriving youth discussion group so that part of it had become centred around his home and Chatham Parish Church where John Wren-Lewis had become a leading member.

Then began a long love-hate relationship with the Church which I began to experience as a repository of beauty and space and of Christian socialism. The home of the clergyman and his wife had books, colour, paintings, good furniture, though they had impoverished themselves by coming to a working class area. The Oxford-educated clergyman himself came from a working class background, while his wife was an upper-middle class parson's daughter. Their home was my first introduction to an all-pervading middle class culture and I liked it. In my wartime town there had been the public library, classical music in the youth group - shreds of culture amid the all-pervading cramped gloom of war. Through the clergy family I came to love the space and symbolism in the Christian liturgy; and to appreciate its meaning for human life. Talk about transcendence and immanence was readily translated by me from the numinous experience I had had in natural scenery, of an enduring otherness which could dispel inner conflict. This was easily transmuted into the space of soaring stone Gothic arches, the changing stability of the Church's year, the ageless words of the James I bible and the prayer book, the mysticism of Julian of Norwich, of St Augustine.

The anti-clerical views instilled by my father were in a way satisfied by the rebellious views of the clergyman centre of our local group, around Chatham Parish Church where I was made a P.C.Councillor soon after I was baptised and confirmed at 18.

Throughout my subsequent life with John Wren-Lewis I became adept at translating Christian statements into language meaningful in mid-twentieth century life. The eucharist satirised by atheist friends at the LSE as ritualised cannibalism became for me mindful of the way women give their bodies for their children's nourishment. I kept quiet about this and would not have dreamt of joining the SCM at the LSE. At the time I had not read Tillich on the place of doubt in faith, but when I did so I understood it very well, feeling myself between the two worlds of religion and scepticism.

The Macmurray-Buber personalism became of course very beguiling; the idea that relationship was part of Being, of a trinitarian God. I nevertheless still saw Christianity as a man-made religion, made palatable to me through the controversial views first of our group priest and then John Wren-Lewis. There was nevertheless always a question for me in the view of God as within the relationship between people, when I thought about it quietly for myself, rather than entering into the exciting conversation of my milieu at the time, Honest to God and all that. Divinity always seemed to me a man-made thing; part of man's imagination. Later, in my thirties, I had the fantasy that, even if I had incontrovertable proof that God and Jesus did not exist, I would conceal it so that the Christian religious rituals could continue their ageless symbolic celebration of man's nature.

I met Eberhard and then Rosemarie Wedell through his interest in the 1950 Group, an association of left of centre MPs with Sir Richard Acland, whose office I ran. Later I came to enjoy the Christian questioning and debate, the drama and the literary criticism explored at St. Anne's Soho under Patrick McLaughlin. I now smile to remember the chorus of a Charles Williams play in which some of us played:

"Not quite thou, and not quite not".

266

Later my life changed completely and I found myself, when the chips were down, driven back onto the refuge of my solitary childhood, the countryside and the sky. The Church had too many associations in which I had ceased to trust. However much credence I had tried to give to relationship as Being, individuals still remained the only animate beings of whom I had had experience. Alone we come into and alone we go out of the world. Between times we seemed to be, au fond, human animals struggling to survive. This interaction of individual human organisms seemed more primary than the Being of relationships, but an affair of chance, depending on the operation of fitful wills.

Reading the Credos of the Chantry Group I find myself closest to the views of Bryan Saunders, though not concurring in his view that we are in at the end of our particular western civilisation. This is not because I am more optimistic, but that I am a constitutional unbeliever, having, in my Christian days, the utmost sympathy for poor St Thomas. Like Bryan I can join in Church rituals with friends despite believing that God is man-made. Like him, I have participated in various "damage limitation" exercises such as work for the CAB and counselling during the last fifteen years of my life. Since then I have been doing things for myself, remedying my mis-spent youth by taking an arts degree, pursuing that world of the imagination which I perceived long ago beneath religious belief.

I live and take part in the ordinary life of a small country town once described as a cross between Clochemerle and Toytown, but have ceased to attend services in its architecturally admirable but impersonal Norman Abbey, where a visiting preacher once warned the congregation that it might find 'togetherness' difficult. The town's centre is small enough to generate its own sense of community, based on propinquity and neighbourliness and that for me is sufficient. I would call myself a humanist, an admirer of the Christian achievement, though I dread its respectability and circumscribed middle-classness. Somehow the faculty of or interest in belief seems to have dropped out of my

267

constitution.   Actions seem more important; mine are concerned with a local bookshop, friends and neighbours as well as family elsewhere; two sons who are senior academics in England and the USA, their wives and my grandchildren.

The psychiatrist, Peter Lomas, once wrote about the aim of therapy being to restore a sense of 'ordinariness'[2]. The sky overarching our world can give a sense of peace and transcendent otherness to troubled lives; as we grow older we can learn to value the otherness of those who have

"an equivalent centre of self, whence the lights and shadows must always fall with a certain difference"[3]

In that spirit I send this present statement of non-belief to those of you known through many years, recognising that my own journey is not yet over.

References;
(1)   Smart, Michael;
      Some footnotes on Faith, p 201
(2)   Lomas, Peter;
      True and False Experience, 1971
(3)   Eliot, George;
      Middlemarch, last paragraph of Chapter 22

PART IV

Ultimate Concerns in the Twenty First Century

What does all this promise for the twenty-first century? The gravamen of the essays in this volume is that Christian faith in the twenty-first century has to stand on its own feet rather than appealing to doctrinal statements originating in the 'ages of faith'.

We have to speak of faith in a world in which so many certainties have disappeared, or have become doubtful; in which the pictures that we drew and the stories that we told have ceased to be regarded as literal truth. This is not a new experience, but it comes to us with a new force when our picture of the universe has changed and our notions of knowledge (both outside ourselves and within ourselves) have become a kind of flux. 'What is truth?' we may ask with Pilate. Yet we and he are left with the question.

This is not to say that previous ways of speech have become false or meaningless: that story and myth and the pictures we try to draw of the world we live in have lost their meaning. Poetry has its own claim to truth. We have to understand more clearly what that claim is. It is clear that the language of factual statement no longer applies. We cannot establish truth by referring to previously accepted factual or logical statements. We have to recognise the truth that the stories and the pictures have always conveyed. For this is the truth that we can know, even if we do not find it in life as we know it. This is the truth that Christians claim to find in Jesus, though it is not confined to the Christian revelation. That revelation, and the manner in which it has been offered, glimpsed, reported and sometimes in part realised has always been the substance of Christian faith.

Most of us share a number of basic experiences. Apart from Robert Mitchell we are over 60 and have lived through the greater part of the twentieth century, reaching adulthood between the 1930s and 1950s. All have had professional or executive jobs and are used to handling ideas, and presenting them in an orderly and comprehensible way. We have also had substantial exposure to Christian belief and practice, either in our upbringing or in later life. However, many of us have developed a degree of unease concerning the Church, largely on account of an excessive or (to us) misplaced insistence on creeds and doctrine. The most common position is one of 'semi-detached' membership or practice, finding something of continuing value, but with a note of reservation. Two or three contributors place themselves definitely outside the Church, but still appreciate certain features of its worship and participate in it occasionally.

The contributions include a number of references to authors who have influenced the writers, the most frequent being Dietrich Bonhoeffer, Don Cupitt, and the Book of Job; followed by John Macmurray, Martin Buber, William James, C.G.Jung, Simone Weil and Wittgenstein. It is noteworthy that the contributors achieve a near balance between men and women.

Four issues stand out in the contributions; God and religion, Jesus, the Church, and Ethics.

God and religion

The central issue for most contributors is the existence of God, a teasing and elusive concept which nevertheless will not let them go. James Mark strikes a note of baffled but inescapable search, writing; 'I have never encountered a theology that succeeds. While it would simplify matters to abandon the search, I shrink from the notion of a meaningless universe. I felt the need to grasp at some meaning, however obscurely perceived in my experience. This can only be a meaning that transcends that experience.'[1] This belongs to the religious attitude in the broadest sense which 'has somehow to be rooted in the life that we know and yet to assume that human beings will look for a fulfilment which that life cannot give; and that we have to look for such fulfilment even if we cannot speak of it.'[2] While such an attitude may seem to be based on wishful thinking, there is no making sense of the world without it. The accompanying 'tension between the conviction that I must trust and a questioning as to how much trust can be justified' simply has to be borne as part of the human situation.[3]

Other contributors take up this challenge in varying ways.

Honor Anthony thinks of God as a person. Another expresses a strongly contrasting view (Dorothy Emmet), pointing out that the idea of God as a person developed during the sixteenth century and was later embedded in the language of evangelical piety. The persons of the Trinity are not persons in our sense, nor should they be thought of like a committee of three. Moreover, 'prayer does not seem like a personal conversation', even if the language of devotion is highly personal. This leads on to the Thomist view that God is unique, having no distinctive property to mark him out as one of a kind. When Moses asks his name, he replies simply, 'I am'. Joan Crewdson believes that God can be spoken of as 'the ultimate form of the Personal' (a phrase used by John Macmurray) and as 'the uncreated source and ground of personal being'.

For most of us (like the men of Athens in the Acts of the Apostles perhaps), God has this obstinately elusive character of 'the only partly knowable' (Honor Anthony), or indeed hardly knowable at all. For some, this is qualified by the rather more definite, though hardly knowable, figure of Jesus. But that does not resolve the primary question of God. What appears to provide continuing motivation to this interest, eccentric as it may appear to many people, is an inward imperative of questioning and search. As James Mark writes, quoting Karl Popper, 'all we can do is grope for the truth, even though it be beyond our reach'.[4] For some, this leads on to the classic Christian stance of 'I believe that I may understand' (Muriel Smith). Others are impatient with 'God talk' (Bryan Saunders, Michael Smart, Shirley Wren-Lewis) but are still inclined to believe that 'man needs his gods', or that a religion starting from the common human experience of 'intimations of transcendence' may be more firmly grounded than a formal theological construction (Michael Smart). One contributor refers to the burning bush that is not consumed and quotes a Czech professor who told her 'as long as man is alive God will not die' (Vera Hodges).

Some relate to a compelling search for order and value, and one notes that 'gods in every part of the world are human-friendly. They often embody also, in one shape or another, principles of evil, dissonance and enmity . . . but these elements are there to represent these parts of human experience, and they never triumph in the end' (Bryan Saunders). This represents a view of God or gods as tribal and relatively accessible. Others stress the littleness of human individuals in the universe, our relation to God being no more than that of a shortsighted worm's view of an elephant (Honor Anthony). 'I am an infinitesimal speck within creation in its never ending flow as it changes, dies and recreates itself. Yet paradoxically, I felt that I matter . . . ' (Olga Pocock).

Vernon Thomas's paper offers us a wide-ranging series of references to writers who all have in common with him some kind of attachment to the transcendent. At the end Thomas is 'mindful to leave our eternal destiny to God "our Creator, Sustainer and End". God is the name we give to the Transcendent.'[5]

David Hughes is concerned to leave room for God in a world fast excluding him. He has provided a spirited critique of Descartes' subject/object standpoint and, drawing on John Macmurray's Gifford Lectures, proposes an alternative standpoint, which avoids the false antithesis between the intellectual rigour of science and the intellectual irresponsibility of post-modernism. This saves human spirituality and moral responsibility from going, along with cartesian dualism, onto the philosophical rubbish heap. He argues that 'the primacy of the practical over the theoretical implies that action is prior to thought.'

Joan Crewdson, who has 'come to believe that the central claims of the Christian faith only make sense when considered within a metaphysical framework', proposes, both here and in a recent book, a personalist metaphysic (inspired principally by the thinking of Michael Polanyi), regarding personal being as the key to the nature of reality. Such a metaphysic 'solves the problem of dualism raised by traditional philosophy, by holding opposites together in a part-whole relation. This gives us a world of both unity and diversity.'

Many of us would probably agree with Wittgenstein's

273

view that religion is a form of life to be simply recognised but not evaluated (James Mark).[6] For some, the most suitable and congenial form of expression is a religion of waiting, movingly described in Robert Mitchell's essay.[7] 'It is not faith in a set of facts or a certain state of affairs; it is faith in the value of an activity. I do not assert that God is, simply that God might be, holding that it is more daring, demanding and fruitful to live with the possibility that God is, than that God is not.' Others testify to the reassurance and renewal that can be found in worship (Elaine Kaye, Olga Pocock, Anthony Pragnell). "There is no 'answer' to the problem of suffering and evil, but the Judaeo-Christian tradition can offer a way of living with it" (Elaine Kaye).

Bryan Saunders takes the view that the God within us does not need to have created the world to be the object of a rich and profound spirituality. Once we have accepted our place in a nature that 'is infinite, remote and indifferent', we can accept the responsibilities of the person who has come of age, and recognize that we can no longer look to God to save us from the consequences of mankind's unwise actions.[8] He does not reject the spirituality of our ancestors. He recognizes the need for faith by entitling his paper 'Credo' and arguing that 'it is possible to be religious without believing in God and possible to believe in God without evidence'.[9] He speaks, however, of beliefs that evolve within our cultures. They will change, as our cultures (our tribes) change; they will not last forever, but they express something valuable, which is to be maintained. He does insist that we must recognise the development of our knowledge and our understanding of our place in our world. And this we must do in a culture which is in a state of decline. Living for others is what makes for life. 'Even in the time of Armageddon the daily round has its value.'[10]

Dorothy Emmet takes a more hopeful line. For her religion is 'a way of life, linked with a view of the world which is intellectually tenable and imaginatively inspiring'.[11] We can live in a world of creative activity that is also a sustaining activity in which we may find we can live religiously'.

Eberhard George Wedell's contribution draws deeply on personal experience as he has observed it in the changing world of our century and, even more strikingly, as he has experienced it in a variety of public posts. He touches on the intellectual challenges involved in social action, quoting Reinhold Niebuhr on the double task of humanity, to reduce the anarchy of the world to some immediately sufferable order and unity; and to get the tentative outcome under the criticism of the ultimate ideal. He has lived through great changes in the life of the Church, both in Germany and in England. This has led him to rate commitment higher than doctrinal niceties. 'It is arguable', he says, 'that the political reasons for credal tests having disappeared almost entirely, they could now be dropped without replacement'.[12] But this would not be because belief had ceased to matter, but because we might show a proper reverence and circumspection in speaking (if we continued to speak) of mysteries. We need cohesion of the Christian community without the imposition of dogmatic affirmations.

Rosemarie Wedell's contribution is even more of a personal one since she tells us at the outset that she is attempting to account for the changes that have taken place in her thinking and feeling during the past decades. She writes about her encounter with other world-faiths and world-views; about her study of some aspects of modern science, and about the influence on her thinking of the feminist movement and feminist theology. She is concerned, above all, with how we are to live rather than with how things are; with morality and the good life rather than with truth in the epistemological sense. But she insists that she is left in a 'state of wonder about the range of the human imagination and its rational mind, world-wide'; 'with a feeling of relief and thankfulness to be adult, at last, and to have reached the state of full autonomy.'[13]

Jesus

Contributors find the figure of Jesus attractive but are in varying degrees reluctant to set him in a traditional doctrinal scheme. 'I have always found it relatively easier to come to terms with the first and the third persons of the Trinity than with the person of Jesus, the Christ' (Eberhard George Wedell). Many draw a distinction between the historical elements in the New Testament and interpretative additions, or what some would see as myth or poetry (Bryan Saunders). An overview of the Gospels and critical study leaves one of us with 'a Christ of whom I can conceive no adequate, or even no coherent, account as being possible; who is both inside and outside history ... ' (James Mark). Most are agnostic on the resurrection as a historical event, and would distance themselves from the doctrine of the atonement, which no contributor actually asserts.

This said, the question, 'what think ye of Christ?' remains insistent and a variety of meanings are put forward. For James Mark, Jesus is an 'icon of love'; for Robert Mitchell, 'a sort of every man, an icon of humanness ... making his claims not on behalf of himself only but on behalf of everyone'. Others find meaning in the cross in which 'the vicious circle of victim and oppressor is broken' (Joan Crewdson), or giving 'an understanding of the re-creative and liberating possibilities in suffering and oppression' (Olga Pocock). At the same time, several are keenly aware of the genuinely religious values of other faiths, which should not be excluded by an allegiance to Jesus (see especially Rosemarie Wedell). 'What we call the resurrection has significance for the whole of human kind, and indeed the whole of creation [but] ... I do not believe that overt faith in Christ within a Christian community is the only path to salvation' (Elaine Kaye).

The Church

Most contributors take an ambivalent view of the Church, one expressing faith in it 'in a somewhat secondary sense' (Robert Mitchell). Another finds that belief in the action of the Holy Spirit together with a natural conservatism allows him to enjoy the fellowship of the Christian community 'in spite of my own, by now laodicean, relationship to the creeds and to some of the more extreme demands of organised religion' (Eberhard George Wedell).

A generally critical view is not inconsistent with appreciation of positive features in the Church which have continuing appeal. One who is firmly outside it really loves it 'for the space and symbolism of the Christian liturgy' (Shirley Wren-Lewis). Another values the many suggestive icons associated with Anglican worship, canvassing the idea of a role for 'Friends' of the Church who could provide sympathetic support without having to take on a formal credal commitment (Michael Smart). Another finds the Church of his dreams in 'a ruined, bombed-out church, a Church with no roof and no doors' and sees the primary task of the Church as 'to preserve a space in which all who come may be held while they wait upon that of God in all about them' (Robert Mitchell).

New points of reference for the Church are suggested in personality or community. 'Religion is a largely cultural matter, but we share a common humanity in God' (Joan Crewdson). Elaine Kaye commends the model of George Fox, who said that he 'walked over the world recognising that of God in all he met'.

Ethics

Contributors share a concern for ethical values but do not necessarily draw a close connection between them and religion. One contributor urges that 'we cannot retreat from the need to know about ourselves, nor from the prudent management of our own dangerous species' (Bryan Saunders). Another affirms a commitment to humanist values of human solidarity, truthfulness, responsibility and self-fulfilment, without any need for religious underpinning (Michael Smart). James Mark explores the idea of a 'Christian humanism', seeing the limitations of being human in accordance with the Christian vision of love. He mentions 'a hierarchy of values, in which the demand of love becomes more insistent the more nearly you approach the Kingdom, and you must give up the lesser for the greater'. Commenting on this, another contributor considers that we have 'to live with uncertainty and with all the responsibility that that entails. We cannot derive ought from is, nor can we formulate absolute values in a way that is at all useful' (Robert Mitchell). The demand is one

277

of action, rather than of theological or philosophical definition. The debate is about morality and a way of life rather than about epistemology. What he has to say is an act of witness, made during a pilgrimage through life to which God has called him, the God on whom he must wait. He adds that the great biblical commandments concern orientation, not specific conduct. 'The harder one tries, the harder it is to know what love really requires, because there is no final definition of human wholeness, only an endlessly enriching succession of kicks in the teeth and glimpses of glory. As with hope, so love turns out to be love of the wrong thing'.

Another looks forward hopefully to an 'emerging European Christian Humanism . . . matched and complemented by the humanism of other faith communities and human societies, setting this in a broad context of historical and contemporary movements' (Rosemarie Wedell).

Some of us continue to live within the Christian tradition. Others have now moved outside it, while still valuing their earlier experience within it. What we all have in common is an experience of continuing pilgrimage in search of truth, and a desire to share this with each other, and through this book, with others too.

Shared preoccupations

The contributors to this volume share various preoccupations. One is the **possibility of speaking of the world in which we live** and therefore possessing the understanding which would enable us to speak of it. It involves facing the challenge both of the extension of our knowledge and of its limitations; of the nature of the language in which we have been used to speaking of it; and of the stories we have used to give a meaning to what goes beyond the limits of knowledge. What is at issue is the dual possibility of speaking of the totality of our experience and of its sequence in what our ancestors thought of as time.

None of us would deny the radical nature of the change that has taken place; our understanding of what we know and how we can speak of it; of our coming to see more clearly than ever before the significance of metaphor and myth, and the purposes which they serve in our language; of the recognition that they do not express literal truth or enable us to get outside our world so as to be able to speak of it as a whole.

The 'man who has come of age', in Bonhoeffer's phrase, is the person who accepts all this; who insists that there is no way back to an earlier phase of human development when we could speak of a reality known to God, and to us by virtue of our faith in him. The person who has come of age is the one who accepts the change; who regards it as revealing to us a world in which we have to do as well for ourselves (individually and in community) as we can; in which we have to recognise that there will always be questions on the margins of experience that we cannot answer and which it therefore makes no sense to ask. In terms of what we regard as human knowledge (actual and potential) this position seems irrefutable. But is this all that there is to be said? Must we remain in the limited existence which seems to be the habitat of the person who has come of age? Few of us think so. We have not questioned either the vast expansion of human knowledge and human power, or the notion of their limits. What we have said could be called, rather, a series of variations on the theme, 'Yes, but . . . '. We all rest, in our different ways, on a conviction (whether explicit or implicit) that there is a dimension to human life which transcends it; which gives it sense and value; without which it would lack what makes for life. Whether and how it can be spoken of, the wish to speak of it or the acceptance of silence remain. This is the main theme on which we have touched in our various ways.

The person who has come of age has to accept that questions about the meaning of the universe cannot be pressed, for the knowledge that would enable us to answer them is forever outside human perception and understanding; otherwise we must accept that a world to which we cannot attribute sense can only be, for us, absurd. In practice our writers have continued to uphold notions of meaning and value even though there is nowadays no agreed metaphysical system to support them. In the end an appeal to faith is necessary.

There is clearly more to be said about our contemporary world than is contained in the concept of the coming of age, however much that concept has been needed. There is more to contemporary (and inherited) experience than can irresistibly be verified. The implication is that the experience of human beings is not to be confined within demonstrable limits. There is a tension between the demonstrable limits of proof and experience which seems to stretch out beyond proof. The notion of the transcendent is still with us, even though it is a transcendence of which we cannot speak.

The collapse of speculative metaphysics is another preoccupation. If it has undermined the proofs of the existence of God, and destroyed Dante's three-decker universe, it is a matter for concern that clergy and laity alike still use this stock description of the eternal verities. Numerous public opinion surveys show that people still put God firmly and instinctively above the clouds, and hell definitely under the pavement. The notion of God within us is both difficult and generally unpopular, probably because it implies a metabolic coinherence which many people find uncomfortable. They would prefer to negotiate with a God-out-there, rather than take him so close to their own persons.

If notions of God "up there" are no longer valid, **Christians need an alternative mode of conveying experience of him**. It is a varied, and often frustrating, problem, as emerges from the section on God and religion earlier in this chapter. More people, in the future perhaps more than in the past, will not be content with religion as a socio-cultural phenomenon. What people want is not phenomena, but to know God. And that difficulty is not surmounted by the fact that the idea of God as a person came in only during the 16th century, as Dorothy Emmet asserts. It may be that Christians can recognise God most convincingly, not in themselves but in each other; and that this is the way the divine presence is most often (appropriately?) communicated today. The commitment to be Christ-to-others requires more attention than we have given it. It could be used in Christian initiation, in confirmation and in the practice of the Christian life. It is essentially a non-verbal activity. It seems to be largely ignored in evangelism, which is mainly regarded as an exclusively verbal activity. If our conclusion is correct, then here is a field that is substantially untilled.

This leads on to the recognition that **language has, in this context, become largely useless.** The employment of words, like water, as though they were in infinite supply has made there use no longer credible. Religious language is metaphorical, the language of suggestion. We have found that it is being rather than telling that matters in the first instance, religious experience rather than religious conversation. Visual and musical experience can convey the presence of God; hence the impact of sense experience. The absence of sense impressions can also be significant. Silence can be as important as noise, an empty space say as much as a well-furnished one.

The template of Christ as the archetype of human perfection has spurred us on, in spite of the impossibility of obtaining an accurate portrait of Christ. The Christ of the Gospels presents both the tough and the tender sides of the response to the realities of human life. We have there "the proper man" (in Luther's hymn), whose response to the demands of life is not sentimental, yet indulgent; is precise and accurate yet infinitely flexible; concerned at all time with substance rather than form.

What is commonly described as "the problem of suffering" will perhaps remain the most difficult challenge to faith in the 21st century. It has not lost its poignancy because massive and often successful efforts are made to avoid or to mitigate suffering. Life for many people in the developed world is no longer nasty, brutish and short. They have less need for the old promise of 'pie in the sky'. Quality of life is available for many in the here and now, rendering redundant faith as an essential compensation for suffering here on earth.

But for more than three quarters of mankind poverty, disease and early death remain the normal expectation. In the

21st century the concept of compassion will take on a more global role. Interdependence is likely to be the continuing motive for being Christ to each other.

Will the recognition of Christ in others, whether next door or in Rwanda, as a motive power for the exercise of compassion run out in the face of inexorable and continuing need? The beginning and end of the Christian vision is not exhausted in helping to meet human suffering, but we know that it determines individual and corporate life-styles; to live in the presence of God is to be blessed indeed.

It is the living in the Samaritan mode that will mark the Christian community in the 21st century. To do so, Christians need to work in the spirit of the Zen master Yûn-men: 'In walking, just walk. In sitting, just sit. Above all, don't wobble'. It is worth remembering that the classic reference to hints and guesses about the Christian life defines it as 'prayer, observance, discipline, thought and action'.[14]

References

1. p. 31 *et seq*
2. p. 51
3. p. 61
4. p. 32
5. p. 232
6. p. 23
7. p. 141
8. p. 178
9. p. 174
10. p. 196
11. p. 106
12. p. 242
13. p. 262
14. T.S.Eliot

List of Contributors

HONOR ANTHONY
Consultant physician (allergies); formerly medical researcher at St James' University Hospital, Leeds.

JOAN CREWDSON
Editor of Convivium for ten years; author of *Christian Doctrine in the Light of Michael Polanyi's Theory of Personal Knowledge* (1994).

DOROTHY EMMET
Professor Emeritus of Philosophy in the University of Manchester; Fellow Emeritus of Lucy Cavendish College, Cambridge. Author of *The Nature of Metaphysical Thinking*, *Rules, Roles and Relations*, and other works on philosophy.

VERA HODGES
Writer on spirituality and prayer

DAVID HUGHES
Management consultant; former personnel manager.

ELAINE KAYE
Lecturer in Church History, Mansfield College, Oxford; Headmistress, Oxford High School 1972-81. Author of *C.J.Cadoux: Theologian, scholar and pacifist.* etc.

JAMES MARK
Retired civil servant in HM Treasury and the Ministry of Overseas Development. Joint Editor of *Theology* 1976-83. Author of papers on Bonhoeffer, Wittgenstein, Simone Weil and others.

ROBERT MITCHELL
Solicitor; Lecturer in Law, University of Exeter.

OLGA POCOCK
Registered psychotherapist; formerly Senior Lecturer in Religious Studies at Stockwell College of Education.

ANTHONY PRAGNELL
Fellow of the European Institute for the Media; formerly Deputy Director-General of the Independent Television Authority; Emil Noel European Prize 1987. Author of *Television in Europe*; editor of *Opening up the Media, Politics and the Media*, etc.

BRYAN SAUNDERS
Retired senior civil servant in the Department of Transport. Honorary treasurer of the Wyndham Place Trust.

MICHAEL SMART
Retired senior civil servant (Department of Employment); Head of the Division of International Affairs, British Council of Churches 1986-90; currently Chairman, Association of Liberal Democrat Trade Unionists. Author of *Labour Market Areas* and pamphlets and articles on employment and general political questions.

MURIEL SMITH
Former Adviser on Community Development to the Home Office.

VERNON THOMAS
Formerly Lecturer in the Department of Overseas Administrative Studies, University of Manchester, Adviser to the International Labour Organisation.

EBERHARD GEORGE WEDELL

Professor Emeritus of Communications Policy in the University of Manchester; formerly Director-General of the European Institute for the Media. Author of *Broadcasting and Public Policy, Broadcasting in the Third World, Making Broadcasting Useful,* etc.

ROSEMARIE WEDELL

Lecturer in World Religions, University of the Third Age; formerly Lecturer in Comparative Religion at the Manchester College of Adult Education.

SHIRLEY WREN-LEWIS

Retired civil servant in the Ordnance Survey.

Other members of the Chantry Group

The contributors to this volume are only some of those who have taken part in the arguments of the group over the years. During the near half-century of its existence others have contributed as actively at one time or another. Those marked with an asterisk have died.

DAVID ANTHONY	Educator
RACHEL BARLOW	Educator and Singer
RUPERT BLISS	Priest and Missionary
KATHLEEN BLISS *	Educator and Theologian
PHYLLIS BLISS	Educator
ELISABETH BROWNE	Psychiatrist
STEPHEN BURNETT *	Canon Emeritus of Sheffield and Head of the Adult Education Dept of the General Synod
JOAN BURNETT	Psychoanalytic Psychotherapist
CLAUDE CURLING*	Deputy Dean of the Science Faculty at King's College, London
GILES ECCLESTONE*	Clerk in the House of Commons; Secretary, Board for Social Responsibility of the General Synod; and parish priest
IMOGEN ECCLESTONE	Educator
JOAN HENDERSON*	Assistant to Leslie Paul
PATRICIA HUGHES	
MICHAEL LETHBRIDGE	Commander R.N. (Retired)
DONALD McKAY*	Professor of Cybernetics, University of Keele
VALERIE McKAY	
PATRICK McLAUGHLIN*	Formerly Director of St Ann's House, Soho
CICELY MEEHAN	Psychologist
SUSAN MITCHELL	Physiotherapist

DEREK PATTINSON	Secretary to the General Synod
JOHN PONSONBY	Lecturer in Radio-Astronomy, University of Manchester
ANN PEARSON	H.M. Inspector of Taxes
CHARLES REGAN	Retired Senior Civil Servant, Department of Health & Social Security
JENNY REMFRY	PhD, Member Royal College of Veterinary Surgeons
MARY SHARP	Senior Lecturer in the History of Art, Manchester Metropolitan University
ELISABETH SMART	Educator
NEIL TYLER	Journalist, formerly Editor BBC Radio 3 News Service
RICHARD WILKINSON	Partner (retired), Binder Hamlyn, Chartered Accountants
MONICA WINGATE*	Principal of Balls Park Training College, Hertford
JOHN WREN-LEWIS	Former Professor, University of Sydney, Australia

Index of Names

Note; The names of the authors are indexed only in Parts I and IV.

A

B

Erasmus 250-251

F

G

H

Hodges, H.A.	110-111, 214-215, 272
Hodges, Wilfrid	112
Hopkins, G.M	167
Hosea	253
Houlden, Leslie	235, 241, 245
Hughes, David	4, 273
Hume, David	119, 127
Hunt, Holman	264

I

Ikeda, Daisaku	256
Isaac	149
Isaiah	261

J

Jacob	149
James, William	202, 204, 206, 271
Janacek, L	52
Jenkins, David	8, 87
Jesus Christ	29, 31, 34-35, 42-44, 47-48, 50, 62, 64-65, 66, 69, 73, 92-94, 96-97, 100, 113, 131-132, 134-136, 142-143, 150-153, 162-163, 167-168, 175, 180, 203, 226-227, 229, 242, 249-250, 254-255, 258, 261, 270, 272
Job	40, 61, 142, 146, 203, 220, 271
Joel	253
John, St., Evangelist	162
Johnson, Samuel	39
Jonah	149
Julian, St. of Norwich	265
Jung, C.G	184, 220, 228, 271

K